1500

MENTAL
HYGIENE

OTHER BOOKS BY KEN SMITH

Ken's Guide to the Bible

Raw Deal: Horrible and Ironic Stories
of Forgotten Americans

The New Roadside America
(coauthored with Doug Kirby and Mike Wilkins)

MENTAL HYGIENE

*Classroom Films
1945–1970*

KEN SMITH

BLAST BOOKS

NEW YORK

MENTAL HYGIENE: CLASSROOM FILMS 1945–1970 © 1999 Ken Smith

All rights reserved.

Front cover photo: Betty and Don suffer post-parking guilt in *The Innocent Party,* 1959.
Back cover photo: Ernie is abandoned by his friends in *The Sound of a Stone,* 1955.
Photos on front and back cover, and on pages 33, 87, 107–110, 113, and 208 courtesy of
Centron Collection, Kansas Collection, University of Kansas Libraries.

Blast Books gratefully acknowledges the generous help of
Owen Dugan, Celia Fuller, Don Kennison, and Ken Siman.

Published by Blast Books, Inc.
P. O. Box 51, Cooper Station
New York, NY 10276-0051

ISBN 0-922233-21-7

DESIGNED BY LINDGREN/FULLER DESIGN

Typefaces in this book are Century 731, Industrial Press, and Twentieth Century.

Printed in China

First Edition 1999

10 9 8 7 6 5 4 3

To Rick Prelinger, founder of the Prelinger Archives.
These films were preserved because of his foresight.
This book exists because of his generosity and kindness.

THANKS

Mental Hygiene would not have been possible without the support, kindness, and friendship of Lia Beard, Anne Bernstein, Michelle Boulé, Toni DeMarco and Don Faller, Owen Dugan, Janis Elko, Celia Fuller, Andy Gosnell, Gaye Gullo, Kathy High, Ronnie and Tim Hill, Jamie Kelty, Don Kennison, Ly Kilm, Julie King, Doug and Susie Kirby, Laura Lindgren and Ken Swezey, Celeste Ries, and Ken Siman.

Grateful thanks to Sebene Selassie at the Prelinger Archives; to Zeva Bellel, Donna Lee, Lee Shoulders, and Jim Trainer at Archive Films; to Pierce Rafferty at Petrified Films; to Kristin Eshelman at the Kansas Collection; and to Becky Jordan and Glenn McMullen at The American Archives of the Factual Film.

I was fortunate to interview a number of the surviving directors, screenwriters, cameramen, and support staff from two of the largest mental hygiene film producers, Coronet and Centron. To these people—Esther Altschul, Pauline Bailey, Abe Blinder, Bruce Colling, Dick Creyke, Lou Garfinkle, Barney Montgomery, Ted Peshak, Tom Rhia, Bill Rockar, Dale Sharkey, Bill Walker, and Mel Waskin at Coronet; and Herk Harvey, Russ Mosser, Norm Stuewe, Trudy Travis, and Art Wolf at Centron—I am deeply indebted. I am equally indebted to independent producers Sid Davis and Earle J. Deems, and to actors Jim Andelin, David Cox, Gene Hardtarfer, Ralph Hodges, John Lindsay, and Bill Mason for their insights and recollections.

Filming the yearbook office scene
for *Effective Criticism*, 1951.

CONTENTS

A MESSAGE FROM KEN

I've often thought of *Benefits of Looking Ahead* while writing this book. That film's protagonist, a likeable guy named Nick Baxter, undoubtedly would have viewed this project with bafflement and scorn—the province of a bum—one of the many small ironies I've noted as I've researched and written *Mental Hygiene* over the past decade.

Benefits of Looking Ahead was a mental hygiene film, one of thousands of similar productions created in the quarter century between 1945 and 1970. They were made to be shown in classrooms. Their topics included table manners, posture, dating etiquette, highway safety, substance abuse, juvenile delinquency, vandalism, and "girls-only" themes. Today, three decades or more since their creation, most people have forgotten them—or aren't aware that they ever existed. They're seen only on late-night cable or on compilation videotapes lumped together with Hollywood exploitation films and drive-in movie trailers. They're considered dumb.

This book is an attempt to change that.

Nick Baxter had a rock-solid purpose and plans: "I want to be happy. Be somebody. Have a good job. Friends. A home. A wife and kids." By those standards all writers are bums, and writing *Mental Hygiene* is nothing short of madness. I don't dispute that. I've written this book instead of getting a good job or buying a home. Its creation is highly unlikely to land me the girl of my dreams and has destroyed whatever small ability I had to relate to the real world. I find myself prefacing my conversations with, "You know, that reminds me of an old educational film I watched the other day...." As my friends will tell you, that wears thin pretty quick.

Writing *Mental Hygiene* first occurred to me in 1990. I was working for The Comedy Channel, an enterprise that chopped funny moments out of funny movies and ran them on television, nonstop, twenty-four hours a

Nick Baxter knows his chances for a happy future depend on looking ahead.

11

day. One resource for its programming was 1950s dating and manners films supplied by Rick Prelinger, an archivist and social historian who had amassed the world's largest collection of old industrials and classroom productions. They were edited for broadcast by a small staff, including me.

The Comedy Channel had tapped Rick's archives because many of his films were naïve and funny. Yet even Rick's universe of material was finite when judged solely on The Comedy Channel's demanding quick-laugh standard. After only a couple of months I found myself altering Rick's films as I edited them, changing them from what they were to what The Comedy Channel wanted them to be, pumping up the laughs. In my search for new material I began screening films I'd seen earlier. I clearly remember watching *Tomorrow's Drivers* (1954) for perhaps the third time, an odd film ostensibly about teaching kindergartners safe driving habits, and suddenly realizing that the kids were just a metaphor; the film was really about suppressing rebellious behavior in teenaged drivers. It was more enjoyable—and frightening—when viewed in its entirety than if I'd chopped it into pieces. That kind of thinking guaranteed the end of my employment at The Comedy Channel and the beginning of a long friendship with Rick Prelinger.

Highway safety in miniature from the strange *Tomorrow's Drivers*.

Mental hygiene films, I have since learned, were tools of social engineering, created to shape the behavior of their audiences. Today they sometimes remind us of *Leave It to Beaver* or *Plan 9 from Outer Space*—and can likewise be appreciated for their cornball innocence and low-budget ingenuity—but that is an accident of time, not intent. The people who made mental hygiene films were not dumb. To view them solely as a source of cheap laughs is, frankly, to miss most of the reason they're interesting.

Mental hygiene films, like a polio sugar cube or a measles shot, were conceived as preventative medicine. Kids would watch them and learn that being selfish, arrogant, undemocratic, or delinquent would make them unhappy or, depending on the producer, dead. Conversely, those who played by the rules and maintained the status quo were rewarded with popularity, fun, and a life span that extended into their twenties.

Potential malcontents and backsliders were spanked with an assortment of cinematic paddles. Fear films—such as *Last Date* and *Keep Off the*

Grass—showed rebellious behavior as self-destructive, scaring teens into conformity. "Busy brain" films—such as *Dinner Party* and *The Prom: It's a Pleasure!*—laid down a lengthy set of constraining social rules and regulations that kept kids too occupied to ask uncomfortable questions. Films such as *Are You Popular?* and *A Date with Your Family* were imitative: you saw teens—clean-cut, obedient team players—who were happy, you wanted to be happy, you tried to act like the happy teens. And then there were "discussion" films, the cutting edge of mental hygiene,

Kay and Nick, role models for their generation, in *What to Do on a Date*, 1951.

with social problems woven into their plots and with characters who tried to solve them. Some of these films even ended without resolution, closing with a messy situation to encourage classroom debate. Most did not.

The people responsible for these films were driven by a sincere desire to guide young people toward behavior that they felt would make them happy. It's no fun to be lonely or physically unattractive. Nor is it enjoyable to be a heroin addict or to have your face torn off in a car wreck.

Unfortunately, responsibility for these problems was not shouldered equally. Society and dogmatic rules were never wrong; it was always the teenagers who were at fault. The frumpy teen in *Good Grooming for Girls* (1956) is unhappy because she doesn't look like Sandra Dee. Is that narrow standard of perfection ever questioned? No; the film simply sets out to transform her into as close an approximation of Sandra as possible. Jeff in *Narcotics: Pit of Despair* (1967) goes to a pot party—and his eventual damnation—because his parents are never home to supervise him. Are the parents called to account?

Director Ted Peshak reviews script changes with one of the leads in *Improve Your Personality*, 1951.

No; Jeff bears full responsibility for his actions. This blame shifting might be understandable in a world where teenagers were allowed a range of options, but they weren't.

Mental hygiene films isolate their issues from the noise and confusion of everyday life. They present a perfect world; even the imperfections are perfectly imperfect, strategically scripted to drive home whatever point the film wishes to make. No dialogue is haphazard, no meaning misunderstood, no timing flawed. Watch enough mental hygiene films, even a half century after

13

A dirty room, a hunk of bread, a moth-eaten sweater: Nick's future if he keeps "drifting."

they were made, and you sometimes forget that. You're thunderstruck by how clear it all seems, how simple and logical. What a dummy you must be; why hadn't you seen the answer before?

Nick Baxter's goals in *Benefits of Looking Ahead* are worthy. Nevertheless, they're not for everyone, and the assumption that they should be is a fundamental design flaw in the soaring architecture of mental hygiene films. Keeping the narrative simple—a requirement of the bottom line and a demand of most teachers—meant reducing all variables. It was as impossible to be a little good or a little bad as it was to be a little dead. This tidy view of life naturally favored stereotypes, resisted unwieldy topics, and perpetuated a simplistic vision of manners and morals in general.

Going on a date is not like assembling a carburetor. Making friends is not like oiling a machine gun. There is no "right way" or "wrong way" to live your life. Nevertheless, these films tried to tell us that there was.

Mental hygiene classroom film production ebbed and flowed with the pronouncements of educational theorists and the demands of the public—a peculiarly American, profit-making approach to social engineering. Dating and manners films had their heyday from 1945 until 1960. Atomic bomb survival films for kids spiked in 1951, juvenile delinquency films in 1955. Antidrug films were fashionable in the early 1950s and again from 1965 through 1970. Highway safety film production blew hot and cold, reflecting the occasionally feverish temperature of popular concern. They were the most evergreen of all mental hygiene films, providing a gore-splattered narrative thread of calamity that continues even today.

The history of mental hygiene films remains fragmentary, but enough information exists to support at least some tentative generalizations. This book is my attempt to set the record straight. Understanding why mental hygiene films were made, seeing them for what they really are, gives us all a glimpse at how information can be manipulated in our society—sometimes with the best intentions.

As Nick Baxter observes at the end of his film, "It's *fun* to do things that come out right."

Everything turns out okay for Nick.

14

> "We pledge...to produce only those films which will motivate constructive student thinking...to maintain maximum interest level through well-paced realism rather than unwarranted artifice...to regard as an honored privilege and a sacred trust our function in aiding in the development of finer men and women to the end that a better understanding may exist among all the peoples of the world."
>
> —"PLEDGE TO THE EDUCATORS OF AMERICA,"
> MENTAL HYGIENE FILMMAKER AD, 1946

A PERFECTLY DELIGHTFUL WAY TO LEARN

February 1946. In the basement lunchroom of a hulking prewar school somewhere in New York City, a hundred teenagers sit quietly, their eyes focused on a nonreflective screen, their ears straining to hear dialogue muddied by cinderblock acoustics and the rattling sprockets of an old DeVry projector.

They are watching something new: a ten-minute "social guidance" film. It was not called a social guidance film then; that label had yet to be invented. Perhaps they'd been told that it was about "attitude enhancement" or "emotional conditioning," or possibly "mental hygiene," a term that had come into vogue during the war.

The film was titled *You and Your Family*. It was directed by George Blake, a veteran 16mm filmmaker whose clients included the War Food Administration and Borden's Farm Products. *You and Your Family* was a low-budget, incidental project for Blake, something to tide him over between his big industrial and government jobs. He probably didn't think much of it.

The stars of *You and Your Family* were Mary, Bill, and George Johnson, a collective vision of the average postwar American teenager. Bill wore a baggy suit and bow tie, George a sweater vest and four-in-hand. Mary, her hair in a shoulder-length curled bob, wore a knee-length plaid skirt and penny loafers. The film opened with a cheery title card reading, "Most family problems can be solved through frank and friendly discussion." It then cut to the Johnson family parlor, where an excited Mary tells her parents about the dance invitation she's just received over the telephone.

Mary, who looks about five years too old to be going through such formalities, is in for a disappointment: Mother and Dad do not approve. "I think we all feel that Mary is still a little young to go out in the evening," Mother says, icily referring to her daughter in the third person. "That's right," echoes Dad over his newspaper. "Sorry, Mary." An off-camera narrator asks, "Has anything like this ever happened in *your* home?" and the film then repeatedly spins backward in time to show Mary's possible responses.

Looking at this from a distance of over fifty years, we can only guess what the teenagers in that chilly New York lunchroom thought as they watched *You and Your Family*. Since nearly all school education in 1946 was conducted through

Mary encounters a problem and resolves it—with Dad's approval, of course—in *You and Your Family*.

classroom drill and repetition, textbooks, and lectures, it's safe to say that they'd never seen anything like it before. "No one in this family wants to have any fun at all!" Mary wails on the screen. "I wish I were dead!" The narrator, not wanting to leave things untidy, coos, "Was that the best way? Or should Mary do this?" An alternative Mary appears—controlled, mature— and smoothly suggests, "Why couldn't I have the gang over here tomorrow night? We could all play the radio and dance and make sandwiches." "Hey! That'd be swell!" cries Bill from somewhere within his large suit. The closing theme song rises and the film ends with the Johnson family well adjusted and on an even keel again.

The students in the audience that February could not have known that, at that moment, a small gear had seized in the social machinery of postwar America. They probably would have laughed had you told them that twenty-five years later their children would be watching school films that could trace their origins to what they had just seen, films such as *For Whom the Traffic Tolls* and *The Pill Poppers,* or that fifty years later their grand-children would watch similar-spirited productions such as *Snowbabies* and *My Daddy Is Seventeen.*

You and Your Family was a hit. Not just in that lunchroom, but in lunch-rooms across the country. *Educational Screen,* the print organ of the instruc-tional film industry, praised its "specific family situations which everyone recognized as authentic," and singled it out for honor "because the situations were presented from the viewpoint of the teen-ager himself." The distribution figures have been lost, but *You and Your Family* evidently played everywhere. Five decades after its release, prints of the film were still to be found in moth-balled state and university film libraries across America. In contrast, many of the thousands of mental hygiene films that trailed in its wake have vanished; with fewer release prints, no survivors remain to mark their passing.

In Hollywood, Edward Simmel took note of George Blake's success. Simmel was a low-budget producer who shot 16mm films in a rented indus-

trial cartoon studio on Sunset Boulevard. His pre-vious year's release, *Dinner Party,* had also been aimed at teenagers, although it dealt with formal etiquette, not everyday social behavior. The film had been warmly received by the educational establishment—a modest success—and Simmel had decided to push his luck by producing more films for the school market. His follow-up, still not quite a mental hygiene film, was almost ready for release. It was titled *Junior Prom.*

In Chicago, David Smart also read the glowing reviews of *You and Your Family.* For seven years he had been try-ing to nudge his fledgling Coronet Stu-dios into the black. Smart was known to the public as the flamboyant publisher of *Gentlemen's Quarterly* and *Esquire,* but his friends knew him as a frustrated movie mogul and an advocate of instruc-tional filmmaking. Smart quickly recog-nized that Coronet's particular strengths were exactly what mental hygiene films required: a pool of teen actors, money,

and a sound stage. Chicago had the teen actors, *Esquire* had the cash, and David Smart had two sound stages, part of a huge free-standing studio he had built in his backyard. What he needed now was experienced directors, cameramen, and writers, and here again he was fortunate. The streets and campuses of Chicago were awash with ambitious young veterans who had cut their filmmaking teeth in

The $75,000 Coronet sound truck records the construction of a two-car garage for *Choosing Your Occupation*, 1949.

the Signal Corps and the Office of War Information and, like Smart, had been bitten by the film bug. Smart called in his chief of production, Jack Abraham, to talk about it.

Edward Simmel and David Smart were neither activists nor idealists. They were hardheaded businessmen who believed they could make money by making mental hygiene films. Any American teacher could tell you why: as a tool of mental hygiene, film was hot. It was hot because the adults of 1946 were scared.

The kids in American schools in 1946 had never known prosperity and peace. Twelve years of economic privation had been followed by five years of domestic upheaval during the bloodiest war in human history. Adults remembered what had happened to American children after World War I. That conflict produced— or at least was popularly believed to have produced—the Lost Generation of the 1920s, young people who viewed the world through skeptical eyes, who abandoned traditional values and responsibility for shallow, hedonistic pleasures. A global economic depression and the rise of fascist dictatorships in Germany and Italy followed. Might not a more involved, selfless generation of Americans have prevented those calamities?

Larry and Dad on the set of *Citizenship and You*, 1959.

To be sure, this was a cut-and-dried view of history. But there was a kernel of truth in it, and with the social and human wreckage that the Second World War had just left behind, the possibility of even greater disasters loomed in the future. Something had to be done to stop them from happening again.

That "something" was the mental hygiene classroom film, a uniquely American experiment in social engineering, the marriage of a philosophy—progressive education—and a technology—the instructional film.

Neither progressive education nor films in the classroom were new. The progressive education movement had been active since the publication of *The School and Society* by John Dewey in 1899. Dewey put his own spin on the theories of English philosopher Herbert Spencer (1820–1903), who believed education should devote itself to what he called the "important things in life" rather than to fields of study not related to human welfare. Dewey felt the best way for schools to do this was to stress "experience" over traditional subjects and to make the curriculum "fit the needs of the child." Schools would not only teach traditional fields of study, but would venture into areas that would later be called "life adjustment."

Educational Screen, September 1926.

The motion picture also had been around since the nineteenth century. Although movies today are synonymous with entertainment, they were developed largely for educational purposes. Thomas Edison was an early advocate of film in the classroom. "Books will soon be obsolete in the public schools," he predicted in 1913. "It is possible to teach every branch of human knowledge with the motion picture."

Making films to fit school curriculums proved more difficult than making predictions. Edison abandoned instructional films in 1918. It took another five years before 16mm became the standard width for nontheatrical films, finally making possible mass distribution of titles and projectors. Five years after that George Eastman of Eastman Kodak demonstrated that film could be valuable as a teaching tool by subjecting more than ten thousand students in a dozen city school systems to instructional movies (which Eastman produced specifically for this purpose) as a regular part of their curriculum. The results were promising: grades went up, kids seemed more interested in their studies, teachers enjoyed their work more.

Nevertheless, both progressive education and classroom films had adversaries.

From its inception, progressive education was viewed with suspicion by conservative educators and parents. To many, the schoolteacher's proper sphere of influence extended only as far as reading, writing, and 'rithmetic. Moral education was seen as the territory of parents and the church. And while progressive programs worked well in carefully chosen schools in cities like Chicago and New York, no one knew how this labor-intensive, child-centered approach would go over in rural areas or in poor, overcrowded schools. Its advocates were worried; how could progressive education be packaged to guard it from corruption by halfhearted school boards and incompetent teachers?

Suspicion also limited the acceptance of instructional films. Many teachers dismissed motion pictures as lowbrow entertainment—to be seen in theaters, not classrooms. Education was not supposed to be fun. Some regarded film as a corrupter of youth, one of the dark forces that contributed to the perversion of the values of the Lost Generation. Movies, after all, meant Hollywood, a place of notorious immorality. Some schools even offered courses in "photoplay appreciation" to show children that the moving image was merely an illusion—a way to counteract its evil influences.

Instructional films that were used before the war were nothing like *You and Your Family*. The two principal producers at that time, Eastman Teaching Films and Electrical Research Products Inc. (ERPI), were aware of prevailing sentiments and obligingly kept their films dry as dust. ERPI even banned all music in their sound productions because music smacked too much of "entertainment." Subject material was limited mostly to natural processes (plant growth, clouds) and faraway lands (Mexico, Kansas).

Classroom films might have continued that way forever. But World War II forced a radical shift in the way most people thought about movies, education, and how the two could work together.

As the war approached, America's army and industry faced the Herculean task of training hundreds of thousands of people in very little time. They turned to film. Training films could communicate standard information to vast audiences, whether they were women on the home front riveting bulkheads or draftees in boot camp disassembling rifles. They proved successful beyond anyone's prediction. By 1944, the last full year of the war, U.S. government films were shown over 700,000 times, to an audience estimated at 67.5 million. It did not escape the attention of social scientists that the film

When the enemy attacks . . .
Our boys remember a movie they saw!

Instructional films were sold as a tool of mass education in World War II.
From an advertisement in *Educational Screen*, March 1943.

shown more than any other was TF 21-2048, known to its viewers as *Military Courtesy.*

Although the public grew to accept film as a teaching tool, it was not always aware of all it was being taught. That was because a second type of film was also being produced during these years, the "attitude-building" film, whose primary purpose was to motivate, not instruct. Carefully chosen visuals were combined with dramatic story lines, music, editing, and sharply drawn characters to create powerful instruments of mass manipulation. Titles such as *Avenge December 7, The Arm behind the Army, Farmer at War, Campus on the March, Price of Victory, Ring of Steel, Conquer by the Clock,* and hundreds of others put backbone into home-front morale and fighting spirit into tenderfoot warriors. Women on the assembly line and soldiers in boot camp learned not only *how* to perform their tasks, they learned to *want* to.

The proponents of progressive education took note of this. Shortly after the war ended they began to demand, through editorials and letters in industry publications, an end to the "antiquated ideas by antiquated methods" then being taught in America's schools. They wanted to "inculcate attitudes and ideals that will enable boys and girls to make their places as efficient and effective members of a democratic society," and to teach kids to "meet the complex problems of modern life." And they wanted to do this using the same supercharged delivery system that had proved so effective during the war: mental hygiene films. These films would be scripted under the watchful eyes of sociologists, psychologists, and Ph.D.s, the high priests of postwar social doctrine. They would be produced to exacting educational standards and distributed to schools nationwide. Guidance, never an easy subject, would be taught correctly everywhere because it would be mass-produced like a jeep or an incendiary bomb.

The persuasive power of the motion picture, so disdained by educators before the war, was now recast as "emotionally derived learning" and praised as an enlightened tool of social engineering. "It's a perfectly delightful way to learn," wrote Ivah Green, supervisor of rural education for the Iowa Department of Public Instruction. "The motion picture...[is] literally knocking at school doors, ready and eager to make learning more rapid, more meaningful, more lasting, and—dare we mention it?—more fun!"

You and Your Family was far from the ideal social guidance film envisioned by some progressive educators. But the adults of 1946 were willing to overlook its limitations. They were grateful for anything that would help straighten out their children, particularly the "teen-agers," a new term that had come into use during the war. By today's standards the teens of 1946 don't seem especially disturbed, but the general feeling of the time, fueled by fretful articles in popular magazines and wartime juvenile delinquency films, was that this new generation was spinning out of control. Defenders of the established social order were especially glum. They saw teenagers as a single-minded, menacing organism, and referred to them darkly as the "youth problem."

"Teen-agers"—particularly those in short skirts—were a popular topic for mid-1940s exploitation films.

The "problem" was that during the war teenagers had tasted personal freedom and liked it. While dad was in the army and mom was in the munitions plant, children were left to fend for themselves—often with money in their pocket from war work. When fend for themselves they did, their "recklessness" and "moral laxity" shocked their elders.

Films such as *You and Your Family* were meant to fix that, to turn back the clock and train American kids how to be kids again. If this had been 1943, Mary Johnson probably would have gone to that dance. But now it was

Mental hygiene films mimicked Hollywood stagecraft to create "emotionally derived learning." Here, gang member Harry is about to commit vandalism in *Right or Wrong?*, 1951.

1946—and mother and dad were back home. The door to early autonomy had been slammed and bolted shut.

Over the next twenty-five years thousands of mental hygiene films would be produced, changing as America's teenagers changed, always with the intention of stopping them from whatever they were up to. Films battled beatniks, nonconformists, loners, bad attitudes, odd habits, independent thinking, loud clothes, and sexual freedom in the name of popularity, democracy, and cultural inertia. They sold citizenship in the icy depths of the Cold War, noninvolvement during the McCarthy era, and the cozy comfort of the status quo in the Eisenhower years. When the teens stopped listening, the films found a new audience in their younger brothers and sisters. When the teens started rebelling, the films fought back with shocking images of what would happen to those who broke the rules. Mental hygiene films preached clean thinking, good grooming, lawfulness, togetherness, sobriety, and safety to wave after wave of young Americans—who often wanted nothing more than to be sloppy, reckless, sullen, high, dirty-minded, independent delinquents.

All this required a far-flung network of production houses, and in that respect mental hygiene filmmaking was as homogeneous as the behavior

The spacious Coronet studio, Glenview, Illinois, circa 1946. More films were shot on its sound stages than in any Hollywood studio before or since.

patterns in its films. The East Coast was home to McGraw-Hill, Caravel, Sound Masters, Knickerbocker, and Audio Productions; the Midwest had Encyclopaedia Britannica, Centron, Coronet, Hardcastle, and Portafilms; and the West Coast boasted Simmel-Meservey, Churchill-Wexler, Gateway, Charles Cahill & Associates, Avis, Bailey Films, Frith Films, Jerry Fairbanks Productions, and John Sutherland Studios. Crawley Productions in Canada produced many of the fifties' most ruthless social guidance titles, while impolite and gruesome topics were the domain of independent *auteurs* such as Leo Trachtenberg (*It's Up to You!*), Dick Wayman (*Mechanized Death*), and Sid Davis (*Boys Beware*).

The quarter century that stretched from 1945 to 1970 was as fertile for industrial America as it was for social engineers. Big business had its own films in schools—free of charge—that offered their own brand of guidance. While educators trained America's teenagers to be well mannered, corporate film divisions groomed them to be happy shoppers. Good citizens, the films explained, spend money. Titles such as *Make Mine Freedom* and *How to Lose What We Have* pitted godless communism against the right to buy breakfast cereals and frying pans, while *Meet King Joe* and *It's Everybody's Business* informed classroom audiences that the founding fathers had actually planned America as a consumption-driven paradise.

By 1952, the dawn of the first Eisenhower administration, mental hygiene films had become an accepted part of America's public school sys-

24

tems, housed and catalogued in special audio-visual libraries under categories such as Social Development, Courtship, and Leisure Time. Guidance films, strictly defined, represented only about 3 percent of the titles produced by the mighty instructional film industry, but that statistic is misleading. Guidance directives turned up in films about punctuation, musical instruments, and soil erosion. Guidance films as we would recognize them today encompassed a broad curriculum: Health and Safety, Sociology, Psychology, Social Science, Home Economics, Civics. Even English classes had films telling kids that "correct" penmanship helped them to "fit in." Five thousand new 16mm film titles were released in 1953 alone. If just 10 percent of them addressed some notion of mental hygiene, it's clear that social guidance in classroom films was dominant and inescapable.

"All education is indoctrination. The real question is whether indoctrination shall be confined merely to the mores and taboos of the past, or whether it shall be directed toward solving the problems of the future. In time, parents will recognize that the hope of a better world lies in such a new curriculum."

—H. M. BARR, DIRECTOR OF RESEARCH, PORTLAND, OREGON, PUBLIC SCHOOLS, 1947

But in 1946 such a far-reaching program lay in the future. Social guidance through classroom films was still the province of New Deal progressives, a very modern and forward-looking thing, the darling of the well educated and open-minded. We may laugh at their pretensions, but we should not dismiss the films they made as shallow or silly, or as a direct reflection of a goofy, innocent past. In fact, the opposite is true. Social guidance films would not have existed had America been like *Leave It to Beaver*. Instead, they thrived in a nation traumatized by war, fearful of communist witch-hunters, terrified of nuclear annihilation, and rocked by fears of a generational rebellion. School boards bought films that showed well-mannered teenagers because, in the eyes of adults, teenagers *weren't* well mannered or well groomed or respectful or polite. Mental hygiene films were popular because they showed life not as it was but as their adult creators wanted it to be.

As those 1946 teenagers shuffled back to their classrooms on that cold February afternoon, they could not have known that the limits of their social freedom, and the limits of their younger brothers' and sisters' as well, had been set in cellulose acetate. America's educators, political leaders, and parents had a sense of moral duty, a hip new technology, and a federal bank account rich enough to put the two together. Mental hygiene through classroom films was going to save America's youth. And there was nothing America's youth could do to stop it.

HISTORICAL OVERVIEW

1940–1945

World War II.

First superhighways open: Pennsylvania Turnpike and Arroyo Seco Parkway.

U.S. government begins producing "attitude-building" films.

Introduction of penicillin sharply reduces VD infection rates.

Philip Wylie's *Generation of Vipers* is published; his theory of "momism" states that poorly educated women are breeding a permanent underclass of juvenile delinquents.

Juvenile delinquency becomes a sensationalized social concern.

Race riots in Detroit and Harlem.

Encyclopaedia Britannica Films, Inc., is founded.

McGraw-Hill's Text-Film Department opens.

U.S. government makes surplus sound 16mm projectors available to schools.

❀ *As the Twig Is Bent; Boy in Court; Dinner Party; The House I Live In; Joan Avoids a Cold; Preventing the Spread of Disease; Sex Hygiene; Youth in Crisis*

1946–1950

Postwar economic and baby boom; rise of suburbia.

Dr. Benjamin Spock's *Common Sense Book of Baby and Child Care* is published.

David Riesman's *The Lonely Crowd* is published; encourages Americans to become "other-directed" (to get along with and adjust to others).

Coronet begins mass production of social guidance films; Sid Davis produces his first cautionary film.

Centron Corporation is formed.

Debut of the high-performance V-8 engine; highway fatalities are at their highest level since before the war.

To combat juvenile delinquency, Santa Ana, California, converts an abandoned municipal airport runway into the world's first drag strip.

❀ *Are You Popular?; The Dangerous Stranger; A Date with Your Family; Dating: Do's and Don'ts; Junior Prom; Last Date; Maintaining Classroom Discipline; Shy Guy; The Story of Menstruation; You and Your Family*

1951–1955

Darkest days of McCarthyism.

David Smart, founder of Coronet, dies; Coronet's studio closes; end of the great postwar wave of social guidance films.

Miltown, Equanil, Thorazine, the first prescription antianxiety "tranquilizers," produced; dawn of the ingestible drug movement.

Despite penicillin, reported cases of VD begin to rise.

Chevrolet introduces a 265-cubic-inch V-8; Chrysler C-300 debuts with a 331-cubic-inch V-8, the first production car with 300 horsepower; 609 people die in traffic accidents over the 1955 Christmas holiday, a new record.

Marlon Brando stars in *The Wild One*, James Dean in *Rebel without a Cause*. *The Blackboard Jungle* causes theater riots in Britain, is banned from the Venice Film Festival, becomes a box office blockbuster. Juvenile delinquency revived as a social concern.

John Clellon Holmes's *Go* is published, the first "Beat" novel.

❀ *Cheating; A Day of Thanksgiving; Drug Addiction; Duck and Cover; Gang Boy; Habit Patterns; How to Say No; Live and Learn; Molly Grows Up; More Dates for Kay; Name Unknown; Skipper Learns a Lesson; The Sound of a Stone; Tomorrow's Drivers; What about Juvenile Delinquency*

1956–1960

Last classroom dating films; first classroom gore films.

Eli Lilly begins marketing Darvon; Roche Laboratories hawks Librium. Over 579 tons of tranquilizers are prescribed in 1959 alone. The police department in affluent Westchester County, New York, identifies a new problem in the community: "teenage drug parties."

J. Edgar Hoover testifies that Chinese Communists are funding the drug trade in an attempt to subvert America; Congress passes the Narcotic Control Act.

Rudolf Flesch's *Why Johnny Can't Read and What You Can Do About It* attacks progressive education, becomes a best-seller when the Soviet Union launches Sputnik.

Dr. Spock revises his *Common Sense Book of Baby and Child Care,* rewriting passages "to emphasize the limits of permissiveness."

Chevrolet introduces the fuel-injected engine; Highway Safety Enterprises produces its first highway gore film.

Congress passes the Civil Rights Act prohibiting discrimination in public places; college students join sit-ins and marches for racial desegregation, but the UC Berkeley student government is forbidden from taking positions on off-campus political issues.

The FDA approves the public sale of Enovid, the first "morning-after" pill.

Reported cases of VD rise sharply.

✹ *As Boys Grow...; The Innocent Party; It's Up to You!; Lunchroom Manners; Safety or Slaughter; Signal 30; The Snob; Social Acceptability; Social Class in America; The Trouble Maker; What about Prejudice?*

1961–1965

High tide of campus idealism and highway mayhem.

Hoffman-LaRoche begins marketing Valium; first reports of LSD being sold on the street; methadone therapy is introduced for heroin addiction. Amphetamines ("diet pills") are the suburban housewife's drug of choice.

U.S. begins bombing North Vietnam; first Marines land in South Vietnam.

First antinuclear and antiwar marches in Washington, DC.

Mario Savio founds the Free Speech Movement at Berkeley; first student "takeover" of an administration building. "Don't trust anyone over thirty."

Draft card burning is made a federal offense.

Detroit drops V-8 engines into its compacts and creates the "muscle" car. Highway deaths skyrocket; physicians picket the New York auto show.

Ralph Nader's *Unsafe at Any Speed* is published.

✹ *Boys Beware; Dance, Little Children; The Dropout; Mechanized Death; Red Nightmare; Seduction of the Innocent; Wheels of Tragedy*

1966–1970

The golden half decade of strident antidrug films.

Student dissidents abandon flower power approach, turn militant; President Richard Nixon calls student protestors (and Dr. Spock) "bums."

Governor Ronald Reagan asks the California legislature to "drive criminal anarchists and latter-day fascists off the campuses" and orders police helicopters to drop tear gas on UC Berkeley.

Congress passes the National Traffic and Motor Vehicle Safety Act; anchored seat-and-shoulder belts are required for all automobiles sold in the U.S.

Vice-President Spiro Agnew blames books, movies, and rock music for leading America's youth into drug use; possession of LSD is outlawed; an estimated eight million Americans smoke marijuana.

Sex education courses begin in many American schools.

Direct cinema and cinéma vérité come into vogue; nonscripted "discussion" films are favored by young teachers; mental hygiene fades away.

✹ *Alcohol Is Dynamite; Highways of Agony; It's Up to You; Keep Off the Grass; LSD-25; Marijuana; Narcotics: Pit of Despair; The Political Process; Red Asphalt*

What makes a film a mental hygiene film?
Mental hygiene films were deliberately made to adjust the social behavior of their viewers. In general, they're preachy and melodramatic. They come from a time when concepts of right and wrong were rigidly defined, and they were primarily used to guide kids toward behavior that was considered proper by adults. During the years 1945 to 1960 mental hygiene was taught through what was called social guidance or life adjustment films, addressing topics such as dating and popularity. From 1960 to 1970 the preachy attitude grew alarmist and was broadcast by antidrug and highway safety films.

What's wrong with teaching kids right from wrong?
Nothing. Unfortunately, mental hygiene films often equated right behavior— as well as other vague concepts such as patriotism and moral correctness— with conformity to a very narrow range of conduct. Which is understandable, since that range of conduct was the one favored by the producers of these films.

Were these films shown just to kids?
Mental hygiene films were produced for audiences of all ages, from preschoolers to senior citizens. However, most of them were made to be shown to kids in schools.

Mental hygiene films were only a very small subset of the tens of thousands of instructional films produced during the years 1945 to 1970. These classroom films covered nearly every topic imaginable, with straightforward titles such as *Graphing Linear Equations, Techniques of Food Measurement, Learning about Your Nose, Oil Films in Action, Rocks for Beginners, The Miracle of Moss,* and *Insects Are Interesting.* Most of these films do not make entertaining viewing today. Well, *Techniques of Food Measurement* does have a few fun scenes.

How many kids actually saw these films?
Millions of American school kids saw mental hygiene films. They were shown in classrooms as a regular part of standard school curriculums.

Did kids laugh at them?
These films look hopelessly cornball to us today, but that's because we can draw from fifty years' worth of media exposure. The kids who saw them back in the 1940s and 1950s didn't have that luxury. They weren't as critical-minded as we are. Also, the people who made these films worked very hard to make them as plausible and realistic to the kids of that time as possible. Mental hygiene films were intended to persuade; they couldn't if they came off as phony.

Were these films made by Hollywood stars when they weren't making movies?
Hollywood had almost nothing to do with classroom mental hygiene films, if for no other reason than that most mental hygiene films were made in the Midwest, not Hollywood. The biggest "star" who ever appeared with any consistency in them was Dick York, aka Darrin Stephens of *Bewitched.* And that was long before he moved to Hollywood and became a star.

Hollywood actors steered clear of mental hygiene films because they paid poorly, and mental hygiene films steered clear of Hollywood actors because they were too recognizable. Educational film producers felt that students wouldn't be able to identify with recognizable actors in films about everyday life.

Some actors in mental hygiene films went on to become successful Hollywood character actors—George Furth and Jim Andelin, for example. But most remain obscure to this day.

How much money did actors earn by appearing in these films?
Coronet, the leading producer of mental hygiene films, paid the union minimum to its teen actors: $25 a day. They budgeted for two or three days' shooting for lead roles, which meant that the teen stars of Coronet films got $50 or $75 for their work. In 1958, teen actor Vera Stough played the starring role in *The Snob,* a fourteen-minute film. She was in nearly every scene. She was paid $100.

No actor ever received a royalty for appearing in a mental hygiene film.

Were these films part of a conspiracy to brainwash kids?
It's important to remember two things about mental hygiene films that may seem difficult to believe today:

1. These films were regarded as the exact opposite of brainwashing by those who created them. In their eyes, films produced by Nazi Germany or Soviet Russia used brainwashing. Mental hygiene films, in contrast, merely provided guidance or stimulated discussion. Again, we have the benefit of history to see that guidance and brainwashing can be two sides of the same coin.

2. Mental hygiene films were not made by conservatives or reactionaries. Rather, they were made by some of the most liberal and progressive-minded people of their time. Their goal was noble: to help children become well adjusted, happy, and independent (within limits). The films look corny and manipulative to us today, but not because the people who made them were evil or stupid.

Mental hygiene, by the way, is still with us, in a myriad of more subtle and perhaps genuinely conspiratorial forms that should be easy to spot fifty years from now. But that's another book.

How come I've never heard of these films?
At least half of all mental hygiene films no longer exist. Film is bulky and expensive to store, and once the companies that made these films went out of business, the films were simply thrown away. Schools and libraries dumped their films when video came in. They were not considered worth saving.

Many mental hygiene films received only limited circulation, and fifty years of neglect have obliterated their provenance. It's often hard to track down even the most basic information about them. Also, most film lovers and preservationists have judged classroom films by the same criteria as feature-length documentaries or Hollywood theatrical releases. By these standards mental hygiene films are boring and inconsequential.

Where can I see these films?
You can't. The few copies that remain are either scattered among university and museum archives or in the hands of private collectors or stock footage libraries. At the moment, neither the public archives nor the private footage libraries seem inclined to release these films for viewing, but perhaps this will change.

Where did you see these films?
+ The American Archives of the Factual Film (Iowa State University of Science and Technology, Ames, IA)
+ George Eastman House Film Archive (Rochester, NY)
+ The Kansas Collection (The University of Kansas, Lawrence, KS)
+ Museum of Modern Art Circulating Film Library (New York, NY)

- ✦ National Archives and Records Service, Motion Picture and Video Branch (Washington, DC)
- ✦ The UCLA Film Library (The University of California, Los Angeles, CA)
- ✦ The Prelinger Archives; Petrified Films; Archive Films; and Streamline Video (all New York, NY); and MacDonald & Associates (Chicago, IL)

How many mental hygiene films were made?
No one knows. From the number I've seen, and from the number I've read about and assume are lost, I would guess somewhere around three thousand.

Were these films effective?
That's difficult to say. School boards obviously believed they were effective or they wouldn't have bought them for three decades. Americans have always had a soft spot for technological remedies for difficult social problems.

Kids undoubtedly learned some things from some films, particularly in the early days when seeing a film about teenage problems in a classroom was something new and powerful. But mental hygiene films were also shown to kids in the 1960s—and those kids were the most rebellious in American history.

Why didn't they work?
For one thing, mental hygiene films usually ran only about ten minutes apiece. It's impossible to present a balanced, reasoned discussion about a topic as messy as sexual morality or substance abuse in so little time.

Also, the films were often improperly used. Teachers were supposed to discuss mental hygiene films with their classes after the films were over, to fix the ideas in the kids' heads. Many teachers did not. Films were used to break classroom tedium rather than as an intense exercise in self-examination and attitude shaping. Without postscreening reinforcement, the messages delivered by these films often failed to sink in.

Mental hygiene films were also hamstrung by the superficiality of youth. Kids immediately turned off to the message in a film, no matter how persuasive, if the teen actors in it used language that sounded old-fashioned or wore clothes or hairstyles that looked out-of-date.

Finally, mental hygiene films had limits to their power. In the late 1940s and early 1950s, when kids wanted to conform, they were effective. In the late 1960s, when kids didn't, they were not.

How did producers choose topics for films?
In theory, the only mental hygiene films made were those that schools wanted to show in their classrooms. In practice, it wasn't that simple.

The big producers, Coronet and Encyclopaedia Britannica, constantly tried to determine what schools would be teaching the following year so that they could produce films that would sell. This was an inexact science at best. Smaller companies and independent producers, such as Centron and Sid Davis, tried to fill in the gaps. The biggest textbook publisher of the time, McGraw-Hill, only made films that would boost sales of McGraw-Hill textbooks. And then there were the universities and corporate producers dumping into the system films that pushed their own private agendas. It was a mess of conflicting interests and degrees of competence, which is why mental hygiene films cover a wider range of subjects, attitudes, and degrees of professionalism than most people realize.

How long were mental hygiene films in circulation?
Highway safety gore films are still shown in classrooms today. Antidrug films are also still shown, although their tone is much less shrill than it was in the days of mental hygiene.

I once found a rental card in a can containing a print of *Shy Guy* (1947) that showed that the film had been screened as late as 1972. That was probably an extreme exception, although many of these films were still in school libraries until the 1980s, when video displaced them—long after students had stopped paying attention to their messages.

Once mental hygiene films became an established, budgeted part of school curriculums, it took years for the bureaucracy to shake them out. David Smart, founder of Coronet—which produced *Shy Guy*—once complained that the educational field "moved like a glacier." He would have been pleased to learn how long and far that glacial pace carried his films.

The Genres

"All these people that you don't like—
aren't they *happier* than you?"

—THE SNOB (1958)

"Sometimes it can be embarrassing to find that you are not conforming."

—JUNIOR HIGH: A TIME OF CHANGE (1963)

FITTING IN

The commandment to conform, or to "fit in," as educational film writers liked to phrase it, suffused practically all mental hygiene films. It lay at the heart of topics such as popularity, responsibility, family togetherness, manners, posture, cleanliness, citizenship. Its flip side—a gut fear of the abnormal—was evident in the postwar obsession with safety and security and was integral to films across a broad spectrum that encompassed everything from *Sniffles and Sneezes* (1955) to *Red Nightmare* (1962). The depth and diversity of this material suggests a nation not quite in its right mind.

Dad advises Phil on how to be popular. "What do the other fellows do? What do they like?"

Shy Guy (1947) was the first mental hygiene film to extol fitting in as a path to social happiness. It follows the trials of teenager Phil Norton (played by a young Dick York), who spends most of his time building a radio in his basement because he can't make friends in his new school. A visit from Dad sets him straight with an odd metaphor. "Maybe school is like your radio," Dad suggests. "This oscillator will do its work well. But . . . you still have to 'fit it in' so it can work with all the other parts." As practical advice toward achieving this goal, Dad tells Phil to "pick out the most popular boys and girls at school and keep an eye on them," so that he can set parameters for his own behavior.

The scriptwriters of *Shy Guy* made all the cool kids in Phil's school friendly and helpful. If they hadn't, a fatal flaw in Dad's social theory would have surfaced: what makes school kids popular with each other is often not what makes school kids popular with moms and dads. Parents in the real world would eventually discover that their teenagers were turning into delinquents thanks to "fitting in."

Phil ponders Dad's advice. "Keep looking around. Try to find out what the score is."

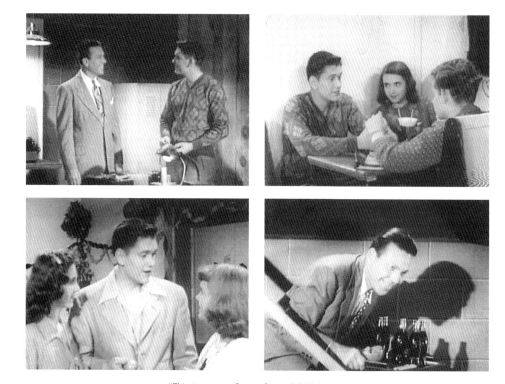

"This is gonna fit in after all!" Phil uses his knowledge to fix the gang's record player and achieves popularity. "He's not really *different*," the narrator concludes as Dad brings Cokes for Phil's newfound friends.

The postwar belief that happiness could only be attained through group bonding had several roots. The war against fascism had just been won in part through the most egalitarian draft in United States history and the shared sacrifice of home-front rationing and battlefront blood. Big business and mass production too had helped win the war and now promised a glorious future. Why be a "selfish" individual when so much that was good had been, and could be, accomplished when the individual operated as a cog in a mega-machine?

> "If you want people to like you, you have to *make* them like you."
>
> —GLENN WAKES UP (1950)

The idea of fitting in with whatever or whoever was popular, when extended to American society in general, meant conforming to a very rigid, conservative status quo. Author David Nye labeled this "cancellation of personality," and it was an accepted fact of life in postwar America. After decades of chaos—the reckless 1920s, the barren 1930s, the bloodstained 1940s—most Americans demanded order and "normalcy" in their world. Films, a uniform delivery system, were ideal for promoting a uniform code of behavior—and for fostering acceptance of that principle. For young audiences, the message was direct. "Know the rules and follow them," barks the narrator in *Making the Most of School* (1948). "If we're going to have any fun, we've got to make some rules!" cheer the disorganized children in *Holiday from Rules* (1958).

For teens, films had at least to pay lip service to freedom of choice. The illusion is preserved in *Student Government at Work* (1953), where seventeen- and eighteen-year-olds expend their energies on the talent assembly and the overdue library books committee, a range of action safely within the system. "They respected the limits of their authority," the narrator remarks. "But they also knew what things they *could* do."

> "If you want other children to like to play with you, you'll have to be a Smiley, not a Sulky."
> —HELPING JOHNNY REMEMBER (1956)

Mental hygiene films never admitted to pushing conformity. Yielding to the wishes of the group was not knuckling under to the status quo; it was "good sportsmanship" and "getting along with people." Wasn't the essence of democracy to seek common ground? To govern by compromise?

Unfortunately, the rules were not made by everyone and there wasn't much compromising by those who did. Large segments of the postwar American "group"—teenagers among them—had no say whatsoever, but mental hygiene films were blind to it. "We have become Americans through the process of sharing," says the proud narrator in *Who Are the People of America?*, the same year (1953) that Separate But Equal laws still ruled in over a dozen southern states.

Fitting in spawned some grotesque deformities. One of these was a national

Smile and Talk to People
Find Good Things in People
Tell Them the Good Things
Do This All The Time

Formula for success. Joe in *Fun of Making Friends* (1950) makes this into a rubber stamp to remind him of what he needs to do—all the time.

fixation on safety and security, fueled by the spread of communism and the bomb. Dozens of films obsessed on the safety of school-age children, the most vulnerable citizens of a nerve-racked nation: *Let's Play Safe* (1947), *Let's Be Safe at Home* (1948), *Why Take Chances?* (1952), and *Let's Think and Be Safe* (1957). *Safe Living at School* (1948) takes the obsession to an extreme as the narrator calls attention to drinking fountains with "no sharp parts" that "are safely constructed to reduce the danger of bumping your teeth while drinking." The tragic consequences of ignoring safety can be seen in *What's on Your Mind* (1946), a Canadian film that suggests that people who cannot face the "strains of living" in an unsafe world will simply go insane.

The quest for security sank the notion of fitting in to its lowest depths. Both the House Committee on Un-American Activities and Senator Joseph McCarthy enjoyed considerable public support in the postwar years, as

In *Habit Patterns* Barbara tries to fit in but is nearly destroyed by her "sloppy ways," evident in the big stain on her sweater.

Americans hid under a blanket of conformity. Fitting in was the only *safe* course of action. Noninvolvement was cast as a social virtue in *Manners at School* (1956), in which the narrator explains, "If we mind our own business, people will like us better." Those who try to fit in and fail, as do teenaged Marion in *Social Acceptability* (1957) and Barbara in *Habit Patterns* (1954), weep in torment, damned by their own individuality. "It's a little late for tears, isn't it, Barbara?" asks the unforgiving narrator of the latter film after Barbara fails to fit in at a schoolgirl party. "Even though you didn't know it would happen today, you've still had your whole *life* to prepare for it." Even worse fates lay in store for those who deliberately challenge the system. In *Are Manners Important?* (1954) young Mickey dreams of issuing a proclamation "abolishing manners forever." This anarchistic dictum is immediately shouted down by Mickey's own kid constituents, who then attack him in a howling mob. Mickey, cowering, disappears beneath the onslaught.

Most mental hygiene films emphasize the positive. In *Developing Friendships* (1950) the teens in the junior citizenship essay contest are happiest when they disappear into the background, allowing their chosen leader to bask in solitary glory. More material payoffs are also possible. Among many examples: Tommy in *Appreciating Our Parents* (1950) is rewarded for his "family teamwork" with a bigger allowance. A nameless teen in *Emotional Health* (1947) hits the jackpot when his positive outlook lands him a cute girlfriend. Another nameless teen in *Body Care and Grooming* (1947) neatens her appearance and wins a boyfriend. Marv's "right attitude" in *Attitudes and Health* (1949) nets him a spot on the basketball team. Jane's selflessness in *Fun of Being Thoughtful*

FIFTEEN FAVORITE FITTING-IN FILMS

Are Manners Important?

Belonging to the Group

Developing Friendships

Feeling Left Out?

Glenn Wakes Up

Habit Patterns

Helping Johnny Remember

How to Say No

Manners in Public

Manners in School

The Outsider

Shy Guy

Social Acceptability

Social Courtesy

The Snob

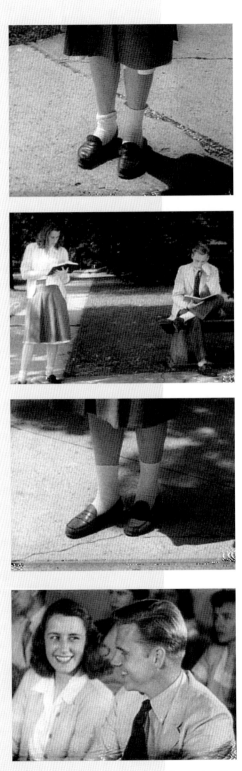

Neatness counts. A girl interests a boy only after she gets new shoes and socks with better elastic. *Body Care and Grooming,* 1947.

A fairy godmother helps preteens learn to be team players. "We'll remember to be clean, neat, and to be on time." *Cindy Goes to a Party,* 1955.

39

(1950) earns her a new dress. Glenn in *Glenn Wakes Up* (1950) apologizes for his antisocial ways and gets a cookie.

The intense desire to fit in gave rise to an equally intense fear of those who did not. Nonconformists were generally seen as either crazy or dangerous in the 1950s. People were expected to follow rules, not make their own. There were no positive role models for rebels, heretics, bohemians, radicals, agitators, inverts, eccentrics, freaks, or eggheads. Teenagers in mental hygiene films who don't fit in are either unpleasant (*The Trouble Maker*, 1957), unhappy (*The Snob*, 1958), or desperate (*The Outsider*, 1951). Ironically, in films about juvenile delinquency or substance abuse, fitting in was bad. "Going along with the crowd" was a sign of weakness, not democratic cooperation, and usually led to a sad end.

Fitting in worked as long as teenagers made only superficial changes to established rules. In *Shy Guy*, for example, Dad tells Phil that it's okay to wear a sweater to school instead of a suit if it helps him fit

> "The fear of social exclusion and ridicule, learned in childhood, remains a powerful motivation for adhering to moral norms in later life."
> —BEGINNINGS OF CONSCIENCE (1957)

in. But when teenagers stopped modifying the rules and started breaking them, mental hygiene filmmakers had to start qualifying their message. In *Understanding Your Ideals* (1950), teenaged Jeff has it made clear to him by his father (and by his disappointed girlfriend) that popularity actually means "loyalty, sincerity, and good sportsmanship." In *How to Say No* (1951) a group of teens wrestles with the delicate politics of *not* fitting in—refusing the forbidden pleasures enjoyed by their rule-breaking friends. And *Responsibility* (1953) shows two candidates for class president: a charismatic, *popular* backslapper with "an attitude toward his work" and a quiet, *responsible* nerd. There's no ambiguity as to which one the film favors.

Fitting in, modified to reflect evolving public trends, remained a message of mental hygiene films into the 1960s. But by then its days as an all-purpose teenage tranquilizer were over. Storm clouds had gathered on the horizon, and a different message—delivered by a different kind of mental hygiene film—would be used to battle the tempest.

"Can't something be done to help these
twisted young lives and set them straight?"
—BOY IN COURT (1940)

CAUTIONARY TALES

Cautionary films painted a bleak picture for those who dared defy the status quo: shame, social banishment, occasionally even death. They sprang from an openly distrustful view of youth held by adults in the postwar years, when it was generally acknowledged that kids, left to their own devices, were a threat comparable to communism or the atom bomb. An old lady encountering a group of polite teens in *Mind Your Manners!* (1953) is so stunned that she stares at them in bemused disbelief. "There's a pleasant, well-mannered group of young people," she tells herself. "Not like *some*."

The mistrust had been building for decades. The earwig of juvenile delinquency—more precisely, a dark fear of the young by the old—first burrowed into the American brain during the Depression, when legions of jobless youths left home to loiter on street corners and in drugstores. Something was needed to sweep all those menacing young people back indoors: "useful education." *Teaching Teens Job Skills* (1940) typified that way of thinking, stressing industrial-arts classes that would give kids a leg up in the job search and "keep young hands too interested and busy for idle recreation."

Adults have little tolerance for rude teenagers in *Mind Your Manners!*

But the answer was not that simple. The teens of the war years had plenty of work to keep them busy—many even dropped out of school to take factory jobs—but with additional income came additional freedom. That made them as threatening to adults as those teens who had been jobless and free. Wartime films went so far as to equate teenagers who had money in their pocket with delinquents who committed crimes. *Children of Mars, Delinquent Daughters, Where Are Your Children?, Youth Runs Wild* (all 1944) sensationalized teen behavior without venturing anything instructive or useful, following the alarmist example set by *As the Twig Is Bent* and *Youth in Crisis* (both 1943), which feature

"Junior," left in a bad environment, becomes a delinquent in *The Adventures of Junior Raindrop*.

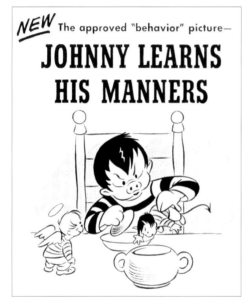

Johnny's uncivil behavior transforms him into a pig-boy until he learns to contain his bad impulses. *Educational Screen*, September 1946.

shocking scenes (faked) of teenaged boys smoking dope and teenaged girls flirting with older men. "To many young girls, even those in their earliest teens, war is opening up avenues of unaccustomed excitement," declares the ominous announcer (Westbrook Van Voorhis) in the latter film. "The adolescent girl, with experience far beyond her age, is beginning, like her brother, to reject parental discipline."

The end of the war forced kids out of the factories and nightclubs and back into the classroom and home. This should have brought the problem to an end; for the most part it did. But the fear of juvenile delinquency didn't end. It remained a popular bugaboo. Even the U.S. Forest Service used it as a metaphor in their film *The Adventures of Junior Raindrop* (1948), in which "Junior" joins a gang of other raindrops "looking for excitement" and runs roughshod over a poorly maintained watershed. If we abandon our responsibility to take care of the land, the narrator warns us, "we can't expect little raindrops to behave."

The Forest Service need not have worried; adults were not about to be caught napping. The postwar years saw the launch of an all-out offensive against delinquency on two fronts: prevention and punishment. The first tried to nip rebellion in the bud, targeting teens who exhibited suspicious "loner" tendencies and teaching them to "get along with people." Films such as *Better Use of Leisure Time* (1950), *Control Your Emotions* (1950), *Social Courtesy* (1951), *Facing Reality* (1954), and *Benefits of Looking Ahead* (1950) all featured teenaged boy protagonists (as do nearly all mental hygiene films about delinquency) who were moody and suspiciously unsocial. In *The Griper* (1954) a frustrated cheerleader asks the disgruntled star, "Oh, George,

Andrew, a "confused" delinquent, tries to bring his dead mom back to life by repairing her radio and later pulls a gun on his classmates. *Age 13, 1955.*

why don't you relax? Why do you keep trying to impress everyone with how *stupid* you think everything is?" Even such an innocuous film as *Shy Guy* was seen by its educational advisor, Dr. Alice Sowers, as preventive medicine against future delinquency. "Self-consciousness can cause one to withdraw from the group," she wrote in a 1947 issue of *Coronews*. "He may fall back upon too much reading or other lonely pursuits...he may accept the companionship of less desirable and anti-social young people.... Shyness can lead to resentments which finally cause him to become a 'delinquent.'"

43

Beer + car + teenager = death. Innocent nonteens are terrorized and killed by uncontrolled young people in *The Bottle and the Throttle,* 1968.

Preventive films far outnumbered those that showed calamitous aftermaths; the intent being, after all, to guide transparently, not to beat one over the head.

> "Teenagers can be such suckers. And for what? A kick? Or a fling? A thrill? You think you're smart enough to get away with it!"
>
> —NAME UNKNOWN (1951)

Then again, sometimes you've just got to knock sense into a kid. This was the role of the "re-education" films, which tried to script happy endings for their youthful protagonists after they slapped them around a little. Jim in *Act Your Age* (1949) is punished after he carves up his desk but forgiven when he creates a "How Old Am I?" chart and asks his parents to rate his recovery. Jerry in *Big Man on Campus* (1963) endures the wrath of an angry principal for his numerous petty crimes, but he's rewarded with a nice girlfriend when he decides to join others in "getting along with authority."

Mike in *Mike Makes His Mark* (1955) is wracked with guilt after he defaces school property (with a pencil), but a timely confession wins him the approval of his guidance counselor and a place in the school band. This forgiving, "permissive" approach to delinquency—a response to teen characters who were driven more by thoughtlessness than lawlessness—was ridiculed by independent producer Sid Davis in *Vandalism*

A guy in a lab coat employs helpful visual aids in *Control Your Emotions*, 1950.

(1953), in which teenaged punks Ben and Dave swipe a car for a joy ride. "It isn't really *stealing*," the narrator mockingly protests. "It's just a Halloween joke." Ben and Dave end up behind bars, where they obviously belong, beyond reprieve or salvation.

Teens in cars brought out the Big Fist in cautionary films: teenagers were basically considered borderline sociopaths anyway, and automobiles were seen as their most powerful tool to spread mayhem. In *The Bottle and the Throttle* (1968) eighteen-year-old Bill downs too many "beach party beers" and runs over a mother and her baby. In *Car Theft* (1956) teenaged joyriders are chased by the police and mow down a little girl. In *Who's Delinquent?* (1947), a liberal-minded film, the town is galvanized into action only after a teenaged boy runs over a police officer. Teenaged Jim in *Alcohol Is Dynamite* (1967) ends his young life on skid row after he plows his convertible—and girlfriend—into a brick wall. Teenaged Harry in *Six Murderous Beliefs* (1955) responds to a warning to drive carefully with a contemptuous (and inarticulate) "Garrragh!" before he barrels into a curve and dies. His bloody hand slides limply down the speedometer as its needle falls to zero.

The most frightening image in all delinquency films was that of normal-looking white kids who have enjoyed all the benefits of free enterprise and suburbia throwing it contemptuously back in adult faces. In *What about Juvenile*

45

Faces of rebellion. Necks are thunked and erasers and apples fly
in *Maintaining Classroom Discipline*, 1947.

Delinquency (1955) a gang of high school hooligans commits the unpardonable sin of beating up a dad. The crime is so heinous that one of the young punks quits the gang (it helps that the victim is *his* dad), but the other thugs remain savage as ever. "You wouldn't catch me mopin' if it were *my* old man," the leader says, sneering.

Juvenile delinquency films lost their cohesion as the 1950s ebbed, splintering into the genres of drugs, highway safety, and syphilis, each carrying varying types of social baggage along with their cautionary messages. By the early 1970s, with the nation mired in a deep recession and filled with a new generation of scary young people, youthful unrest was again seen as an economic issue, and prevention sounded a familiar Depression-era note. "These young people take their leadership attitudes and pride in their trade to the marketplace!" yells the leather-lunged narrator in *Skills Build America* (1973), a film praising an Olympic-style competition "aimed at helping young people develop respect for the dignity of work."

> "Nightlife in rural precincts has altered considerably since taffy-pull days."
> —WHO'S DELINQUENT? (1947)

Mental hygiene juvenile delinquency films had come full circle.

"Your physical urges fight against your reason.
In the height of emotion it's not always easy to think things through."

—HOW MUCH AFFECTION? (1957)

DATING

Dating films, viewed today, come across as stiff and small-minded. But they represent a tough admission on the part of late-1940s parents: the old, adult-supervised rituals of courtship had become outmoded in the postwar world, and kids were now free to roam, hang out, and chart their own social course through life.

That freedom, however, did not extend to the serious business of hanky-panky. Postwar teenage courtship may have escaped the watchful eyes of mom and dad, but it had not escaped the adult-dictated customs of society, which were just as unyielding and vigilant. Dating films served as a way to remind teens of that. They also allowed adults to present their views on teenage dating habits through the films' teenaged characters. It often wasn't a pretty picture. "You can't help getting into situations where petting's likely to start," cautions Lucy in *How to Say No* (1951). "Just give him half a chance, alone, and there's no stopping him!"

Dating films tackled three deep-seated fears of nervous post–World War II parents, none of which they felt comfortable discussing with their kids. The first was that their children, bereft of guidance, would end up as social misfits. The second was that they might rush into marriage without thinking things through, setting the stage for almost inevitable future divorce or lifelong unhappiness. The third was sex, either reluctantly agreed to by daughters ("Some girls think they *have* to permit it," Lucy explains, "for 'date insurance'"), or genuinely consensual and leading to unwanted pregnancy.

Coronet director Ted Peshak preps Jack and Nora for their passionate hand-holding scene in *How Do You Know It's Love?*, 1950.

47

High-school romance blossoms over the telephone in *What to Do on a Date* (1951), above, and *Dating: Do's and Don'ts* (1949), right. Nick and Kay end up sharing Cokes with the gang, while Woody and Ann demonstrate the right and wrong way to "say goodnight."

PSYCHOLOGICAL DISTANCE→

Sometimes romance goes too far. Mr. Hall—aided by Coronet's props department—
cautions Sue and Larry against early nuptials in *Are You Ready for Marriage?*, 1950.

These were not irrational concerns. Although the postwar years are often portrayed as a period of no-holds-barred baby making, early marriage and young families were, in fact, discouraged. Most adults were embarrassed by the "necessity nuptials" of World War II and the scandalously high divorce rates that followed. (In 1946, for example, the courts in Reno, Nevada, granted eleven thousand divorces—an average of over thirty a day—still an all-time high.) Furthermore, the middle class looked down on early marriage as a lower-class phenomenon, an indulgence of the under-educated, often triggered by unplanned parenthood.

Dating films seemed ideally suited to tackle these thorny issues, which were beyond the range of experience of most moms and dads. More than any other form of mental hygiene, they were relied on by parents as a magic new technology, crafted by experts, impossible for an older person to understand. All you as a parent had to do was to make sure your kid went to school when they showed the dating film. *Presto!* Everything was taken care of in the comfort of a darkened classroom.

Unfortunately, it didn't work out that way.

Dating films, at least the ones dealing with the early stages of courtship, are the most beloved of all mental hygiene films today. It would be unfair to accuse the people who made them of lacking a sense of reality, although the films certainly lack it now. We can't travel back in time and view *Are You Popular?* in a classroom in 1947, or *Dating: Do's and Don'ts* in 1949, or *What to Do on a*

**TEN CLASSIC
DATING FILMS**

Are You Popular?

Are You Ready for Marriage?

Beginning to Date

Date Etiquette

Dating: Do's and Don'ts

Going Steady?

How Do You Know It's Love?

How Much Affection?

Junior Prom

What to Do on a Date

CHUCK: "All lined up for the party?"
ALAN: "All except for the clean-up committee. I just can't get anybody to do the dirty work..."

Date in 1951, so we will never really know if their audiences found them enlightening or just dumb. They were shown in schools into the 1970s, which suggests at least some measure of identification and acceptance.

Dating films cover a wider range of social situations than most people realize. The popular image is of films such as *Date Etiquette* (1952) and *Beginning to Date* (1954), in which a typical date unfolds for our edification: a boy nervously asks a girl out, a destination for their date is agreed upon (always a well-populated place), a return deadline is set, the boy meets the girl's parents, the boy and girl make awkward conversation, the evening ends with a heartfelt handshake. "Considerate escorts," notes Mary in *The Prom: It's a Pleasure!* (1961), "make sure their dates don't have to remind them that it's time to go." These films are filled with warmhearted, reassuring images, but they were only the first tier of dating films, aimed at social greenhorns. Older teens, wise to the messier aspects of relationships, saw darker films that addressed thornier issues.

> "I hope Jeff doesn't feel that he has the right to—take liberties."
>
> —GOING STEADY? (1951)

KAY: "What dirty work? Can I help? I'll do it! I'll be *glad* to!"
Setting out the boy bait in *More Dates for Kay*, 1952.

For example, in *Going Steady?* (1951) Jeff and Marie encounter non-stop unpleasantness: their parents frown on their exclusive relationship, their friends offer unwelcome advice, and they aren't even sure they want to go steady anyway. "I'd rather go out with Jeff—but I wish the others wouldn't ignore me so!" Marie wails in frustration. The solution to their predicament is simple: they back off. It's the same advice that's given in films such as *How Do You Know It's Love?* (1950) and *Social-Sex Attitudes in Adolescence* (1953): keep circulating. One-on-one relationships only lead to trouble.

Those young people who refused to heed these warnings had to contend with "marriage-training" films, the adults' last line of defense. Some of these films featured wise teens, such as Larry and Sue in *Are You Ready for Marriage?* (1950), who decide to put things off when an on-screen adult counselor explains: "There's more to marriage than just this *boing*." Others showed the unwise, such as Viv and Rex in *Worth Waiting For* (1962), who end up living with mom and a screaming baby. Even young couples who forged successful marriages apparently enjoyed only meager happiness, especially the wife. In *Marriage Is a Partnership* (1951) newlywed Dottie

51

Joe ignores his homework to ponder a possible lifemate
in *Choosing Your Marriage Partner,* 1952.

spends all her time in the kitchen, learns to enjoy eating liver because her husband likes it, and is elated when he drags a finger through her cake icing. "Believe me, a wife *does* appreciate her husband's appreciation."

The great outpouring of mental hygiene dating and marriage films ended by 1958. Only occasional stragglers appeared thereafter, usually sponsored by businesses (who only used them as a cover for product promotion) and churches. A new crisis had arisen in October 1957—the launch of Sputnik and the apparent technological superiority of the Soviet Union—that demanded the attention of America's educational film producers. Dating films were shunted to a back burner and the rapidly changing social climate of the 1960s ensured that they would stay there. Culturally defunct, hopelessly hokey, they were the least adaptable of all mental hygiene films. Like dinosaurs, they became extinct.

"If a girl doesn't dress right—the way everyone else is dressing—
well, she's just out. She might as well be dead!"
—TEEN-AGE GIRLS (1945)

GIRLS ONLY

Mental hygiene filmmakers knew what they liked: teenagers who were polite, clean, and just like everyone else. An important part of this—50 percent, in fact—was defining the social limits of girls. Of course, mental hygiene films never identified the goal as limitation; they simply stressed that women were better at certain things than men: cooking, caring for children, organizing things, listening and understanding, appreciating beauty, being supportive. These skills—sometimes recast as the pleasant-sounding "talents for living"—encompassed the whole of a woman's world. The development of these talents was the proper focus of her energies. The idea that women might have other priorities—business, politics, ambition, leadership—never intruded.

World War II transformed women into a threat to the established order by giving them freedoms and equality with men unmatched in American history. Over six million women had entered the work force during the war. No longer just secretaries, floorwalkers, and switchboard operators, they built tanks, wore slacks, and were guaranteed equal pay for equal work by the federal government (although the federal government rarely gave women work equal to men—and hence rarely had to make good its promise—and private industry did not offer the same guarantee). Women also made up more than half the student population on college campuses.

This state of affairs was tolerable to a male-run society during a global holocaust, but it quickly disappeared with the war's end. The proportion of female students in college shrank to less than a third. Women were fired from their jobs and replaced by returning servicemen. Both Washington and the major trade unions supported the turnover; there were, after

In *Treasures for the Making* (1951) Susan finds all the satisfaction she needs by cooking jelly.

53

all, only so many jobs to go around. Women were expected to return to their roles as housewives and mothers. Girls were expected to be better-trained versions of exactly the same thing, and films were expected to help make that possible.

The Woman Speaks, a series of news-reels produced from 1945 through 1947, set a baseline of behavior. Worthy examples of American womanhood were show-cased, including the mayor of Portsmouth, New Hampshire ("an efficient and pleas-ant woman in public office"), members of the Chicago Water Ballet, the first woman in twenty-five years to hold the World Profes-sional Typing Championship, a "moulder of lifelike dogs," and the Northwestern Uni-versity Marimba Co-eds. Selected subjects from this series were shown by the U.S. War Department in Germany, Austria, Japan, and Korea to help explain woman's role in a progressive democracy.

This was as good as it got. The lady mayor of Portsmouth may have proved useful in overseas public relations, but no mental hygiene film encouraged American girlhood to follow in her footsteps. More typical was the role presented in *American Women: Partners in Research* (1960), in which the "partnership" extends only to offering suggestions for improvements in a proposed coffee percolator.

"Be considerate of your employer." *Office Etiquette* (1950) uses women as examples of bad employees who snack and make personal telephone calls on the job.

Classroom films bombarded bobby-soxers with similar messages of domesticity and subordination. A few exam-ples: In *A Date with Your Family* (1950) "Daughter" is expected, apparently every day, to help cook a multicourse dinner, set an elaborate table, and then change into something "festive" to look "more charming." "Brother" is left free to study. In *Social-Sex Attitudes in Adolescence* (1953) teenaged Bob drinks beer in a speeding car, gropes a girl in the backseat, yet escapes criti-cism, while teenaged Mary is shown fending off similar advances and is mocked by the narrator when she attempts to "be more sophisticated than

> "He may originate the ideas to be communicated, but she is the one who specializes in putting those communications into permanent and perfect form."
>
> —TAKE A LETTER...FROM A TO Z (1967)

she actually is." In *Tell It Like It Is* (1968), a vocational guidance film, boys are groomed as salesmen and future executives while girls learn to design store windows and operate a cash register. In *Men of Tomorrow* (1962) the "future leaders" of West Virginia are bussed to an exclusive retreat where they learn political prowess. No girls are invited.

Girls were not supposed to bother with leadership, since they had their own practical skills to learn—limited to the area of "home engineering" and the vocations of secretary, receptionist, and stenographer. *Office Courtesy: Meeting the Public* (1953), *Duties of a Secretary* (1947), *Take a Letter...From A to Z* (1967) encouraged girls to be tactful, courteous, poised, alert, personable, efficient, prompt, neat, and orderly. The idea of career growth was nowhere to be found; a job was just a way to earn a living until a girl found a husband and moved on to her proper role of home engineer. The prevailing sentiment, bluntly expressed in *All about the Fair Sex* (1968)—a film made for men, not women—was that "Boys go out to work while girls stay home and go shopping."

Staying home and going shopping, however, were far from simple tasks—at least according to mental hygiene films. The role of home engineer and purchasing agent—much more so than that of the outside wage earner—was cloaked in a mantle of serious study. "If I'm gonna be a homemaker the rest of my life, I want to know what I'm doing!" cries teenaged Janice in *Why Study Home Economics?* (1955). This view was serviced by films about sewing (*Zip Zip Hooray*, 1949), decorating (*Color Keying in Art and Living*, 1950), and cooking (*Techniques of Food Measurement*, 1955). The fast pace of modern life, the wonderland of new gadgets in the home, and the abundant variety of consumer choices in the postwar world could not be entrusted to unschooled girls.*

Kay and her lampshade. A reflective moment from *The Home Economics Story*.

Films sounded the clarion call of education in productions such as *The Home Economics Story* (1951), in which college freshman Kay learns how to

---

*Curiously, films made for adult women took the exact opposite approach, stressing how brainless and effortless homemaking could be with the appliances of the sponsoring companies.

prepare cream of tomato soup in her applied chemistry class, and *Treasures for the Making* (1951), in which home ec major Susan is shocked by sister Ellen's opinion that homemaking requires "no great demand for talent or brains." "Does Bill know he's marrying a can opener instead of a wife?" Susan retorts and goes on to illustrate her point

> "The women of this family seem to feel that they owe it to the men of the family to look relaxed, rested, and attractive at dinner time."
>
> —A DATE WITH YOUR FAMILY (1950)

with a twenty-minute lecture on jelly preparation. In *Why Study Home Economics?* young women peer at cloth swatches through microscopes and stretch them on a mechanical rack. "Present-day textiles," the home ec teacher cautions, "cannot be judged with confidence just by casual examination."

Social skills were considered—after the role of wife and mother—a woman's most important contribution to society. Entire films were made addressing subjects such as personal appearance, public rituals, dealing with men, and the sad consequences if rigidly distinct gender roles were allowed to blur.

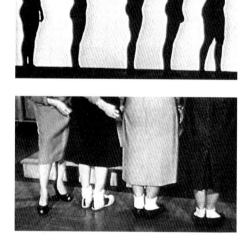

Body types and skirt lengths are carefully studied in *Clothes and You*, 1954.

Poise, charm, and the self-discipline necessary to make them automatic were stressed in *Fit and Fair* (1945), *Sitting Right* (1946), and *Posture* (1961), while "appropriate" dress was the focus of *How to Be Well Groomed* (1948). *Good Grooming for Girls* (1956) pushed clean underwear and nail polish "that's not too bright." The social agenda behind *Making the Most of Your Face* (1958) is evident in its title; in *Body Care and Grooming* (1947) the narrator tells a sloppily dressed teen, "You aren't exactly the type to make this guy act like a human being." She instantly becomes attractive to the same young man after she tucks in her blouse and pulls up her droopy socks.

Although a bobbysoxer in *Teen-Age Girls* (1945) asserts, "The most important thing for a girl is being popular with the other girls," the makers of mental hygiene films disagreed. The true benchmark of success in girls-only classroom films was a boyfriend. Girl-to-girl relationships were often depicted as vicious (*Social Acceptability*, 1957), vengeful (*The Gossip*, 1955), and cruel (*Habit Patterns*, 1954). *The Way to a Man's Heart* (1945), a home ec film sponsored by the livestock industry, shows dour Jane Heywood landing her man after ditching her eyeglasses and developing a flair for cooking

Jane successfully woos her professor by downplaying her brains
and uplifting her bosom. *The Way to a Man's Heart.*

"variety meats." *More Dates for Kay* (1952)—perhaps the most disturbed
film ever made for teenaged girls—takes the position that social happiness
is unattainable without constant male companionship. No task is too menial,
no approach too degrading if it can eliminate "dating slumps." Kay's schem-
ing, groveling, and bulldog tenacity are held up as examples of "letting the
boys know you're around" and provide her with "a long list of dating
prospects."

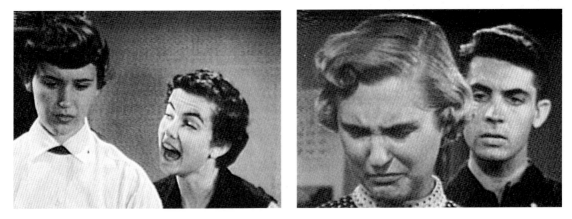

No sisterhood here. Frieda spreads misery among her weak-willed gender in *The Gossip.*

57

Once a boyfriend was hooked, however, it was a maiden's responsibility to set the limits of behavior. As the narrator states plainly in *Are You Popular?* (1947), "Girls who park in cars are *not* really popular." In *How Much Affection?* (1957) Mary bursts into tears when she describes how she nearly succumbed to temptation in a lover's lane: "We were so *close*." In *Toward Emotional Maturity* (1954) Sally recognizes that "it isn't always easy to think things out in the heat of the moment" and tells her prom date to take her home. But not all girls were as mature as Mary and Sally, and the consequences of premarital nooky could be brutal. Ginny, the parking girl in *Are You Popular?*, is shunned afterward in the school cafeteria by everyone, even by "the boys she parks with." (Although, to be honest, Ginny seems not to care.) Betty in *The Innocent Party* (1959) yields to her boyfriend's desire and ends up with syphilis. Ethel in *Name Unknown* (1951) thinks she's "too sophisticated for boys her own age," allows herself to be picked up by a guy with a car, and is raped on a lonely back road. Similarly, Mary in *Girls Beware* (1961) submits to the will of a truck-driving jarhead she meets at a hamburger stand. A few months later, the narrator says remorsefully, "She had to tell her parents. But now it was too late for advice."

EIGHTEEN ENLIGHTENING FEMALE FILMS

Clothes and You: Line and Proportion

Girls Beware

Good Grooming for Girls

The Gossip

The Home Economics Story

It's Wonderful Being a Girl

Let's Give a Tea

Molly Grows Up

More Dates for Kay

Name Unknown

Office Etiquette

The Story of Menstruation

Take a Letter: From A to Z

Teen Togs

Teen-Age Girls

Treasures for the Making

The Way to a Man's Heart

Why Study Home Economics?

"Why not?" Ethel (right) is about to suffer for her relaxed attitude toward men in *Name Unknown*.

The most legendary girls-only films are those about menstruation. Like all films addressing basic human sexuality before 1970, they were less common than is generally remembered, primarily because no American educational film producer would touch the subject. *Educational Screen* tried to put some backbone into the industry by touting the classroom film as "the ideal medium to impart sound information and to develop a wholesome mental attitude concern-

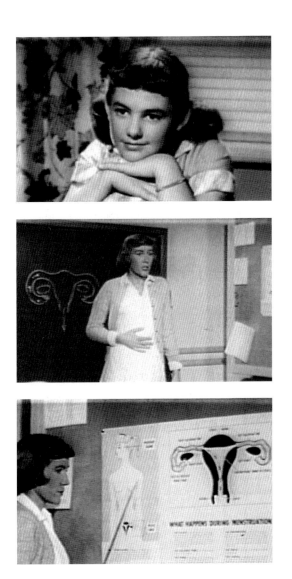

Same subject, different styles.
Miss Jensen uses diagrams and charts
to teach a rapt twelve-year-old in
Molly Grows Up, while *The Story of
Menstruation* employs Disney animation
and a lengthy list of do's and don'ts.

ing this function." Among its positive attributes, *Educational Screen* pointed out, "It is impersonal. It is run in a darkened room which prevents embarrassment. Furthermore, a trained commentator speaks from the screen without self-consciousness."

Nevertheless, no American instructional film producer took the bait, which left the field open to manufacturers of tampons and sanitary napkins. Kotex was first into the fray with *The Story of Menstruation* (1946); Modess responded with *Molly Grows Up* (1953) and *It's Wonderful Being a Girl* (1960). Booklets describing each manufacturer's products were distributed during each film, transforming personal hygiene education into a sales pitch. Product placements in the films helped things along as well. Mom holds up a napkin in *It's Wonderful Being a Girl* and explains, "See this blue polyethylene on the side? That's a special moisture-proof shield."

The lead actors in menstruation films are always perky, attractive, and downright joyous about the new routine that had entered their lives. "Mom, guess what? I started my first period!" Molly tells her mother cheerfully, echoing her film's position that "growing up is fun." Negative attitudes are dismissed as old-fashioned. Supporting characters—moms and school nurses—are always present to caution Molly or Mary or Libby against strenuous dancing or "anything that bounces you around a lot" and to encourage spirited use of the sponsor's feminine-hygiene products. The disposal problems created by such energetic consumption were never addressed in American films, although the English film *Growing Girls* (1949) recommended that its viewers save their soiled napkins and burn them in the kitchen stove.

> **"You *can* have fun while you're menstruating!"**
> —IT'S WONDERFUL BEING A GIRL (1960)

"Take a trip from Squaresville. Get with the countdown.
Shake this square world and blast off for Kicksville."
—NARCOTICS: PIT OF DESPAIR (1967)

DRUGS

Mental hygiene drug films—that is, any drug film made before 1970 for classroom viewing—bloomed in a shadow world. Very little was written about them in the educational literature of the time. Like films about menstruation, they were shunned by the large educational film producers, which meant the field was left open to obscure independents such as Larry Frisch, Alan Kingsbaugh, and David W. Parker, who don't seem to have produced much else besides drug films. Apparently the mainstream considered drug abuse too messy to discuss and too fringe to be profitable.

That, of course, did not stop mental hygiene drug films from being made, sometimes with amazing results. Given the perceived evil nature of their foe and a general lack of hard facts, school drug film producers were able to stretch the truth—and sometimes ignore it entirely—as long as what they created showed drugs in a bad light. Thus was nurtured, for example, the "crazed weedhead" character, played in *Drug Addiction* (1951) by a stoner who laughs hysterically as he cuts his mouth to ribbons drinking from a broken Pepsi bottle, or in *Marijuana* (1968) by a guy who looks in a mirror and sees his face replaced by a rubber monster mask. Another popular horror was the "time-bomb-in-the-brain acid flashback" that occurs at inconve-

nient moments in films such as *Trip to Where* (1968) and *Curious Alice* (1969). Acid trippers are also prone to staring at the sun until they go blind (*LSD-25*, 1967) and running into traffic because they "believe they are God" (*Drugs and the Nervous System*, 1972).

Sensationalizing drug use in films was nothing new. Hollywood had used morphine and opium addiction as lurid plot devices since the nineteen-teens. Marijuana took center stage in the 1930s in films such as

End of the line for another know-it-all teen. *The Pill Poppers,* 1971.

61

"Why do you think they call it 'dope'?" Sonny Bono's laid-back delivery and lamé suit provide some unintended laughs in *Marijuana,* 1968.

Reefer Madness and *Marijuana: Weed with Roots in Hell,* but these were commercial movies that were never shown in classrooms—something that cult cinema devotees often aren't aware of today—as was true also of 1960s LSD exploitation films such as *The Trip* and *Psych-Out.* What's astonishing about mental hygiene drug films is that they were advertised as objective and instructional, yet they were often indistinguishable from their melodramatic, profit-driven theatrical brethren. The gut fear of drugs, deeply rooted over many decades, had produced a mythology so pervasive that the image shapers seem to have believed it themselves.

> "I'm one with the universe!
> I'm God and Jesus!"
> —TRIP TO WHERE (1968)

Youth in Crisis (1943) was probably the first "educational" film to show teenage drug use (i.e., pot smoking), but only briefly as an incidental part of its horrors of modern life montage. The earliest known mental hygiene drug films designed specifically for classroom use that supposedly met rigorous standards of educational content were films such as *The Terrible Truth* and

One of acid's most horrifying hallucinations showcased in *Trip to Where?*

Pot, heroin, withdrawal, happy ending. Early drug films like *The Terrible Truth* crammed a lot of melodrama into ten minutes.

H: The Story of a Teen-Age Drug Addict (both 1951), which featured dramatic stories of the decline (marijuana), fall (heroin), and resurrection (clean and sober) of misguided teens, the whole drama unfolding over a period of a few weeks. It's unlikely that these were shown anywhere outside the most progressive, urban schools, and then only to carefully chosen audiences as a kind of shock therapy.

Producers and distributors of these early films probably expected nothing more. Drug use outside the cities was virtually unknown; to most Americans of the time, the word *drug* brought penicillin to mind. It wasn't until the introduction of pill tranquilizers in the mid-1950s—an aseptic, easily concealed delivery system—that recreational drugs began to find favor among the suburban and middle class. The earliest mental hygiene drug film to show teenaged "pill poppers" was probably *Seduction of the Innocent* (1961); until then it had all been about reefers and horse in gritty downtown

"A person that has to cop out on drugs, a person that has to escape, can't face reality, can't face his problems, this person is emotionally weak. They have a psychological problem."
—KEEP OFF THE GRASS (1970)

"Turn on! Tune out of the rat race and its square problems!" A bemused Tom watches helplessly as his glassy-eyed friends smoke pot and suffer "wholesale abandonment of goals and ambitions."

settings such as in *Subject: Narcotics* (1951) and *Monkey on the Back* (1955). Because mental hygiene drug films were typically urban centered, they are one of the few places in early 1950s education where blacks appear.

Most mental hygiene drug films promote two major themes: 1) drug use is a character flaw, entirely the fault of spineless users; 2) pot smokers end up either as acid casualties or heroin junkies. Both loosely fall under the definition of what the late author Gerald Klerman called pharmacological Calvinism: "A general distrust of drugs used for nontherapeutic purposes, and a conviction that if a drug makes you feel good, it must be morally bad." Mental hygiene drug films exploited this relentlessly, showing teenaged users invariably being stripped of their "moral fiber" and sinking to a life of theft, prostitution, and the corruption of ever-younger victims in their lust for kicks.

> "I couldn't see anything except *colors* and I thought this was supposed to be reality but it wasn't! It wasn't anything except *things* that weren't *objects!*"
>
> —LSD-25 (1967)

The "stealing from mom's purse" scene, featured in *Narcotics: Pit of Despair* (1967), *Assassin of Youth* (1957), *Narcotic Evils* (1955), and many others, usually marks the beginning of the end.

This approach to visual guidance education, more akin to a 1930s gangster movie than *Dating: Do's and Don'ts,* ended abruptly in the mid-1960s and was replaced by an approach that was radically different, although no more insightful. In this new wave of films, LSD became the ultimate evil. Heroin was shunted to the background.* The locale shifted from the city to the suburbs. Drug use was no longer blamed on urban decay and poverty; it was a willful act of generational rebellion and, ironically, fitting in. Ominous bongos and twangy sitars fill the music tracks, handheld cameras dip and weave amid beatifically smiling teenagers at pot parties, and characters "rap" to the camera and each other about the relative merits of the drug experience. "It's a groovy way of relaxing," says one teen in *Keep Off the Grass* (1970). "It's like John Glenn trying to explain what he saw in outer space," says another in *LSD-25* (1967). But this

---

*Heroin did not, however, disappear. The film *Scag* (1972) showed that heroin use was thriving among inner-city blacks. But *Scag* was a rare exception. The profitable market for drug films was well-funded suburban school districts, where the principal bugaboos were LSD, pills, and pot, pot, pot.

TEN FAVORITE DRUG FILMS

Don't Smoke Pot

Drug Addiction

H: The Story of a Teen-Age Drug Addict

Keep Off the Grass

LSD-25

Marijuana

Narcotics: Pit of Despair

Seduction of the Innocent

The Terrible Truth

Trip to Where

Belting booze in *None for the Road,* 1957, and sniffing glue in *Drug Abuse: The Chemical Tomb,* 1969. As the years passed, drug abuse films used harder drugs and younger abusers to unsettle their audiences.

new breed of drug film was just new packaging surrounding the same old carefully scripted approach. The quotes were fake; the groovy camera work was imitative technique.

The really odd thing about mental hygiene drug films is that their know-it-all attitude allowed no room for error. If any kids who watched them ever did use drugs, even pot, they'd realize that the alarmist position taken by these films was based on myth, not fact.

Attempts to curb drug use through moving images continue to this day, although scientific data and appeals to reason have supplanted horror stories. But the message seems no more advanced than it was in 1951, when the narrator of *The Terrible Truth* concluded, "The answer is a simple one." A title card appears on the screen. It reads, innocently, GOOD SENSE.

SEX EDUCATION

Sex ed mental hygiene films are about plumbing, not sex. They were rarely seen outside of senior biology class. Most are dull. *Your Body during Adolescence* (1953) is typical: ten minutes of blotchy outline art of male and female bodies, an abstract monologue on the process of fertilization, and a lot of dry information about hormones and endocrine glands. Nothing at all about sexual intercourse, which is not surprising, since sexual intercourse was something that teenagers were not supposed to know about. *Wonder of Reproduction* (1961) ignores humans altogether, instead favoring the parallel example provided by Uncle Bob's aquarium of Egyptian mouthbreeders, which undoubtedly confused a lot of kids. The basic formula is the same no matter what decade the film was made in: *In the Beginning* (1937), *Human Growth* (1947), *You're Growing Up* (1956), and *A New Human Life* (1968) all hint at something larger though none explain it.

There were, of course, a few quirky exceptions. *Social-Sex Attitudes in Adolescence* (1953), a film intended for parents, not kids, includes a scene where Mom discovers a crude drawing of her son and his girlfriend on the couch, naked. "(Bob & Betty) WOW!!" reads the caption. However, it's clear that the drawing depicts a

A liberal teacher explains sex to six-year-olds in *Human Beginnings,* 1950. The painting at bottom is supposed to depict a pregnant woman.

67

Bob's leg-locked fantasy girl in
Social-Sex Attitudes in Adolescence.

boyish fantasy, not a fond memory. *As Boys Grow...* (1957) is a true oddity, a sex ed film in which members of a track team get to hammer their coach with blunt questions about wet dreams and sperm. It was shot in San Francisco on a shoestring budget by the same company that produced an even more liberal film, *Human Beginnings* (1950), shot in New York City. This latter production caused a furor when released because it showed breast feeding and featured adults explaining childbirth to six-year-olds ("The baby comes out through this opening, called the vagina"). While both of these films make entertaining viewing today, they are wildly atypical of their time, and their progressive producers never even hinted at the possibility of teenage sex.

The beast with two backs was openly acknowledged in only one group of films during the mental hygiene years—films about syphilis. This bleak marriage of sex and disease was justified with the following syllogism: Sex outside of marriage was wrong; teenagers were not supposed to be married;

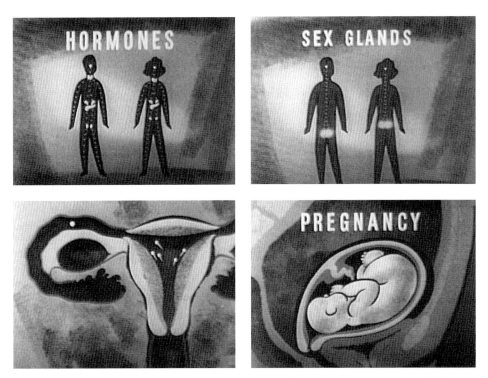

Bing, bang, boom. Few films have made sex as unappealing as *Your Body during Adolescence.*

therefore any teenager who had sex was probably not married and was certainly wrong. Syphilis merely served as a club to pound home the message that sex between teenagers was s-i-n-f-u-l. It produced symptoms that were terrible, often disgustingly visceral (a real plus for a visual teaching aid), and at first invisible. Films exploited this by implying that it was only during the

Coach Douglas in *As Boys Grow...* spells it out for his curious track team.

earliest, asymptomatic stage that syphilis was curable (which is not true). The message was clear: even if teenagers had sex and felt fine, their bodies might still carry a deadly disease. They either had to tell an adult whenever they had sex, or they had to abstain.

> "Oh...you want to know about sexual intercourse? Well, that happens like this...the erect penis enters here...."
>
> —AS BOYS GROW...(1957)

Certainly syphilis is a disease no one should take lightly. But the choice of syphilis as a poster plague to fight the war against teen sex is curious, considering that no mental hygiene teenage VD films were scripted around gonorrhea, which was seven times more prevalent than syphilis but has less terrifying symptoms. And of course there was a simple way for teens to have sex during these years and drastically reduce their chance of catching syphilis: condoms. But they were never mentioned.

The first syphilis films were produced for servicemen as far back as World War I. The Second World War unleashed the disease on a new generation, and mental hygiene producers unleashed syphilis films on new audiences: GIs (*Sex Hygiene*, 1941), educated liberals (*To the People of the United States*, 1944), blacks (*Feeling All Right*, 1949). There was even a precocious syphilis film, *The Invader* (1954), that treated the disease as old news and boasted, "The end of VD as a peril is now in sight!" But syphilis infection rates grew steadily despite the widespread availability of penicillin. Teenagers—horny, condomless, and obviously ill informed by classroom biology films—were spreading the bug. It's perhaps not coincidental that the first known syphilis film aimed directly at teens, *The Innocent Party*, was released in 1959, the same year that the first highway safety gore

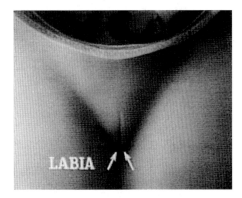

LABIA

Human Reproduction (1947) has many helpful illustrations.

"I got some sort of sore—down *there*."

"You get it through your head that you're dealing with a deadly disease! Not some common cold or a case of the chicken pox...."

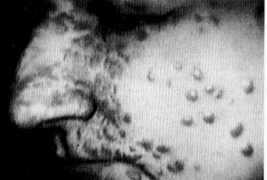

"Syphilis can cripple you, blind you, destroy your brain."

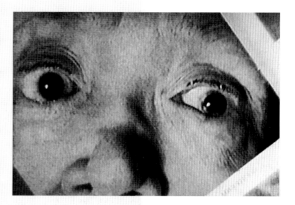

"She'll never know until it's too late. She goes insane or becomes a hopeless cripple...."

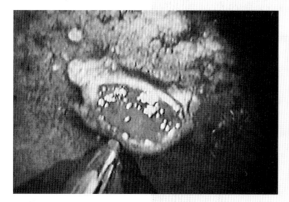

DOCTOR: "These germs enter the body when you have sexual intercourse. They burrow into the skin...."

DON: "Boy, that's pretty awful looking."

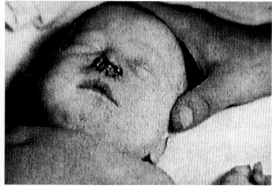

"Look at this baby. Its mother infected it before it was born—because she had syphilis and didn't get treated...."

Syphilis films made it their business to portray sex as upleasantly as possible.
Few did the job with such aplomb as *The Innocent Party*.

70

film, *Signal 30*, reached the classroom. Old cautions no longer deterred the young. The calamity bar had to be raised.

**FIVE FAVORITE
SEX ED FILMS**

As Boys Grow...

Dance, Little Children

Human Beginnings

The Innocent Party

Sex Hygiene

The Innocent Party and *Dance, Little Children* (1961), both sponsored by the Kansas State Board of Health, featured virtuous maidens who became infected by sex-crazed dates. Both films took the position that teenagers—boys and girls alike—were lusty automatons who would go over the brink when outside stimuli went too far. A warm night, a convertible, and a John Wayne movie were the root of disaster in *The Innocent Party;* in *Dance, Little Children* it was a succession of spicy lingerie ads, pulp novel covers, and bad surf-rock music. "Who is to blame," the narrator of the latter film asks, "if they respond to what an anxiety-ridden world seems to be telling them?"

Nevertheless, once the deed was done the sledgehammer of social condemnation came down swift and hard. Lynne in *Dance, Little Children* contracts syphilis and is later cured, but the narrator remarks that "she may never be free of its emotional consequences." Pete in *Where the Girls Are*

"You've never had a girl before.
I could make you happy...." Jim falls for
smooth Luanna and adds several links to the
chain of infection in *Summer of '63.*

"You have syphilis, Jim."

"I couldn't!"

"We'll have to get your parents' consent."

"Oh, you're kidding!"

An unintentionally suggestive frame from
Meaning of Adolescence, 1953.

(1969) has to break off his engagement to his high school sweetheart because "You can't promise a girl like Julie you'll be true to her and show up with a case of syphilis." Don and Betty are so sickened by sadness in *The Innocent Party* that through most of the film they look as if they are suffering from intestinal cramps. "You took a risk by doing something that society condemns," the school doctor explains as the two former lovers grimace, eyes downcast. "Perhaps you didn't realize some of the penalties involved."

In the end, it made little difference. However well received these films may have been by adults (both *The Innocent Party* and *Dance, Little Children* won numerous awards), their message of extramarital chastity was ignored by their target audience. By the early 1970s reported cases of syphilis and gonorrhea were at their highest level since the introduction of antibiotics.

BLOODY HIGHWAYS

Highway safety films are a durable genre in mental hygiene. They were in classrooms before menstruation films, dating films, LSD films, fitting-in films, and they outlasted them all. A few classic titles were still being shown in schools into the 1990s.

Highway safety films are also the bad cop of mental hygiene. They are the only genre that grew not more refined and sympathetic as the years passed, but cruder and more brutal.

Like most areas of mental hygiene, highway safety is a broader field than most people remember. Highway safety films were made for kids (*Dick Wakes Up; The Talking Car*), pedestrians (*When You Are a Pedestrian; Dead Right*), bicyclists (*The Bicycle Clown; Drive Your Bicycle*), and adults (*Fatal Seconds; Driven to Kill*). A whole subgenre was devoted to the evils of drunk driving (*Alco-Beat; The Bottle and the Throttle*), another to school bus safety

Virtual reality, 1954. Drive-o-Trainer classes were the carrot of teenage highway safety education. The stick was mental hygiene shock films.

73

(*Priceless Cargo; Safety on the School Bus*), and a third to slow-motion footage of test dummies crashing (*Crash and Live; Safety Belt for Susie*). There were also mental hygiene films for teenagers that were not shocking but merely conformist and coercive (*Tomorrow's Drivers; Jaycee Teen Age Road-E-O*), which is typical of most guidance films of that period.

But these are not the highway safety films that most people remember.

What people remember are films such as *Highways of Agony* (1969), which opens with an artfully composed shot of a shoe, a wrecked truck, and a pile of human meat on asphalt. Or *Mechanized Death* (1961), whose opening sequence, complete with audio, is of a dying woman hacking up blood as a pair of state troopers pry her from a wrecked car. Or, going way back, *Last Date* (1950), which was promoted with the teaser: "What is Teen-a-cide? See *Last Date*...see how!"

How did things get so weird?

It helps to understand that the roads really were deadly in the heyday of highway safety films, although not only because of teenaged drivers. Traffic engineering had remained dormant since the 1920s, when cars were slow and scarce. Poles, rocks, trees, and ditches lay just off the shoulder, if there was a shoulder. Passing lanes were rare, curves sharp, and guard rails had blunt ends that skewered anyone unfortunate enough to hit them head on.

If you hit something, you would probably die, for there were no air bags, shoulder belts, and very, very few seat belts in cars. There were no roll bars, headrests, antilock brakes, child safety

Six-year-olds demonstrate that "bad driving habits are childish" in *Tomorrow's Drivers,* 1954.

Susie is safe, but the other dummies are not, in *Safety Belt for Susie*, 1962.

seats, or "crumple zones." Steering wheels were rigid steel and would crush your chest on impact if you weren't impaled on the steering column. Many people were killed simply by being thrown through the windshield or out of doors that easily sprang open. Worse still were the older cars on the road, the kind frequently driven by teenagers—jalopies that were made before the war, little more than motorized coffins even by the lax standards of the day.

Detroit blamed the carnage on poor highway design and "the nut behind the wheel." No one blamed Detroit, even as it crammed bigger, more powerful engines into its all-steel behemoths every year. Styling and performance sold cars. No American automobile manufacturer had a safety department.

In this uneven world, where minor auto accidents were often fatal and the driver shouldered all the responsibility, highway safety films flourished. Their purpose varied: those sponsored by insurance companies and the auto industry tried to shift blame onto drivers; those produced by independents tried to provide a media counterbalance to Detroit's siren song of power and speed. The inability of either to meet these objectives eventually drove them to extremes never seen in classroom films before or since.

Teenagers were dragged into the bloody battle in 1949. The lightweight overhead-valve "rocket" V-8 engine debuted that year; teenaged boys dropped them into heaps to turn them into hot rods. It is perhaps no coincidence that highway fatalities jumped 20 percent in 1950, or that the focus of highway safety films

75

shifted that year from the vague "reckless driver" to the specific "thoughtlessness of youth," i.e., the teenager.

Last Date was the film that did it, the first classroom film to brand teens as a highway menace. It was sponsored by an insurance company, and it touched a nerve. *Last Date* told the story of Nick, a teenaged sociopath (played with gusto by twenty-two-year-old Dick York) whose uncooperative philosophy of driving ("Just give 'em the horn and make 'em get out of the way!") leads to a bloody end. By portraying teenagers as thrill-crazed maniacs, the film offered the public a familiar and acceptable scapegoat. *Last Date* was enthusiastically supported by business interests, who saw to it that the film played in downtown theaters as well as in classrooms and high school gymnasiums. It was reportedly seen by three million people in its first eight months of release. *Business Screen*, the print organ of the business film industry, was so impressed with *Last Date*'s success that it ran an entire special section on highway safety films. "It is to the everlasting credit of the industry," the magazine cheered, "that it has helped hold down the toll of needless sacrifice caused by the indifferent drivers as well as the maniacs of speed."

More crash-test-dummy mayhem.
The Automobile-Pedestrian Collision, 1966.

"It is appalling how much that is awful can suddenly be packed into such little pieces of time."
—FATAL SECONDS (1948)

Actually, *Last Date* and subsequent other similar-minded films such as *Borrowed Power* (1951), *Car Theft* (1956), and *What Made Sammy Speed?* (1957) did little or nothing to stem the carnage on the roads. Death tolls continued to climb as engine horsepower increased. That relationship was ignored; new scapegoats were sought. "Permissive" education was the next target. Accidents continued to happen, the argument went, because teenagers no longer believed the predictable shocks delivered by highway safety films. A tough new approach was needed.

It came in 1958.

As often happens, the idea blossomed independently in the minds of two very different people. One was Budge Crawley, who owned a family-run

Jeanne's pretty face is about to meet Mr. Windshield in *Last Date* (above). The result, however, is left to the viewer's imagination—as is the bloody end suffered by the protagonist in *What Made Sammy Speed?* That line of discretion would soon be crossed.

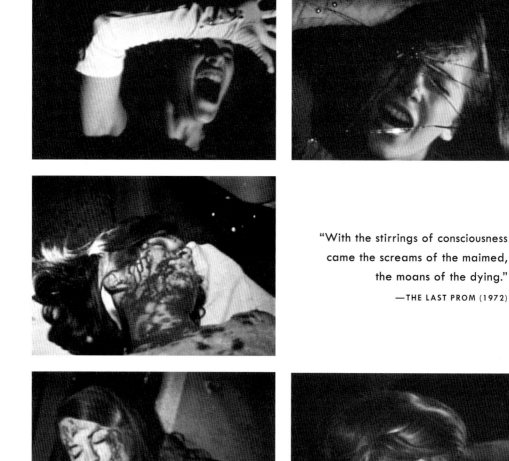

"With the stirrings of consciousness
came the screams of the maimed,
the moans of the dying."

—THE LAST PROM (1972)

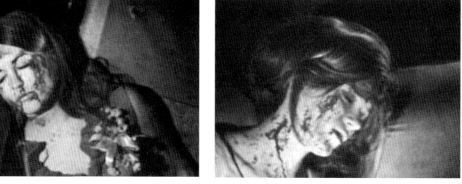

More pretty girls, less tact. By 1972's *Last Prom,* gore had become
an accepted staple of highway safety shock films.

production house in Ottawa, Canada, that had made several classic mental
hygiene films in the preceding ten years (e.g., *Age of Turmoil; Is This Love?;
Social Acceptability*). By the late 1950s Crawley films had developed a distinct depressing quality, so perhaps it's not surprising that Budge Crawley—who reportedly later went insane and killed himself—was the first to
insert footage of a real accident scene in a highway safety movie. The result
was *Safety or Slaughter* (1958), the first educational gore film. "I'd like to

show you a few statistics," says the deadpan narrator as the camera pans a wreck littered with bodies. "That man is a statistic. So is that girl."

The other person who had this idea was Richard Wayman from Cleveland, Ohio, a partner in the prestigious accounting firm of Ernst & Ernst (later Ernst & Young) and an extremely puzzling character. He lacked the filmmaking talents of Budge Crawley, but the films he would make didn't require talent. What they required was single-minded determination, and Wayman apparently had plenty.

According to his business partner, Earle Deems, Wayman became interested in highway safety after a friend was killed in a car crash. Wayman's job required him to drive frequently between Cleveland and Columbus, the state capital, so he had a police scanner installed in his car, tossed a camera in the backseat, and began snapping pictures of auto accidents and victims whenever he heard of one nearby. The resulting labor of love was assembled into a highway safety slide presentation that he distributed free of charge to every state trooper post in Ohio.

"The stuff out on the highway was shot by [freelance] cameramen. I appreciated that because I shook so bad it would be hell if I ever shot anything without a tripod."

"My wife went out on some of them... we'd get a phone call, ten o'clock at night — or later. Often I'd go with her. I really never did much, but sometimes I would be corralled into helping the troopers. I remember one particularly that was only a few miles out. There were four people killed in this car; it was a head-on accident. There were two mammoth, big women in the backseat that were killed. And the trooper asked me to help him. I wasn't accustomed to that kind of stuff, you know."

"We had some of them that were just so bad we couldn't even imagine putting them in a film. They were just that bad."

"Some of these films that I directed, they didn't take much to direct. You don't need a director to tell the ambulance people to get the victims out."

—Earle Deems

The police were impressed. One of the patrol superintendents learned that Wayman also owned a 16mm motion picture camera and reportedly asked, "Did you ever think about making a movie?" Apparently Wayman hadn't, but the idea appealed to him. Although one would think by now he had seen enough dead bodies to last a lifetime, Dick Wayman, who earned an estimated $300,000 a year, bought another movie camera and gave it to a newspaper reporter he'd met at accident scenes. Between the two, and with contributions from troopers who had filmed the aftermath of bloody accidents on the Ohio Turnpike, he spliced together a thirty-minute film, joining its segments with a narration of broad injunctions—"Death is forever"—and lurid descriptions—"His occasional moments of semiconsciousness are filled with agonizing screams." He titled the film *Signal 30*, the Ohio State Highway Patrol's code for death on the highway, and released it in 1959.

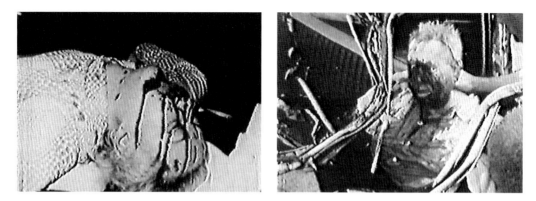

Real-life dead people were the stars of *Signal 30*, the first highway safety gore film.

"You are there when stark tragedy strikes," bragged *Signal 30*'s brochure copy. "It is an ugly film. It is meant to be. It is designed to drive home to those who see it that an accident is not pretty." The brochure playfully noted that the film was shot "in living (and dying) color."

> "Almost every bone in his body is broken. He is very, very dead."
>
> —SIGNAL 30 (1959)

Whether or not *Signal 30* was an instant hit (accounts vary), it did win an award from the National Safety Council—and it had the full endorsement of the Ohio State Highway Patrol. Encouraged, Wayman pressed on. He organized a production company, Safety Enterprises, Inc., and a nonprofit corporation, the Highway Safety Foundation (HSF), hired a staff, and solicited submissions from more freelance cameramen and -women. There was no shortage of material; footage rolled in. In 1961 a second thirty-minute film, *Mechanized Death*, was released, which added live audio to the horrible visuals thanks to some of Wayman's freelancers who carried tape recorders. A third film, *Wheels of Tragedy*, followed in 1963, in which local dinner theater performers reenacted the mistakes of victims up until the accident scene gore footage took over.

Wayman had picked an auspicious moment to begin his crusade. The 1960s turned out to be highway safety's bloodiest decade, with Detroit—beginning in 1964—cramming 400-horsepower engines into compacts and marketing them as "muscle" cars. The death toll skyrocketed. So did sales of Dick Wayman's films. (By the early 1970s Safety Enterprises boasted that its films had been seen by

TEN CLASSIC HIGHWAY SAFETY FILMS

Highways of Agony

Last Date

The Last Prom

Mechanized Death

Options to Live

Red Asphalt

Safety or Slaughter

Signal 30

What Made Sammy Speed?

Wheels of Tragedy

forty million people.) Proponents of visual education, never fans of Wayman's work, quietly admitted that the artlessness and barf-bag realism of Wayman's films might be the only effective way to send cautionary messages to a generation that seemed hell-bent for highway anarchy.

What the kids really needed, of course, was safer cars. They finally got them thanks to Ralph Nader, not Dick Wayman. Nader's 1965 book, *Unsafe at Any Speed*, exposed the deadly design of Detroit's products and provided the evidence Congress needed to demand lap and shoulder belts in all American cars. Rising gas prices and the need for a better public image forced Detroit to quietly abandon the muscle cars, and the OPEC oil embargo of 1973 finally ended the era of the gas-guzzling high-performance V-8 for good.

Meanwhile, strange things had been happening at the Highway Safety Foundation. Martin Yant, in his book *Rotten to the Core*, reports dark talk of ambulance services kicking back money to HSF executives and allowing Wayman's cameramen to ride to accident scenes in order to get more calls from the Highway Patrol. There was still darker talk that Safety Enterprises was making pornographic movies on the side. The talk grew pitch black when Wayman's former mistress, who was on the HSF payroll, was discovered dead in her bed under mysterious circumstances. Wayman, who had continued to collect his six-figure salary from Ernst & Ernst all these years, suddenly decided he'd had enough of highway safety. He left Ohio for good, reportedly moving to California to become Sammy Davis Jr.'s business manager.

> "There are no words to express agony. There are only sounds. Agonized sounds."
> —MECHANIZED DEATH (1961)

Safety Enterprises, Inc., was taken over by Earle Deems, who continued to make bloody safety films through the 1970s. His first, *Highways of*

Mechanized Death, Dick Wayman's sequel to *Signal 30*, includes audio of dying accident victims.

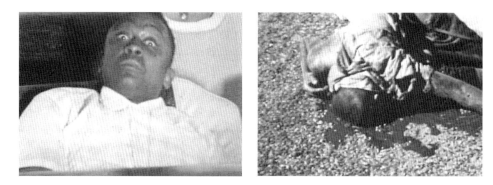

Dick Wayman hired local actors to add melodrama to his third film, *Wheels of Tragedy*.
This man's face is reduced to pulp when it hits the asphalt.

Agony (1969), upheld the ghastly standards of his mentor. His last, *Options to Live* (1980), is a "best of" film that proudly—and fondly—showcases past footage highlights: dead babies, extra-crispy truck drivers, housewives with their faces ripped off. Parts of the film were shot in the Highway Safety Foundation bus, which Yant claims was also used as a set for some of Safety Enterprises's porno films.

Dick Wayman died in obscurity in either 1982 or 1983, no one is sure. Exactly what did and didn't take place at HSF died with him, but his films—the highway safety kind—were untarnished by the rumors of shenanigans that swirled around them. They still stand as the ultimate in school shock cinema.

"Gee, there sure are a lot of things I'd like to buy for better living!"

—WISE USE OF CREDIT (1960)

SNEAKY SPONSORS

While educators tried to save America's children, big corporations tried to indoctrinate them.

Business-sponsored films for schools praised diversity in products, not people, and insisted that the greatest freedom in America was the freedom to consume. Regardless of their stated purpose, their mission was to sell a product or a political system that made possible the selling of the product. "Just think what it would be like if all this were taken away," says the narrator of *What Is Business?* (1948) as the camera pans across exteriors of grocery stores and gas stations. Before we can think, however, the narrator answers, "It would mean living like *this*," and the camera shows a Navajo woman pounding corn with a rock. In *How to Lose What We Have* (1950) the narrator praises "our free choice as customers" but cautions that too much freedom—particularly freedom from free enterprise—is really no freedom at all. "What price freedom?" he asks. "You talk about full security, full employment; why, you could have that in a penitentiary!"

Midge and Tom come face-to-face with the Master State in *How to Lose What We Have* ...

Industry's version of classroom mental hygiene films fell into two broad categories. One promoted the profit motive and showed kids how they could participate in it, "planting seeds"—as *Business Screen* put it—that it was hoped would later blossom into a hearty faith in market forces. The other was more directly self-serving; it mimicked social guidance films in the hope that schools would use them as such and overlook the product placements within. Both

...and end up jobless and homeless. "Where government is not limited, no man is free!"

83

had no qualms about manipulating the minds of their young viewers. In the words of Jam Handy, one of the top producers in this field, audiences who saw sponsored films were people "whose minds are to be reconditioned."

Business-sponsored films first appeared in classrooms in the nineteen-teens and were shown because they were free. A few industry groups prior to World War II, such as the Milk Board, sponsored school films because their products were consumed by school-aged people, but until the war ended the concept of marketing directly to kids through classroom media was still unknown. Most sponsored films shown in schools before 1945 were funded by big industrial manufacturers like Curtiss-Wright or Willys-Overland. They sold awe, not consumer goods, and their sponsors wanted their products hawked on-screen, loud and clear and frequently.

Bob becomes peppy—and popular—when he eats more dairy products in *It's All in Knowing How!*, 1954.

That changed after the war. Schools, now supplied by full-time educational film producers, no longer showed just any movie simply because it was free. And corporate public-relations directors had learned from wartime propaganda that a film need not be shrill to be an effective selling tool. Selling by association—deftly placing products in familiar everyday scenarios—proved more effective and usually passed muster with school film review committees.

In order for these kinds of films to work, however, the idea that happiness could be purchased had to be programmed into the young. That job fell to persuasion and "image-building" films, directed at school kids whose adolescent opinions could easily be shaped. Cartoons were an obvious way to achieve this, and big business sponsored dozens of them: *The Dawn of Better Living* (1945, Westinghouse), *Destination Earth* (1956, American Petroleum Institute), *It's Everybody's Business* (1954, U.S. Chamber of Commerce), to name a few. Some of the slickest were those in the *Fun and Facts about American Business* series, sponsored by The Alfred P. Sloan Foundation, founded by a former chairman of General Motors. *Make Mine Freedom* (1950) shows a giant beefy, green fist representing "ism" (fascism, socialism, communism—take your

Mary, star of *The Prom: It's a Pleasure!* (1961), somehow manages to talk on the phone and drink Coca-Cola at the same time.

pick) crashing down on a worker, manager, farmer, and politician. "No more private property. No more *you*," a booming voice shouts as the manager is hurled out the window of his factory. In contrast, *Meet King Joe* (1949) touts the sunny skies of capitalism, explaining that Joe is "king of the workers of the world" because free enterprise has enabled him to "buy more with his wages than any other worker on the globe." Americans, the narrator points out, own 54 percent of the world's telephones, 92 percent of the world's bathtubs, "and practically all the refrigerators in existence."

Colonel Cosmic, a Martian, learns that competition and oil are what make America great in *Destination Earth*, 1956.

Image-building films are characteristically packed with vague bromides, usually delivered over images of pie-eating contests and wind-rippled American flags. "Only the American system of free enterprise will give the young people of today the freedom of opportunity to develop ideas that will make a better way of life for the children of tomorrow" (*Going Places*, 1950). "As long as we keep the foundation of our business system strong, we shall be able to maintain and improve the way of life our forefathers conceived and established" (*It's Everybody's Business*, 1954). "Our way of life... exists because Americans before us met the exciting challenges in marketing that continue to upgrade our standard of living" (*Tell It Like It Is*, 1968). "Working together to produce an ever greater abundance of material and spiritual values for all—that is the spirit of American prosperity" (*Make Mine Freedom*, 1950). The sponsors apparently hoped these empty maxims would fog the minds of kids whenever they were tempted to save money.

> **"This little old dryer sure gets clothes done in a hurry—man, oh man!"**
> —YOUNG MAN'S FANCY (1951)

Business-sponsored mental hygiene films tried to sell products by associating them with successful, attractive teenagers and often went to strange extremes to disguise their ulterior motives. In *Mr. B Natural* (1957, Conn Instruments) a Peter Pan–like "spirit of music," cheerful to the point

TEN FAVORITE MENTAL HYGIENE BUSINESS FILMS

A Date for Dinner

Focus on Junior Achievement: Learning by Doing

Make Mine Freedom

Mr. B Natural

The Prom: It's a Pleasure!

Skills Build America

Tell It Like It Is

The Way to a Man's Heart

Wise Use of Credit

Your Permit to Drive

This forward-thinking and suspiciously mature-looking teen in *Mother Takes a Holiday* (1953) equates women's emancipation with a Whirlpool home laundry.

of dementia, links band instruments to dating popularity. *A Date for Dinner* (1960, Kimberly-Clark paper products) and *The Well Mannered Look* (1964, duPont fabrics) push paper products and wrinkle-resistant polyester clothes using social taboos that were already dated when the films were made. On a broader social front, *Your Permit to Drive* (1952, General Motors) uses a talking driver's permit to contrast the dark world of juvenile delinquency with the happy world of shiny new GM cars. And *Tell It Like It Is* (1968, American Vocational Association) tries to convince Love Generation teens that what they really want is a career in marketing.

With the end of the war came a new generation of relatively affluent suburban kids, and influencing these children was considered smart business. Not only were they the future champions of the free market, they were also, as Vance Packard wrote in *The Hidden Persuaders*, "surrogate salesmen"—the path of least resistance to the family purse. They also were little consumers themselves and could be expected to develop into major purchasers by the time they reached adulthood. Brand loyalty, burned into the brain of a twelve-year-old, would pay dividends for decades to come.

The invisible "spirit of music" in *Mr. B Natural* tells youthful Buzz that high school popularity lies in domestically manufactured band instruments.

The Producers

Trudy Travis, Norm Stuewe, and Herk Harvey of Centron.

"Since the whole class can't go to Kansas
to see the wheat farmer, the motion picture
will bring the wheat farmer to you."

—USING THE CLASSROOM FILM (1945)

CORONET FILMS
Social Guidance Gothic

Drawing of the Coronet studio from the late 1950s.

Coronet set the standard against which all social guidance classroom films were measured. Their productions were the first in America to use character development and drama to teach social lessons. They were more like little Hollywood movies than classroom films, and thus they remain entertaining to watch even today. That, alas, has served them poorly, since these films—lionized in their time—are the ones most frequently used by contemporary social critics as fodder for cheap laughs. *Dating: Do's and Don'ts, Are You Popular?, Lunchroom Manners,* hundreds of others: when you think of a 1950s dating or manners film, it's likely a Coronet production.

Coronet was the dream of David Smart, one of the overlooked entrepreneurial talents of the twentieth century. Contemporary writers described him as "brilliant," "imaginative," and "grandiose." He slept on a motorized circular bed (an idea later appropriated by one of his young employees, Hugh Hefner) and enjoyed posing for photographs with his shirt off. He had made millions in publishing, founding both *Apparel Arts* (which later became *GQ*) and *Esquire*, and by the late 1930s was looking for something new to do.

Two passions stirred his soul: making money and making movies. Tradition has it that Smart, then an amateur filmmaker, visited Germany in the 1930s, possibly during the 1936

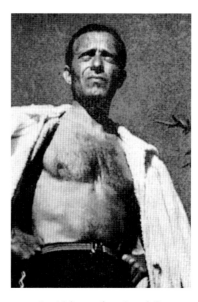

David Smart, founder of Coronet, strikes a regal pose in 1945.

Munich Olympics, and saw how the Nazis used films in their schools to shape the behavior of young people. A less dramatic version of the story has it that Smart simply read an account of someone else's travels to Germany. Whichever is true, there's no doubt he was convinced that the Nazis had hold of a powerful new instructional tool. He also realized that he'd stumbled onto a great way to write off his hobby.

In 1938 Smart announced that he was forming a company, Coronet Films, to produce state-of-the-art educational films. In those days that meant films that had live sound—delivered by the actors on-screen, not an off-camera narrator—and that were shot in color. People thought he was nuts. America was still reeling from the Great Depression; only a thousand schools in the country owned sound projectors; color film processing and live sound production were prohibitively expensive. But Smart had cash and foresight. He banked on an affluent future for America, one in which school boards would be eager to buy his movies in bulk—which they had better, since each Coronet film would have to sell three hundred prints just to break even. Smart broke ground for a million-dollar studio on his estate in Glenview, Illinois, a well-to-do suburb of Chicago. The studio would eventually sprawl over two acres, the largest privately owned motion-picture production facility east of Hollywood, housed within pink stucco walls. Smart specified that it be built to overlook Glenview Country Club, which had barred him from membership because he was Jewish.

Then—nothing happened. World War II shut down all nonmilitary, non-Hollywood film production. Smart seemed content to play moviemaker, giving tours of his empty studio to Hollywood celebrities passing through Chicago. But he was merely biding his time. When the war ended Smart

On the set of *Everyday Courtesy*, 1948.
Sweater-clad John Lindsay went on to star in
the classic *Dating: Do's and Don'ts*.

hired a no-nonsense production head, ordered him to recruit a staff of low-budget scriptwriters, cameramen, and directors, and set out to fill the void of films in America's classrooms. He announced that Coronet would release an "outstanding new educational film every four working days." Again people thought he was nuts, but time proved David Smart true to his word. From August 14, 1945, through the end of the decade, Coronet averaged a film release every 4.2 working days.

The studio was what made this possible. Modeled after the Warner Brothers lot in Hollywood, it had two sound stages; a scene shop; editing, art, and sound recording facilities; a film lab; offices; producer conference areas; and a cafeteria. Films could be punched out at an assembly-line pace. The studio never sat idle. Sometimes Smart had three crews filming in it at one time, tripping over each other.

Among their productions were the first Coronet social guidance films, *Shy Guy* and *Are You Popular?*, released in 1947. Coronet recognized that social guidance was a bankable formula, fashionable with educators at the time, and educators showed Coronet films because they were desperate for

Script girl, cameraman, director, gaffer. These four-person crews—here on location shooting *Good Sportsmanship*, 1950—typically cranked out five films a month in Coronet's heyday.

91

Caroline meets the lunchroom gang in *Are You Popular?*, 1947, Coronet's first classroom film about dating.

Cameraman Bill "Rocky" Rockar poses with his favorite ingenue, Marilyn Fisher, who played Caroline in *Are You Popular?*

social guidance material. And some educators (though not all, at first) loved them because Coronet broke the taboo that educational films should not be like Hollywood movies.

The best way to appreciate Coronet's achievements in the late 1940s is to compare its films with those of its contemporaries:

+ Encyclopaedia Britannica Films (EBF) was the biggest studio at the time. "Encyclopaedia Britannica brings the world to the classroom" was its imposing slogan, one that also defined the boundaries of traditional educational film philosophy in 1947: films should be used only to show the strange and unfamiliar. EBF made travelogues about foreign countries and time-lapse studies of plant growth and cloud formation. They were made in the traditional dry, detached, static, way; an illustrated lecture more than a movie, with everything shepherded by an off-camera voice of authority.

+ Unlike EBF, Simmel-Meservey produced social guidance films, but their films showed none of the pizzazz of their hometown of Hollywood. While Simmel-Meservey dared to show the familiar—teens eating and dating—it also tried to portray everything as "nice" as possible by placing the teens in unrealistically stiff, formal situations: proms, teas, dinner parties. Guidance in films like these could cover only specific

"The pictures in those days... it was so square, oh my God. I mean, even then we thought, 'Hey, the kids don't talk this way.' You know, 'Golly,' 'Gee whiz.' Everybody was too damn nice.

"The point was to be a role model, of course. But, I mean, at the time we thought, 'Do they really talk this way?'"

—Jim Andelin (Mr. Parks in *Law and Social Controls*)

social rituals, not everyday life. Characters were one-dimensional, either good or bad, and there was no drama, no development. Like EBF films, Simmel-Meservey films were shot silent. Everything was explained by a narrator.

✦ B. K. Blake had produced several social guidance films in New York, among them *You and Your Family*. Blake used live sound, made his teen characters middle class, and created everyday situations for them to confront: coming home late from a date, gossiping about friends, cleaning up after dinner. In many respects they were superior to any social guidance film produced for the next ten years, particularly because they ended with multiple resolutions, leaving it to the audience to discuss and decide which was best. But Blake's films were mostly disconnected vignettes that dropped viewers into the middle of the action, leaving no room for character development. And, although Blake's sponsors had promised to produce more, in the end he made only three or four titles.

David Smart, we can imagine, looked at these films and thought he could do better. He didn't want to make dull illustrated lecture films anyway. He wanted to make movies like Hollywood, with drama and emotional impact. He had the facilities and the capital to do it. And, for better or worse, he did.

> "Coronet films boiled down to a compromise between real life and life as it ought to be."
> —Ted Peshak (director)

Coronet's scriptwriters created flat teenaged characters—white, middle class, clean-cut, good-hearted—but they still had more depth than those

E. J. McQuade, script girl (left); Ted Peshak, director (center); Dale Sharkey, cameraman (right), on the front porch set of *The Solar System*, 1950.

Sue and Larry "get all the facts" before getting involved, typifying Coronet's problem-solving approach to teenage turmoil, in *Are You Ready for Marriage?*, 1950.

in any previous social guidance films. Coronet's problem-solving formula introduced character development into its guidance films, something that had never been tried before. Here were "real" teens acting like real human beings (or something close to it), learning, thinking, growing as the film progressed. "People will accept learning from that kind of person," director Ted Peshak later explained. "That's the key to whole thing."

Coronet social guidance films also used the manipulative techniques of Hollywood filmmaking: background music, dramatic lighting and editing, montages, fades, dissolves. Educational films that bordered on "entertainment" were condemned by companies like EBF, but Coronet took the position that Hollywood techniques were not, of themselves, evil. Instead, they made possible "dramatic learning." It was exactly what the Nazis had done in the 1930s—shaping social behavior

> "We were supposed to be as good as Hollywood; we just wouldn't be paid as much."
> —Ted Peshak (director)

in classrooms through the emotional power of film—but Coronet was using social guidance films for well-intentioned, democratic purposes. The teachers of America, somewhat chary but shouldering the burden of saving children from a chaotic postwar world, embraced it.

David Smart's million-dollar studio was no longer written off as a white elephant. Smart was able to make state-of-the-art classroom films that

"Chuck! Don't talk with your mouth full!" To make its films believable, Coronet built sets of middle-class homes and filled them with ordinary-looking people. Dad in *Good Table Manners* (1951) was played by the next-door neighbor of the director.

Coronet associated each of its films with an "educational collaborator"
who theoretically upheld rigid scholastic standards. Here,
Margaret M. Justin, Dean, School of Home Economics, Kansas State
College, checks napkin placement in *Good Table Manners*.

no one else could, because no one else with money had believed that American teachers would use films that had Hollywood-quality production. Coronet had an exclusive on the market. It quickly became known as "the social
guidance studio" and began punching out films at David Smart's promised
brutal pace.

Coronet not only had the personnel and facilities, it had access to
Chicago, which meant a vast pool of potential child actors was at hand, as
well as progressive educational advisors who would keep Coronet abreast of
the latest trends in social education. Other film companies might make two
or three guidance films a year; Coronet had the resources to make twenty-
five to thirty. This dominance led to a homogenization of style, as other social
guidance filmmakers applied Coronet's successful formula to their own productions. Even EBF, after some stalling, began to produce social guidance
films—and they looked like Coronet social guidance films.

Every Coronet social guidance title was the product of a stable of
film specialists. There were no *auteurs* at Coronet, no writer-directors or
cameraman–set designers. Tasks were separated, as in a factory. This resulted
in a consistent product: bare-bones productions that were mass-produced
like Levittown houses, often unrecognizable from each other. You were not

supposed to look at a Coronet film and remember its cinematic technique. You were supposed to remember what it was trying to teach you.

Coronet's state-of-the-art facility allowed its production team to build an artificial yet everyday world: bedrooms, living rooms, classrooms, locker rooms, kitchens, soda shops, front porches for evaded goodnight kisses. Populating these sets were teen actors cast to be as "average" as possible. Visually, Coronet strove to create a universe indistinguishable from the one in which its audience lived.

"We had to deal with school teachers who saw these films many, many times. They picked on everything. We once got a comment about an actor wetting a stamp with his tongue; that was unsanitary. So we were given a rule that people in our films had to wet stamps with a sponge."

—Ted Peshak (director)

Conceptually, it did not. Coronet crafted a perfect world: clean, carefully managed, script-driven. Coronet films presented the embodiment of the current educational theories, because it was curriculum correlation that sold films, not reality. "Every word must be pronounced correctly," instructed a 1948 article in *Coronews*, the Coronet house organ. "Every bit of writing or lettering must be done in the best acceptable style. Every actor must maintain good posture. Every set, prop and costume must be in good style and taste, yet nothing must look rich or glamorous." Because the characters and sets in

The Coronet staff Christmas party, 1945. David Smart stands center holding a teacup—without wearing gloves.

the film *looked* real, the audience was supposed to believe that the problem-solving techniques shown in the film were real as well. "If problems and learning seem personal and real, they will be remembered," explained the 1948 Coronet catalog.

The "Coronet style," as it came to be known, had turned social guidance on its head. Every subject—from dating etiquette to table manners—was pared down to a lifelike problem that a teen protagonist would have to solve by the end of a ten-minute film. And the problem *would* be solved; there were no messy endings to Coronet films.

It need not have been. B. K. Blake's films had been open-ended, encouraging discussion; why not Coronet's? The answer is lost to time. But at some point in 1946, perhaps at the urging of well-meaning Chicago educators, a decision was made that Coronet social guidance films would not be messy. Positive role models in each film would undertake what *Coronews* called "motivated self-analysis" and resolve whatever everyday difficulty they were experiencing: bad study habits, flawed social skills, improper personal hygiene. It was all organized and "systematized," a dispassionate, nuts-and-bolts approach to life that reflected Coronet's linear approach to filmmaking. Post-screening discussion would not be necessary: a problem would be recognized, then it would be resolved. The experts had spoken. All the kids had to do was take what they had seen and apply it to their own lives.

It would be unfair to say that all Coronet social guidance films were completely tidy. A few later films, like *How to Say No* (1950) and *Right or Wrong?* (1951), at least tentatively explored darker issues and left some wiggle room for classroom discussion. The Coronet style did evolve, though barely. But Coronet was hamstrung by its own success. With a proven formula, tight production

TWELVE FAVORITE CORONET FILMS

Are You Popular?

Beginning Responsibility: Lunchroom Manners

Benefits of Looking Ahead

Dating: Do's and Don'ts

Friendship Begins at Home

Good Table Manners

How to Say No

More Dates for Kay

Shy Guy

Social Courtesy

What Makes a Good Party?

What to Do on a Date

"We didn't have any carpets or rugs on the floor of the studio. So when any of these kids walked through, you could hear it a mile away. It loused up the sound. And I fought and fought to get something; they finally got a cheap rug and they sprayed it. They sprayed the rug and gave it a green color. But they used cheap, water-base paint, so once it dried, every time you walked through there was this cloud of dust. The camera was covered, the lens was covered; we had a hell of a time."

—Bill "Rocky" Rockar (cameraman)

schedules, and rigid cost accounting, Coronet was locked into an approach that could not easily be changed. A smaller, independent studio—Centron—eventually came along to make more ambitious films that explored pre-1960s teenage problems in all their unresolvable glory.

David Smart didn't live to see that happen. In October 1952, less than two weeks after his sixtieth birthday, he died on an operating table during surgery. Smart suffered from pathophobia—the fear of disease—and had ordered an operation to inspect his colon against his doctors' wishes. The chief surgeon reportedly diagnosed Smart's death as "mental suicide."

Two years later, the studio mechanics at Coronet struck to form a union. In response, the company—now run by Smart's younger brother—simply closed the studio. Lighter cameras, faster film, and portable lights and sound-recording equipment had made it possible to farm out work to freelance directors who could film in the real world. The postwar passion for social guidance was spent, and changing social values would soon render Coronet's carefully crafted productions obsolete. The studio, whose facilities had been so invaluable, had become a burdensome overhead. Coronet would occasionally release social guidance titles into the 1970s, but its days as "the social guidance studio" were over.

David Smart's pink stucco studio stood for another twenty years, housing a succession of smaller film and television production companies. More films had been produced in it than even in any Hollywood studio before or since, but it had outlived those who appreciated it. The Smart estate was subdivided for suburban housing, and in 1974 the studio was razed by a bulldozer. All that remains today is its old street number—now on a private home—and the street name—Coronet Road—as a reminder that Glenview was once the mental hygiene capital of the world.

> "I remember the day I was about to leave. David Smart came by and told me how nice it had been to have me there, and I stuck out my hand and he took it and—I forget who—somebody whispered, 'He doesn't have a *glove* on!' He was evidently so scared of germs that he would never shake your hand without a glove."
>
> —Kathy Kingery (script girl)

ENCYCLOPAEDIA BRITANNICA FILMS

No Music Allowed

Encyclopaedia Britannica Films (EBF) was Coronet's closest rival, both in content and proximity. EBF's offices and studio (an old bank building and a vaudeville theater) were only a ten-minute drive from the Coronet studio, a straight run down Glenview Road into downtown Wilmette. EBF and Coronet production staffs could have easily lunched together, had they chosen to.

The dizzying EBF logo from the title sequence of *Color Keying in Art and Living*, 1950.

The start of EBF can be traced to 1936, when William Benton, cofounder of the Benton & Bowles advertising agency, a friend of David Smart, and a multimillionaire at the age of thirty-six, retired from advertising and became vice-president of the University of Chicago. The University of Chicago had been America's center for progressive education since John Dewey's tenure there at the turn of the century, and consequently an early advocate of visual education. Benton wanted to get involved. On his first day on the job he asked the Rockefeller Foundation for a $4 million grant to produce classroom movies. They refused. Benton waited.

Marty, stoned on pot, unknowingly cuts his mouth to ribbons in *Drug Addiction*, 1951.

Then, in 1943, Sears, Roebuck & Co., which had bought Encyclopaedia Britannica after World War I, decided to dump it. They offered it to the University of Chicago, but the school's conservative trustees balked at the $100,000

FIVE FAVORITE
EB FILMS

Are Manners Important?

Beginning to Date

Care of the Hair and Nails

Drug Addiction

Getting Along with Parents

asking price. Benton did not. He put up the capital out of his own pocket, with the proviso that the university would buy it back from him at cost. Now, as chairman of Encyclopaedia Britannica, he bought the ERPI collection of sound classroom films from Western Electric—which had been trying to unload it since 1937—for $1 million. He then talked the Eastman Kodak Co. into donating all of its old silent productions from Eastman Teaching Films to the university. Presto. Without shooting a foot of film the newly formed Encyclopaedia Britannica Films, Inc.,

had a catalog of almost five hundred educational films that it could sell to schools. By 1946 the university had repaid Benton his $100,000 and was averaging more than $300,000 a year profit from his new corporation.

With its network of contacts with independent producers, EBF was able to release films at a pace even faster than Coronet: 373 in the 1940s, 475 in the 1950s, 433 in the 1960s. The company took its work very seriously* and concentrated on mainstream subjects such as geography, history, and science. EBF made only a handful of social guidance titles, most of them in imitation of the Coronet style. Perhaps dating and etiquette films seemed beneath EBF. According to Coronet director Ted Peshak, "The joke was, 'Encyclopaedia Britannica brings the world to the classroom; Coronet brings the classroom to the classroom.' "

Today the old EBF buildings house offices for companies such as Career Strategies and Tom Rangars Yachts & Travel.

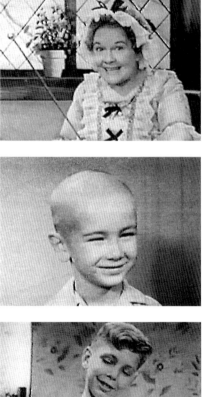

EB films never got mental hygiene quite right. *Care of the Hair and Nails* (1951), for example, features a fairy godmother and a bald kid with pinworms.

---

*Until 1951, all EB films used the same narrator, James A. Brill, who also had narrated all the ERPI films since 1931. He was a former news reporter and university instructor in art with an extremely monotonic voice.

"You can never find the right words to tell a mother
her daughter has been murdered."
—GIRLS BEWARE (1961)

SID DAVIS

The King of Calamity

By the late 1940s social guidance filmmakers were in a quandary. The world they had created in their films was brimming with positive role models and happy endings, but real life was not so clean and simple. In dark alleys and less-desirable neighborhoods there existed a world of unspoken unpleasantness: substance abusers, sexual perverts, juvenile delinquents. Good kids had to be warned of the dangers; bad kids had to be shown the consequences of bad behavior.

Sid Davis and his Bolex
camera, circa 1954.

Social guidance filmmakers wouldn't make films about such things. As social engineers they believed that kids would imitate what they were shown, hence films should show only uplifting images. As profit-minded businesspeople they feared that films about disagreeable subjects would upset prudish educators, hurting sales for the rest of their product line. It would take someone else, an outsider, to get to the grim task of making mental hygiene films about the nasty things in life.

That someone was Sid Davis.

Sid Davis was a child of Hollywood, an on-and-off employee of the movie industry since the age of four. By the late 1940s, as he was approaching middle age, his main source of income came from working as a stand-in for John Wayne. His was not an upwardly mobile career path. He wanted to direct his own films, but how on earth would a Hollywood stand-in ever be given that opportunity?

It came, as it sometimes does, at the misfortune of someone else. In this case it was a little girl who was molested in Los Angeles in late 1949. The story made the papers and Davis, who had a little daughter himself (who would later appear in several of his films), was deeply affected. He tried to

101

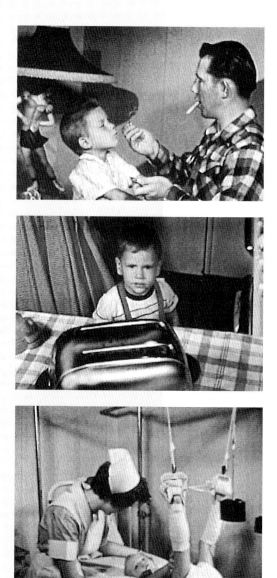

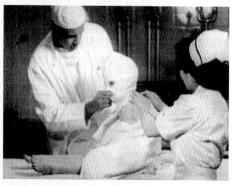

Tough love. Kids never fare well in Sid Davis films. In *Live and Learn,* 1951 (left), Jill—played by Davis's real-life daughter—impales herself on scissors, Bill falls off a cliff, and everyone ends up in the emergency room. A similar fate awaits the children in *Too Young to Burn,* 1954 (above), brought to their sorry state because they "did first and thought last."

"When Jimmy got out Ralph gave him a friendly pat." *Boys Beware,* 1961.

warn her about the dark side of human nature. But, as he later recalled, "it went in one ear and out the other." Frustrated by his own child's inability to see things as they really were, full of noble intentions and back-to-the-wall bravado, Davis asked John Wayne for money to make a 16mm classroom film about child molesters. John Wayne liked the idea, loaned him a thousand dollars, and Sid Davis made his first mental hygiene film, *The Dangerous Stranger.* It was released in January 1950.

Hyped by a print ad campaign that declared, "It should be seen by every schoolchild in America!" *The Dangerous Stranger* sold well—so well that Davis realized he'd tapped into a totally undeveloped market. Here was an opportunity not only to be a director, but *the* director. Davis used the profits from *The Dangerous Stranger* to make more films about youthful miseries: injury (*Live and Learn*), drug abuse (*Seduction of the Innocent*), prejudice (*Skipper Learns a Lesson*), social anarchy (*Gang Boy*). His willingness to probe forbidden territory made him ideal for the job. He was genuinely fascinated by unconventional behavior, regarded most of it as evil, and was willing to dedicate his professional life to stamping it out.

"What Jimmy didn't realize was that Ralph was sick...a sickness of the mind. You see, Ralph was a homosexual...."

Society's discomfort with Sid Davis's dark world gave him the freedom to do pretty much whatever he wanted. No committee of educational advisors oversaw his work, no peer group condemned his excesses. If Davis wanted to accuse the Soviet Union of promoting drug use in the United States, as he did in *The Terrible Truth,* it went unchallenged. If he wanted to assert that smoking marijuana brought on "wholesale abandonment of goals and ambitions," as he did in *Keep Off the Grass,* that was okay too. In his films Davis placed full responsibility for the calamities on the "wise guy" kids who

"All homosexuals are not passive. Some resort to violence...."

103

suffered them, and no one suggested that external forces might share the blame. Chaos lurked around every corner; cruel fates overwhelmed teens who mocked the system. It was a brutal world devoid of gray areas or relative truths, and it apparently was endorsed by the local law-enforcement agencies with whom Davis routinely worked.

Off-camera horrors. Mary's mom discovers her missing daughter in an abandoned refrigerator...

Sid Davis took pride in his ability to produce entire films, from idea to answer print, for $1,000 or less. Even in the early 1950s this was rock-bottom filmmaking. The result was a trancelike style, stripped of anything even remotely approaching drama or human emotion, as instantly recognizable as that of any feature film *auteur.*

Most of Davis's films—and he made over 150—possess the visual dynamism of a pancake. *The Bicycle Clown, Dead Right, Alcohol Is Dynamite, Girls Beware,* and dozens of others—all appear to have been shot at noon. Their characters squint in the bright southern California sunshine; casting no shadows, they wander a flat landscape of tract housing and hamburger stands before being run over by cars, molested by perverts, or arrested by the police.

"John Wayne financed *The Dangerous Stranger;* he was my silent partner. I remember when I finally first got some money—like a little kid who sells papers, I walked into the dressing room where they were putting on his makeup, and I put a check in front of him for $5,000. He looked down at the check and said, 'What's this for?' I said, 'It's your first dividend check.' And he said, 'Fuck you; put it back in the business!' That was his way of saying, 'I don't need this,' you know."

—Sid Davis

Many of the horrors featured in Sid Davis films were too complex to stage on a thousand-dollar budget. Instead, the camera pans away at the last moment before tragedy strikes or cuts to a shot of horrified onlookers—a power of suggestion technique necessitated by financial constraints. The gaps in action sequences are filled by the narrator—relentless, judgmental—hammering away with all the anger in Sid Davis's soul, not at the drug pushers and child molesters but at the hapless kid victims. It's the voice of a stern father trying to talk sense into an uncomprehending child: "There's a difference between good fun and being stupid" (*Vandalism*). "You youngsters can save yourselves a lot of pain if you just stop and think" (*Live and Learn*). "Can you continue the way you're going and stay out of trouble? You *wish you knew*" (*The Dropout*).

...and Jimmy's playmate learns why "caves" should not be dug in hillsides. Both from *Why Take Chances?*, 1952.

Looking back on how he became involved with the genre of cautionary films, Sid Davis explained, "I made a whole series of child-molestation-type films. The first one, *The Dangerous Stranger*, was for the fourth, fifth, sixth grades. Then I made it for the first and second grades, then I made it for the third and fourth grades, then I made another one for the fifth and sixth grades, then went into junior high with *Boys Beware*, then I made another one for the girls called *Girls Beware*. Then I made films for young adults in high school on how to protect yourself. You know, besides just being molested there's also rapists and so on.

"I called them 'youth guidance' films. That was part of the curriculum then, youth guidance. And having been somewhat of a delinquent myself as a younger kid, I understood their thinking. So it was right up my alley.

"In 1952 I went to a California State Juvenile Officers Association meeting in Hollywood. This one guy who was there walked over to me and said, 'Oh, so *you're* Sid Davis. Boy, I'm sure glad to meet you. You know, your films saved one of my kids' lives.' He went on to tell me that his daughter's school showed *The Dangerous Stranger* and on the way home from school that day some guy tried to pick up his little girl. In the picture, we showed how to write a license plate number on the ground. But she had a camera. She took a picture of the car, went home, and told her mother. They took the camera to the police station, they developed the film, and they couldn't read the license plate but the car was such that there was only two of them in the whole city of that type. So they went to this one guy—I think he worked at the railroad yard—and they confronted him. And he said, 'I never tried to molest that little girl.' Then they showed him the picture and said, 'Well, this is your car, isn't it?' Well, he

SCREAMING NEWSPAPER HEADLINES IN SID DAVIS FILMS

VAST SEARCH FOR MISSING GIRL BABYSITTER
—*A.B.C. of Babysitting*

KID KILLERS AT THE WHEEL
—*The Cool Hot Rod*

"DUST OF DEATH" H-BOMB HINTED
—*Gossip*

BABYSITTER SLAIN BY UNKNOWN ASSAILANT
—*Name Unknown*

NAB 16 IN TEEN AGE DOPE RING
—*The Terrible Truth*

YOUTHS STEAL CAR FOR "GAG"; JAILED
—*Vandalism*

got so panicked that he admitted it. And not only that, but he admitted molesting other children! And as this guy is telling me this story, for the first time in my life as an adult I started to cry. Tears came to my eyes. And at that point I dedicated my life to making films for youth."

Social Armageddon is a broad subject, so Sid Davis had to pack a lot of tragedy into his ten-minute films. His narrators had to read quickly to squeeze it all in, and Davis refused to pay enough to get anything better than bottom-of-the-barrel, atonal talent. The effect is hypnotic, often rendering invisible whatever mayhem is on the screen. All you can recall in the end is the robot narrator barely pausing for breath between sentences, properly enunciating every self-satisfied condemnation.

TEN FAVORITE SID DAVIS FILMS

Alcohol Is Dynamite

Big Man on Campus

Boys Beware

The Dropout

Keep Off the Grass

Live and Learn

Name Unknown

Seduction of the Innocent

The Terrible Truth

What Made Sammy Speed?

"Everybody keeps talking about teenagers as if we were
a bunch of *freaks* or something."
—WHAT ABOUT JUVENILE DELINQUENCY (1955)

CENTRON

Hollywood in a Likeable Town

Centron was born, lived, and died in Lawrence, Kansas. It was the child of Russell Mosser and Arthur Wolf, two boyhood chums from Topeka. Both had received degrees from the University of Kansas and set their sights on a career in filmmaking, which they wanted to pursue right where they were, in Lawrence. It was, to all appearances, a stupid decision. Film production rarely strayed outside of New York, Chicago, and Los Angeles. Who would ever pay two nobodies from Topeka to make movies in Lawrence, Kansas?

As it eventually turned out, lots of people would. Mosser and Wolf were not only good filmmakers, they were resourceful businessmen. Their first film, *Sewing Simple Seams,* shot in 1947 in the living room of Mosser's boss (Mosser was working in the KU film library at the time), served as a calling card that was eagerly grabbed by Young America Films (YAF), one of the top three educational film distributors in the country. YAF was in desperate straits. In the frantic days following World War II, when everyone was clamoring for educational films, YAF had signed a contract with a New York company to produce a hundred titles. After ten months the company had delivered only one.

Until mid-1955 Centron shot all of its films in the back of this camera shop.

Mosser and Wolf, now known as Centron, promised YAF that they'd meet their deadlines—which they always did, film after film, year after year. By the early 1950s, operating out of an old vaudeville theater in the back of their camera shop, reliable Centron had made such consistently well received movies that it had become the sole producer of classroom films for YAF.

The set for *The Sound of a Stone*, 1955.

On the set of *The Snob*, 1958.
Centron productions grew more complex
as their studio space expanded.

Mosser and Wolf shot on a shoestring budget. Their cameras were spring-wound, their camera dolly was a modified toy wagon, and they had to calculate parallax correction with a ruler. They had to stop sound shooting whenever a train rumbled through town or a truck made deliveries next door. But their proximity to the university—it was just two blocks away, on Massachusetts Street—meant they, like Coronet, had a bottomless well of actors and educational collaborators to dip into. It also put them in contact with the creative flotsam that naturally drifts around a university, people who were willing—like Mosser and Wolf—to work hard for modest pay in order to do the kind of work they liked in a town they liked. Soon cameraman Norm Stuewe was on staff, followed by edi-

> "I took a vacation and shot *Carnival of Souls* in two weeks. I've been to festivals and people always ask, 'How come you made only one film?' And I say, 'Hell, I've made over four hundred.'"
>
> —Herk Harvey (director)

tor Chuck Lacey, writer Margaret "Trudy" Travis, and director Harold "Herk" Harvey, who would later direct the film *Carnival of Souls* on a two-week vacation from work at Centron. Isolated in Lawrence, where no one expected them to do anything in particular, driven by the desire to produce better films than their more well known competitors, the crew at Centron made movies the way they saw fit, and they themselves served as their harshest critics.

Herk Harvey strikes a meditative pose in his Centron office. A theater major in college, he often played bit roles in his films.

The creative reins of Centron were held by Art Wolf and Trudy Travis. Travis,

Art Wolf and Trudy Travis collaborated on most of Centron's best mental hygiene films.

Script conference with (from left) Herk Harvey, an educational advisor, Trudy Travis, Art Wolf, and Russ Mosser.

a young housewife who yearned to write, initially became involved with Centron out of curiosity. She couldn't understand why Art, whom she'd often see through the storefront window of the camera shop, was sitting alone at a little table in the shop's cavernous space, typing on a typewriter. (Centron couldn't afford to buy a desk.) She soon learned that Mosser and Wolf were doing more than selling cameras, and she realized that their fledgling company could provide an opportunity for her own considerable talents. She and Wolf became a scriptwriting team, happiest when they could write about what Wolf called "the human stuff," sharing the vision that mental hygiene films should stimulate discussion and that showcasing human emotions was the best way to do that.

Social guidance titles began to appear on Centron's production list: *Glenn Wakes Up; The Other Fellow's Feelings; A Day of Thanksgiving.* Not every mental hygiene film written by Wolf and Travis was a classic. Centron produced its share of social guidance clunkers. But when Wolf and Travis and the others got it right, they made the greatest mental hygiene films of their time: *The Trouble Maker; The Snob; The Sound of a Stone; The Outsider.*

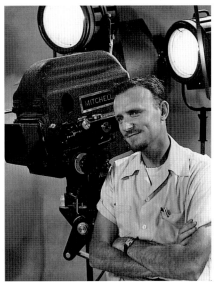

Cameraman Norm Stuewe and his beloved Mitchell, circa 1953.

Most of Centron's best mental hygiene films were part of its *Discussion Problems in Group Living* series, produced from 1951 through 1959. The "problems" Centron chose to depict were not the kind that could be resolved through rational thought. Centron

109

C
E
N
T
R
O
N

"The Never-Squeal Code." Early considerations for Centron's *Discussion Problems in Group Living* series, 1951.

Unlike Coronet, Centron often depicted teenagers as dark-minded and fallible. *The Trouble Maker,* 1957.

films made problem situations unavoidably complex and human by using malcontents as their protagonists: the class bully; the school gossip; the self-serving cheater. Centron did not paint them as one-dimensional "wise guys" (as would Sid Davis) or box them into a tidy story line (as would Coronet). Instead, Centron dragged its audiences into uncomfortable intimacy with its on-screen misfits, exploring their maladjusted lives and complex inner feelings in all their painful human glory. This was usually accompanied by unflattering close-ups and one or more characters bursting into tears.

Teenagers cry frequently in Centron mental hygiene films. They also yell, sulk, brood, bring shame on themselves, and occasionally threaten to beat each other up. In Centron's view, happiness was not a component in discussing social problems. The characters in Centron films were made

"Chalky" in *Manners in School* (1958) comes to life and teaches Larry to be a "regular guy."

to suffer without resolution, so that teenagers in the real world would be led to recognize and, it was hoped, resolve similar problems in their own messy lives.

Perhaps the most remarkable thing about Centron was that it was not exclusively an educational film-maker. Centron produced everything, from *Operation Grass Killer* (Monsanto) to *Pork: The Meal with a Squeal* (John Deere) to *Tomorrow's Spark Plug Today* (AC Delco). Big business paid big money. Centron was responsible for the wretched *Tell*

110

The Outsider, 1951. This grim film portrays the path to popularity as littered with misunderstandings and heartbreak, yet worth the effort nonetheless.

It Like It Is and *Take a Letter: From A to Z,* films that aped mental hygiene so that corporate sponsors could weasel their way into the classroom. The creative staff at Centron took these projects as they came, viewed them with detached professionalism, and made them into the best propaganda they knew how.

Ironically, the mix of business and social guidance helped Centron make better mental hygiene films. The varying clients and subjects, and their varying demands, kept the creative staff from getting stale. Fees paid by large industrial clients kept Centron from getting locked into the five-films-a-month grind that kept Coronet going.

Centron had entered the mental hygiene field late, but this, too, proved beneficial. Its best guidance films were not produced until the latter half of the 1950s, after Coronet and other educational producers had burned out.

TEN FAVORITE CENTRON FILMS

Cheating

Dance, Little Children

A Day of Thanksgiving

The Gossip

The Griper

The Snob

The Sound of a Stone

The Trouble Maker

What about Juvenile Delinquency

What about Prejudice?

Centron followed "The Uncle Henry Principle," named after one of Mosser's farmer relatives, which holds that the best crop to plant is the one that the neighbors aren't. As Coronet and EBF scrambled to produce science films in the wake of Sputnik, Centron released films like *What about Prejudice?*, *Understanding Others*, and *Teenage Manners Made Easy* to a wide-open market.

It was too good to last, and it didn't. The concept of mental hygiene changed when the 1960s arrived, and Centron was not inclined to produce the drug and driver-safety films that would carry the torch of social engineering into the next decade. Centron would continue as a studio for another twenty years, producing hundreds of films for Fortune 500 companies, state and federal agencies, the armed services, and a jumble of foundations, commissions, and associations. One of its classroom productions, a documentary titled *Leo Beuerman*, was even nominated for an Academy Award in 1971. But Centron's days of making gut-wrenching mental hygiene films were over. The company was eventually bought by Coronet— to get hold of Centron's backlist of educational films—and then both were bought by Gulf + Western Industries. Centron was then slowly allowed to die.

The original Centroners are now long retired or deceased. Most still live in Lawrence, a town they like, critical of the films they made that failed to meet their standards and fiercely proud of those that did.

"When I was in ninth grade, which was many, many years ago, they used to show us these so-called educational silent films. The teacher'd just put them up on the wall and go out and come back twenty minutes later. We'd been sitting there looking at these dumb films that didn't mean anything and even at that age I said to myself, 'Someday I'm gonna change this.' There's no reason an educational film can't be interesting. You know, capture your imagination. And that was the basis we tried to work on. We wanted to make something that wasn't just another dumb educational film."

—Art Wolf (cofounder)

The Films

"Where do you get this stuff Ernie?
A 'recreation center' for juvenile
delinquency. A recreation hall isn't
gonna do *you* any good."

—THE SOUND OF A STONE (1955)

Given the scope of this book and the limitations of a single volume, I've had to be somewhat arbitrary in choosing films for this review section. It would have been impossible to include every noteworthy mental hygiene film, even if limited to the genres of dating, safety, sex, and drugs.

With occasional exceptions all of these films still physically exist in public collections and private archives, although sometimes only a single battered print survives. Beyond that, titles such as *Charm and Personality, Coed Courtesy, A Date with Death, Teen Queen, Fast Way Nowhere,* and hundreds of others—seen, collectively, by millions of schoolchildren—are simply gone. Some were sold for their chemical content, most were simply thrown in the garbage when their upkeep became too expensive or inconvenient. The total number of these missing films undoubtedly exceeds that of those that have been preserved. We will never know what has been lost.

ACT YOUR AGE
Coronet Instructional Films, 1949, 13 minutes

High schooler Jim gets mad and carves his initials into his school desk. He's caught and sent to Mr. Edmunds, an unusual principal who tells Jim that "growing up is a problem." "Why can't our young people act their age?" he asks, and then punishes Jim by confiscating his prized mechanical pencil. As Jim slowly erases his vandalism with sandpaper, he begins to accept that he does exhibit a lot of "infantile reactions," and so do a lot of his

friends. To reinforce this message, the film moves to a surreal sequence where bratty teenagers are transformed into little kids. Not wanting to suffer this fate, Jim devises a "How Old Am I?" chart to keep track of his emotional development and asks his parents to rate him. Mr. Edmunds applauds this sign of maturity and gives Jim back his pencil.

AGE OF TURMOIL
Crawley Films for McGraw-Hill Book Co., 1953, 19 minutes

Culled from the book *Adolescent Development*, this film was produced for the parents of teenagers, not the teenagers themselves. It tries to be scientific and objective as it shows that "annoying" teenage behavior is perfectly normal. This odd goal, revealing the generation gap that already existed in 1953, is hamstrung by Lorne Greene's narration, which often belittles the "childlike" teenagers and presents them as, well,

> **"Sometimes young adolescents appear to enjoy utter uselessness."**

dumb. Girls are chided for their "excessive" behavior, their "unrealistic ideas of their

own future," and for giggling. Boys are criticized for being "impressed by material possessions" and for the way they "seem to spend hours in completely useless activity." And when girls and boys do get together—as in this film's memorable "beginnings of sex adjustment" sequence—nothing happens. The girls throw soda straw wrappers at the boys, then go to a movie without them. Nothing to worry about here, Mom and Dad.

AGE 13
Arthur Swerdloff for Sid Davis Productions, 1955, 27 minutes

Andrew's mom is dead. The death of a mother, the narrator explains, is "the nearest experience to the agony of death" that a child can suffer. "It may lead to juvenile delinquency, to a mental institution, or to a fiendish crime." Andrew—age thirteen—cries out at the graveside, "Don't leave me! Don't be dead! Mother!!!"

Andrew is a poor kid whose clothes are literally falling apart. His stepdad is a total goon who would rather shower affection on the cat than Andrew. In this bleak environment Andrew becomes convinced that he can bring his mom back to life if he can repair the radio she used to listen to. He tosses the cat into an outbound freight car, then brings his stepdad's gun to school and threatens the kids on the volleyball court. Andrew is sent to a psychologist. He stares at a Rorschach blob that looks like a dish of ice cream and sees—a dish of ice cream. "This suggested his hunger not for food, but for love," the narrator insists. "There was hope for Andrew."

The evil stepdad gets mad at Andrew for stealing money out of the teapot—to buy radio parts—and smashes the radio with his boot. Andrew goes over the edge, "deeper than ever into the distorted world of his mind." He throws an 8 x 10 glossy of his stepdad into a muddy puddle, sinks it with a rock, and becomes a runaway. "One high-pitched, piercing note away from real tragedy," the narrator cries, as a montage of Andrew, running, is superimposed over shots of bongos, billiard balls, and a bare lightbulb. "At this point, Andrew was an animal."

Age 13 wraps up very quickly. Andrew shows up at the house of his aunt because he's hungry. She decides to adopt him. He returns to the psychologist who finds "his answers improved." The school counselor gets him back into the volleyball game at school, and no one complains that their new teammate tried to shoot them only a month earlier.

ALCO-BEAT
Charles Cahill and Associates for Independent Insurance Agents of Northern Nevada, 1965, 12 minutes

"These people are deliberately getting drunk—with the later intention of driving automobiles!" Party balloons fly and middle-agers gyrate to groovy saxophone music as the Alco Drivers' Test, staged in Reno, begins. "Guinea pig drivers" are liquored up in a trailer under police supervision, then dressed in orange safety suits and motorcycle helmets and forced to drive through an obstacle course of hay bales and plastic cones while bleachers of jeering spectators laugh. "This time, he's only going to be embarrassed," the narrator points out. "He's lucky. After running that red light, he could have been *embalmed.*"

ALCOHOL IS DYNAMITE
Sid Davis Productions, 1967, 10 minutes

Bud and Jack are two "wise-guy" teens who want to buy some booze at a local liquor store. However, a big sign—STATE LAW PROSECUTES ALL MINORS—stands between them and their fun. Up walks Tom Olman, a sports reporter from the city paper. The kids ask him to buy them their liquor. They get a ten-minute Sid Davis lecture instead.

Tom tells the story of Paul, Jim, and Tip, high school boys remarkably similar to Bud and Jack. Paul is a musician, and you know how they are. He guzzles whiskey from a full fifth he supposedly keeps hidden in his blazer pocket and quickly turns his good friends Jim and Tip on to the stuff. "Alcohol is a violent narcotic!" narrator Tom exclaims as the three boys each take one swig and end up either unconscious or doubled over in pain. Alcohol's remarkable addictive properties are quickly apparent, since after the boys wake up they keep right on drinking and become alcoholics.

Tom tells Bud and Jack that alcohol turns you into an "animal" by removing your inhibitions. As pulsing horns and nervous strings fill the soundtrack, the three boys sit in a bowling alley with their dates (in beehive hairdos and minidresses). "Like dope addicts, our drinker can't stand the sight of somebody not drinking," Tom comments, as Paul

116

spikes the Cokes of his companions with his ever-present bottle. Jim, thoroughly drunk, plows his convertible into a brick wall and kills his girlfriend, Judy (played by Sid Davis's daugher, Jill). "Just another victim of a drunk driver," Tom sighs, as Judy's body lies in the street, covered by a sheet.

Jim went to jail, Tom explains, then went back to drinking and ended up on skid row, "a hopeless derelict." Paul joined Alcoholics Anonymous and "now he has a chance to save himself." Tip made a vow never to touch a drop of liquor again, and he hasn't. "How do I know?" Tom asks. "Because Tip is *my son*."

Tom gestures toward the sign and declares, "Every boy and girl should be glad they put it there. Because alcohol is dynamite!" Bud and Jack, exhausted, nod numbly.

APPRECIATING OUR PARENTS
Coronet Instructional Films, 1950, 10 minutes

Although young Tommy's parents are slaves to their gender roles—Mom cooks and cleans while Dad tinkers in a musty basement—this film takes the position that they shouldn't be slaves to their son, too. Tommy, the narrator insists, must be "a real member of his family team" and, if he pitches in and picks up after himself, he'll be rewarded. With what? "A bigger allowance! That's mighty good!"

> "Wouldn't you like to do things for your parents the way Tommy does?"

ARE MANNERS IMPORTANT?
Encyclopaedia Britannica Films, 1954, 11 minutes

Good manners "keep things running smoothly" and are "just as important as laws."

The film opens with several shots of courteous children. One even holds a door open for adults. But then there's Mickey Taylor, a rude boy who insists, "Kids don't need manners! Manners are just for grown-ups!" Mickey "hasn't stopped to think," the narrator says, but his mother warns him, "You'll never be happy with others until you learn to be considerate of them."

Mickey begins to suffer because of his rudeness. No one will sit with him at lunch. "He begins to wonder," the narrator reflects, "whether the others may not be passing him by."

With no one to talk to, Mickey imagines himself as president, and he makes a proclamation "abolishing manners forever." But Mickey can't escape the Big Fist of 1950s conformity even in his own daydream. His young subjects refuse to obey and attack him like zombies! "Yaaaggghhh!" Mickey returns to reality, shaken, and as the film ends, is starting on the road to becoming a better-mannered boy.

The music track makes good use of minor strings and horns to foreshadow impending calamities and dream sequences.

ARE YOU A GOOD CITIZEN?
Coronet Instructional Films, 1949, 11 minutes

Alfred Heineman, named First Citizen of Midvale on Citizenship Day, has one of his living-room windows broken by the softball of young teen Jim Foster. Jim tells Al he's sorry, then complains that his gang has to play ball in the street because their old vacant lot was posted off-limits by its owner.

Al suggests that Jim quit griping and work through the system to get the town to buy the lot as a playground. Jim wonders why he has to go to all that trouble. "Don't be a part-time citizen," Al responds, indignant, "thinking only of your rights and neglecting your duties." Jim is still leery; won't something like this be too complicated to pull off? "You're like a lot of other citizens in this town and everywhere," Al sighs. "You haven't taken the trouble to inform yourself about how democratic government operates. The way is wide open for citizens to get what they want from their government! If," Al adds, they're "willing to work for it."

Jim is willing. He returns to his buddies and tells them that if they circulate a petition, the town will hold a referendum and they'll get their ballfield. "Gee, that's great!" the boys agree. They do as Jim suggests, the town cheerfully approves their suggestion, and everything works out swell.

ARE YOU POPULAR?
Coronet Instructional Films, 1947, 10 minutes

This was the first social guidance dating film.

Caroline Ames—"the kind of girl you'd like to know"—is popular with the gang because, among other reasons, "they've heard no scandal about her." On the other side is Ginny—"a crude looking and acting girl," according to *Educational Screen*—who "dates *all* the boys" and is shunned even by those who take advantage of her gen-

erosity. "Girls who park in cars are *not* really popular," the narrator explains, as a table of teens in the lunchroom ignore Ginny and instead invite Caroline to sit with them.

Wally Johnson, one of the gang, decides that he really likes Caroline and calls her for a date:

WALLY: "I—I was wondering if you'd like to go to the Strand and see a movie Saturday night. And then go over to Teen Town, maybe."
CAROLINE: "Well—yes, I..."
WALLY: "Or, if you'd rather go with the gang for a skating party and weenie roast..."
CAROLINE: "Oh, the skating sounds like loads of fun!"

Having agreed on a safe group activity, Wally comes to Caroline's house, shakes hands with her parents, and is invited to come back after the party for milk and brownies. "Gee, that sounds *good!*" he exclaims. "I'll take you up on it, Mrs. Ames!" The film ends as Caroline and Wally run merrily down the street, hurling snowballs at each other.

118

Are You Popular? took thirty days and cost $11,000 just to shoot, which brought the wrath of Coronet's accountants down on its studio staff. They never spent as much time or money on a social guidance film again.

Cameraman Bill "Rocky" Rockar had a soft spot for seventeen-year-old Caroline (Marilyn Fisher), which perhaps explains why *Are You Popular?* took so long to film—and why Caroline looks so angelic in many shots.

The teacher evaluation committee of *Educational Screen* praised Caroline and Wally: "Both present excellent examples of good grooming, good posture, interest in and consideration for others, good manners both in public and in the privacy of their homes, regard for their parents, well-modulated voices, promptness, and foresight in making arrangements."

ARE YOU READY FOR MARRIAGE?
Coronet Instructional Films, 1950, 16 minutes

Larry and Sue, a couple of fresh-scrubbed high school seniors, want to get hitched—but Sue's parents disapprove. The two lovebirds decide their only hope is to visit Mr. Hall, a marriage counselor with incredibly wide suit jacket lapels.

Rather than help them elope, Mr. Hall shows them something he calls a "psychological distance board"—a crude chartlike thing on which he pushes around tiny wooden dolls tied together with piano wire and shoelaces. Somehow—it isn't really clear—this helps Larry and Sue understand that they don't know much about each other and should wait until they're older to tie the knot. As the music swells and the film ends, the happy couple reads a copy of *Marriage and the Family* and helps Sue's parents dry the dishes.

Educational Screen remarked, "The producers are to be complimented on creating an atmosphere of life-like situations."

Sue also starred in *How to Be Well Groomed* and Larry went on to play a heroin junkie in *Drug Addiction.*

AS BOYS GROW...
Medical Arts Productions, 1957, 16 minutes

Medical Arts Productions specialized in frank, plainspoken sex ed films in the 1950s, something people in the 1950s desperately needed but probably didn't appreciate. This

one, a film designed expressly for teenaged boys, is unique.

Gene Douglas, a perpetually smiling coach, is the on-screen host and a font of reproductive system knowledge. The freshman track team hammers him endlessly

with questions about masturbation, menstruation, wet dreams, erections, ejaculation. Coach Douglas, who has infinite time and a bottomless supply of helpful diagrams, matter-of-factly answers every one. "Oh...you want to know about sexual intercourse? Well, that happens like this...the erect penis enters here...."

This cheaply made film looks as if it were shot through gauze. The actors shout their lines because the questions and answers, which supposedly take place in a gymnasium, sound as if they actually *did* take place in a gymnasium, with all its resounding echoes.

AS OTHERS SEE US
Social Science Films for Hardcastle Film Associates, 1953, 10 minutes

The stated purpose of this film is to spare teenagers "the embarrassment of doing the wrong thing." It does this by filling their heads with a nonstop barrage of "simple rules"—to be followed in a restaurant, at a formal dance, in the cafeteria line—read at breakneck speed by a bouncy narrator. "The boy is presented to the girl the boy always  rises when introduced boys always shake hands girls

may if they choose." Teens are instructed to "put your napkin in your lap quietly," and it's made clear that "popular girls devote themselves to pleasant conversation."

Because of the high-intensity lighting used in the production of this film, the teenagers—students of Webster Groves, Missouri, high school—look like walking corpses.

AS THE TWIG IS BENT
Motion Picture Bureau of the Affiliated Aetna Life Companies, 1944, 10 minutes

The dawn of delinquency filmmaking—and by extension social guidance filmmaking—arrived with this film. The title suggests an audience familiar with the writings of Alexander Pope and able to understand analogies, which shows just how old this film is.

The narrator, with a voice like Criswell, quickly gets into the spirit of things. "These are America's future citizens," he says as cute kids sing in church and dance on a playground. "The boys and girls to whom we must look for leadership in our postwar democracy. America's hope for the future."

Then the visuals shift to grimy-faced thieves, gamblers, muggers, and bums. "These are the boys and girls of *yes*-terday," he explains, "whose fathers fought the *first* world war." You get the idea. "Behind every hardened criminal is the shadow of a youthful lawbreaker!"

It's happening all over again, the narrator laments. Uprooted factory families are living in trailer parks and slums; nobody's home to supervise the kids. Young people with "impressionable young minds" are leaving school for menial jobs to earn money. The film cuts to staged shots of kids shooting craps and smoking cigarettes and of girls "confused by the hero-worshipping spirit of wartime" flirting with GIs and men in suits. These kids are enjoying the "dangerous thrills" of freedom! It must be stopped.

And happily, it can be, as parents active and involved in their children's lives demonstrate while the narrator urges moms and dads to teach lawfulness, piety, wholesome reading, and thrift to their kids. "Insist on meeting your daughter's dates." "Train your children to attend church services regularly." "Show them how a systematic

savings program"—close-up on an Aetna life insurance policy—"will help them attain the things they want."

The film returns to the cute kids on the playground, grinning into the camera. "As parents, you can render no greater service to your country than by providing a wholesome, normal home life for your children!"

ATTITUDES AND HEALTH
Coronet Instructional Films, 1949, 10 minutes

Marvin Baker is "an average fellow from an average home in an average town." When he fails to make the high school basketball team, Marv consults a doctor who explains that Marv may be suffering from "improper attitudes" and that "right attitudes are vital to good health." To drive the point home, a montage of people with bad attitudes ensues, including a fat-faced man with a violent nervous tick.

Marv certainly doesn't want to end up like that man. By the end of the film he's adopted a "better perspective" and has made the first team in basketball.

THE AUTOMOBILE-PEDESTRIAN COLLISION
University of California, Los Angeles, Extension Media Center for Institute of Transportation and Traffic Engineering, 1966, 11 minutes

Does the world really need a film to tell it that people who are run over by cars get hurt? The UCLA traffic engineers who sponsored this film thought so. But rather than show any honest-to-goodness mangled bodies, this film showcases pseudoscientific parking lot crash tests. A narrator who spits out consonants like Rod Serling resonantly intones about "impact load," "lift force," and "angular velocity" as test-dummy families are run down in slow motion by car after car. The "mass of moving metal" is remorseless, the narrator comments, and "few children [are] presumed to have survived." Shots follow of earnest young engineers in Brooks Brothers suits, pencil-thin neckties, and pomaded hair hunched over data sheets and computer printouts, eagerly searching for undiscovered truths. Their conclusion? "These controlled collision experiments demonstrate that a pedestrian is no match for even a small motor vehicle." Duh.

BE YOUR OWN TRAFFIC POLICEMAN
Portafilms, 1958, 10 minutes

Most of the screen time in this film is taken up by cheaply animated, garishly colored, late-fifties blob artwork with giant-headed people, cars that look like battered bowler hats with tiny wheels, and backgrounds consisting of a horizon line and the skeletal framework of office buildings.

The film is hosted by the narrator of such Portafilms classics as *Holiday from Rules* and *Helping Johnny Remember.* Here he plays Officer Maxwell and, accompanied by two overly agreeable children (also refugees from those films), tells the audience that good citizens need to "learn all the rules."

But youngsters can't count on adults always being around to show the way. "Boys and girls who want to be considerate of others and avoid getting hurt must learn to be their own traffic policemen." This strange concept is demonstrated inside the blob-art universe, as kids are

121

shown about to commit thoughtless acts on the street—jaywalking, skating on the side-walk—when in their oversized heads a tiny traffic policeman appears, yelling at them to shape up and be sensible.

BEGINNING TO DATE

Encyclopaedia Britannica Films, 1953, 12 minutes

The Teen Club has organized a Winter Frolic at the Community House. Short, eager George, who's never been on a date, wants to ask much taller Mildred—a mismatch appar-

ently made by poor casting, not design—but he doesn't know how. What should he do? The swimming coach—played, some claim, by a young Studs Terkel—knows the answer. He reminds George how frightened he was when he first stepped onto a diving board and tells him he should similarly be ready to "make the plunge" into the world of dating. George is as unsure of the applicability of this analogy as he is of his dating skills, but the coach is insistent. "Try it again!" he orders when George's first efforts fail. The narrator concurs: "Party skill, like diving skill, is gained by just one thing—by practice and more practice."

The high point of the film is, of course, the date. George combs his hair and wonders what he should talk about. Thanks to the Encyclopaedia Britannica optical printer, sug-

gested topics for conversation magically appear super-imposed above George's short head. These include COMIC BOOK and MILDRED'S NEW DOG. George easily keeps the conversation flowing with Mildred as they arrive at the Winter Frolic—where all the boys wear identical black suits and the music is supplied by a matronly woman on piano accompanied by an unseen snare drum.

George arranges with his dad to drive Mildred home and his "first plunge into the social scene comes to a successful end." With no kissing, of course.

Educational Screen commented on the "marked awkwardness" of the cast, but couldn't decide if it made the film less effective or more realistic.

BEGINNINGS OF CONSCIENCE

Knickerbocker Productions for McGraw-Hill Book Co., 1957, 15 minutes

James Brice, an average guy, drives his snappy convertible to work. As he passes a beehive the narrator talks merrily about the lifestyle of the "social insect." "If only you weren't a human being," he chuckles. "No moral problems, no troubles, no rebels, no criminals, no nonconformists in a beehive!" Jim, who apparently is none of those things, stops at a stop sign even though there isn't a car in sight. Why? The film spins back in time to find out.

Now Jim is a little boy. He's a brat, no question: messing up his classmate's finger painting, crossing the street against his father's orders, giving in to "the life of forbidden joy" whenever it suits him. Little Jimmy must be cured of this "cockiness," the narrator insists. He must learn "moral rules," "moral norms," and "social education." How? Through "the educational aspect of punishment."

As Jimmy's parents scold him and send him to his room, the narrator remarks that "the fear of social exclusion and ridicule, learned in childhood, remains a powerful motivation for adhering to moral norms in later life." It certainly works; the film now shows an older, wiser Jimmy who no longer crosses the street whenever he feels like it. The purpose of punishment, the narrator explains, is "to reaffirm the moral standard for everyone else."

Back in the present, Jim is snug and secure in his shiny car. "You're James Brice," the narrator says. "A social being at long last. Because your parents, teachers, and group did a good job of socialization. Without this socialization, and without the sanctions used to achieve it, there would be no basis for moral order in human society."

BENEFITS OF LOOKING AHEAD
Coronet Instructional Films, 1950, 10 minutes

Nick Baxter is a sloppy teen with greasy hair and a poorly knotted necktie. He can't even build an end table in shop class. His clean-cut, obviously successful friend Don cheerfully tells Nick that he's bound for skid row if he doesn't come up with some detailed plans for his future. "A guy without any purpose or any plans—you're liable to end up just being a drifter. Maybe even a bum."

Nick is stunned by Don's prediction and forces himself to "look ahead" to his destiny—a choice of only two extremes: a cigarette-smoking derelict in a filthy hotel room or a successful businessman in a crisp suit. "Hello, Dad," says the good-future Nick, grinning, into a phone. "I've been elected chairman of the community club." The fantasy ends, and the film returns to teenaged Nick staring wistfully into space. "Yes," his voice echoes, "I want a future that's something like that."

THE BICYCLE CLOWN
Sid Davis Productions, 1958, 10 minutes

A suburban street corner. Young Jimmy is being packed into an ambulance, his bicycle lays in the street, battered by the car that hit it. Why? His big brother pedals off to find out.

Jimmy, it's soon clear, was always "clowning and showing off on his bicycle." He possessed a "foolish and dangerous it-won't-happen-to-me attitude" and "was more interested in flashy ornaments" than in keeping his bike mechanically sound. This all comes out in a relentless, nonstop monotone narration delivered by Jimmy's nameless brother, who sounds as robotic as any adult Sid  Davis narrator. "He wanted to draw attention to himself and he foolishly thought this childish showing off was the way to do it."

The film mercifully draws to its end and finally shows why Jimmy had his accident: as he was riding he had his thumbs in his ears and was wiggling his fingers while he stuck out his tongue at a couple of girls on the sidewalk. The poor sap never knew what hit him.

BIG MAN ON CAMPUS
Sid Davis Productions, 1963, 10 minutes

"This is Jerry Warner. And he's in trouble." Jerry is the "big man" of this film's title, although the actor portraying him looks like he's thirteen, and the voice on the soundtrack

123

(Sid Davis never shot with sync audio) sounds like he's ten. Jerry is sitting outside the principal's office, about to be suspended from school; the film goes us back in time to show how he got into such a mess.

Jerry believes that rules are "silly" and "sissy stuff." "Nobody's gonna tell me what to do," he snorts. Jerry pulls a series of "stunts," such as riding his bicycle in traffic and spilling milk on a classmate in the cafeteria, in the strange belief that this will make him more popular. "That's the way to be somebody, rather than nobody," he explains.

As the BMOC, Jerry has the adulation of four (count 'em) of his fellow students. He brags that Carol, a girl who uses too much hair spray, is "pretty impressed with me, all right." Yet Jerry also has doubts about his success. "I wonder if she's really the kind of girl I could go for," he reflects. "She's always *around*. She isn't really that good looking, either. Kind of flashy. And it's certainly true that she isn't very smart."

Jerry also isn't satisfied with his mediocre level of malevolence, so he walks into an empty school science lab, grabs a convenient can of spray paint, and starts vandalizing a white lab coat.

Jerry, of course, is caught, and the film returns to the present, where he still awaits his appointment with the principal. This gives Jerry a chance for more anguished self-examination. He acknowledges that he "refused to listen to anyone with authority." He observes that "most of the other kids were getting along with authority okay, and it did seem to pay off for them." He then concedes, "Everyone has a boss. I guess it's about time I learned that too."

Since Jerry has come around to an acceptable, subservient point of view, Sid Davis rewards him. Even though the narrator points out that Jerry "called the tune" and consequently must "face the music," the final shot shows him walking with a good girl (wearing a sensible dress and not too much hair spray) as string music swells to fill the soundtrack. The narrator proudly announces, "He is taking the first step toward growing up!"

BODY CARE AND GROOMING
Audio Productions for McGraw-Hill Book Co., 1947, 16 minutes

A serious young man in a tie and sport jacket sits outside studying a textbook, oblivious to the lovely spring day. He's also oblivious to the "beauties of nature" who walk past— teen girls wearing plaid skirts, white socks, and penny loafers. The narrator, doing his best to make the guy put down the book, becomes annoyed when a sloppy-looking girl walks past and ruins the mood. "You," he tells the girl, "aren't exactly the type to make this guy act like a human being."

"A good appearance is a must."

The boy makes a sour puss, slams his book shut, and walks off. "Wait a minute!" the narrator cries. The scene of the boy walking off is run backward: he again looks up from his book, but now he sees the girl neatly groomed and lovely. "*Now* look at the skirt," the narrator says with approval. "And the socks." The boy straightens his necktie and chases after the girl; happy violins play.

The rest of the film is more typical of the genre: grooming tips, animation of hair roots and oil glands, and a narrator offering nuggets of hygiene wisdom such as "most everyone sweats" and "many men ignore their cuticles."

BORROWED POWER
Pennsylvania State College Productions for AAA Foundation for Traffic Safety, 1951, 16 minutes

Jerry Thomas has big ears, a big nose, and more important, a "bad driving attitude." While he's rocketing past a weaving car at an intersection in his '51 Ford, a pedestrian is killed. But was Jerry the real culprit?

Jerry is hauled into court by a cop who tells the judge, "We've been watching this young man for some time." Jerry is guilty of a litany of offenses dutifully recorded by the town's Big Brother police force: cutting in and out of traffic, "shaving the red light," blocking crosswalks. Jerry's future really looks bleak when the officer tells how Jerry didn't give proper respect to the "brake reaction detonator" demonstration put on for his driver ed class at school. "I figured it was only a matter of time," the cop snorts.

It wasn't always this way. The judge remembers that Jerry was a safe walker and bike rider. It was only "when he started to borrow power not his own" that his moral character hit the skids. "It was not yours to do with as you please," the judge tells him. "It was only yours to control. A powerful machine does not do its own thinking!"

The judge lambastes Jerry for his lack of "good judgment" and "unsportsmanlike driving," and it seems as if his goose is completely cooked when his girlfriend Nancy, asked to describe the incident, recalls "when we hit that big bump." However, it's eventually proved that the driver of the car that Jerry was passing—a worthless drunk—actually killed the pedestrian. Jerry is set free, a changed teen.

"I didn't drive that car—it drove me!" he exclaims. "From now on when I borrow this power, I'll furnish the brain! That ought to make a good team! A good, safe team!"

THE BOTTLE AND THE THROTTLE
Sid Davis Productions, 1968, 10 minutes

"Not too many minutes ago that young woman and her child were happy and healthy. Now their young bodies are crushed and wracked with pain." Sandy-haired Bill looks on, remarkably unconcerned, even though his Mustang was the car that plowed over them.

Turns out that Bill had one too many "beach party beers" and, as Sid Davis's narrator points out, young drivers are more impaired by alcohol than old drivers. "The latest driving skills mastered are the first to go under the influence of liquor." The things you learn in Sid Davis films!

Bill passes his sobriety test (barely), but he can't escape the Big Fist of Sid. "The report just came through. The little girl died on the way to the hospital. And the mother will probably never walk again." As Bill is handcuffed and stuffed into a squad car, the narrator gloats, "No matter how your trial comes out, you'll always have to live with those facts, won't you, Bill. A child dead. A mother crippled. Not a pleasant future to face at the age of *eighteen*." Dramatic bongos up and out.

BOY IN COURT
Willard Pictures for National Probation and Parole Association, 1940, 10 minutes

This early juvenile delinquency film takes the position that juvenile courts "can make good citizens out of wayward youths." That certainly seems possible in the world created here, one in which every kid has his or her own parole officer with so much time to devote to the case that he becomes a surrogate father.

Johnny Marvin, who always looks painfully bored, is the protagonist—a "sullen, misguided fifteen-year-old," according to the narrator. Johnny and his punk pals steal a car, it crashes, and he's caught and hauled into court. "Can't something be done to help these twisted young lives and set them straight?"

Enter clean-cut probation officer Brenton in a snappy hat and double-breasted suit. The judge tells Johnny, "I could send you to the industrial school until you're twenty-one, but I don't want to do that," and Johnny is instead placed into officer Brenton's manly care. And what a difference it makes! Officer Brenton quickly learns that Johnny really isn't to blame for his wayward ways, as he lives in a "world of squalid homes, dirt, and confusion" and has a "nagging mother." Before long Johnny is fresh-scrubbed, happy, and flying model air-

planes with the ever-present officer Brenton. "Intelligent and friendly guidance has accomplished what mere punishment could never do," the narrator explains. "Johnny has found a new world and ambition. The gang is forgotten. He's looking ahead to the things he really wants!"

The film ends as Johnny returns to court, now wearing an identical father-son suit to officer Brenton's. He has a brief conversation with the judge.

JUDGE: "I guess you won't steal any more automobiles, will you."
JOHNNY: "Gee, that was dumb, wasn't it."
JUDGE: "It certainly was, heh-heh."

BOYS BEWARE
Sid Davis Productions, 1961, 10 minutes

Leave it to Sid Davis to go where no social guidance filmmaker had gone before—or would ever go again.

As jaunty strings and happy flutes play, the film introduces Jimmy Barnes. Like countless kids in Sid Davis films, he makes one "thoughtless" mistake—here accepting a ride home from a bald guy wearing sunglasses named Ralph—and ends up suffering for

it. "When Jimmy got out, the stranger gave him a friendly pat," the narrator says, but Jimmy is oblivious to the obvious. "What Jimmy didn't know was that Ralph was sick. A sickness that was not visible like smallpox, but no less dangerous and contagious. You see, Ralph was a homosexual."

Ralph and Jimmy begin to hang out together: fishing, hunting, playing miniature golf. "By now, Jimmy felt a fondness for Ralph. Ralph was generous and he took Jimmy many interesting places and did many nice things for him. He bought presents and even gave him money." The happy flute finally is replaced with ominous strings and horns as Ralph and Jimmy climb the steps of a motel.

"Payments were expected in return," the narrator explains. "Jimmy hadn't recognized Ralph's approach soon enough."

This film's only half over. Next comes Mike, doomed in a different way. "All homosexuals are not passive. Some resort to violence." A stranger wearing a suit and bow tie shoots some hoops with Mike (which Mike finds perfectly acceptable), then offers him a ride home. "He probably never realized until too late that he was riding in the shadow of death." Mike, of course, is killed, and the film careens forward, informing viewers that "public rest rooms can often be a hangout for the homosexual"; cautioning them to be wary of men "if they are too friendly" or "if they become overly personal," whatever that means; and warning that "one never knows when the homosexual is about. He may appear normal and it may be too late when you discover he is mentally ill."

"The decision is always yours," the narrator concludes. "And your whole future may depend on making the right one." Have a nice, nonparanoid childhood, boys.

THE BULLY
Centron Corp. for Young America Films, 1951, 10 minutes

Centron's *Discussion Problems in Group Living* series provided social misfits with lots of screen time during the 1950s. The malcontent in this one is Chick Allen, the school bully, who holds an unquenchable grudge against all the good—and much smaller—kids in his class.

Chick resembles a pro football lineman more than a high school student and is always grabbing people by the shirt and throwing them to the ground. He wants to mess up the class picnic, but his plans are leaked by Skipper, one of his small lackeys, who has an asymmetrical head and big, floppy ears. "If it was a picnic for his own family, he'd just as soon bust it up." The class decides to thwart Chick and, at the same time, offer him a last chance to bond with society. Chick stomps menacingly toward the picnicking teens and the film ends, as did all *Discussion Problems* films, with a big question mark filling the screen. "What do *you* think?"

CAR THEFT
Bray-Mar Productions for Buffalo Youth Board, 1956, 14 minutes

Eddie, Mike, and Joe wear T-shirts and jeans, smoke cigarettes, and read hot rod magazines. "Just hangin' around, waiting for something to happen," the narrator says.

In another part of town lives innocent little Shirley Johnson, helping her mom at a backyard clothesline. "This is going to be a big day for Shirley," says the narrator. "A very big day. But she doesn't know that yet."

The film cuts to an unnamed blonde driving a two-tone '55 Pontiac convertible, then to Sally, who thinks that Mike's "a pretty cool character." "This might have been a real serious thing if it weren't for what happened that day," the narrator sighs. "This is the last time she'll say goodbye to him without that certain look in her eyes. The very last time."

Two ominous timpani drums begin a funerary "bum-bum" on the soundtrack; tension mounts. The nameless blonde parks in front of an art gallery, leaving her keys in the ignition. Eddie sees the keys. "This is where it all begins," the narrator says. "This is the point of no return. After this bit, you don't go back any more." Eddie hops in, backs the car toward the camera for a close-up on its YOUR CAR: LOCK IT, YOUR KEY: POCKET bumper sticker, then picks up Mike and Sally. "So long, Sally," the narrator says, his voice dripping with sarcasm. "Have a nice ride."

The film races to its climax. The police spot the stolen car, a chase ensues, Eddie swerves onto a side street—and straight into innocent little Shirley!

The camera pans. A cop stands slowly shaking his head; Eddie and Mike, handcuffed; Sally, weeping. Cymbal crash! Timpani roll! Fade to black.

CARE OF THE HAIR AND NAILS
Encyclopaedia Britannica Films, 1951, 10 minutes

A very atypical EB film, *Care of the Hair and Nails* opens with a drawing of a boy with wild, lion mane hair and clawlike fingernails. The camera pulls back to a grandmotherly woman wearing a lace cap, seated in a room filled with Colonial furniture. "I always keep that picture on my wall," she says, "just to remind me how many boys and girls still need my help."

Who is she? The hair and nails fairy? Apparently so, although this film never explains why she exists or why she's dressed like Betsy Ross instead of a fairy. Instead, a slew of camera tricks—swish pans, freeze-frames, high-speed reversed film—progresses as the lady introduces a bald-headed kid with pinworms and a boy named Stanley with dirty nails (that's bad) who washes his hair once a week (that's good).

Scalp diseases figure prominently in this film, as they would in a world where people wash their hair only once a week. The lady warns about "nits"—the eggs of hair lice—and instructs, "Don't use anyone else's comb but your own. And don't wear anybody else's hat."

CARE OF THE SKIN
Encyclopaedia Britannica Films, 1949, 11 minutes

Care of the Skin shows the daily grooming rituals of three terrible child actors—Fred, Billy, and tubby Virginia—as it tries to encourage young viewers to keep their "living coat of armor" clean. Interspersed between shots of soapy washcloths and toenail clipping are animation of sweat glands and skin pores, gruesome footage of kids with disgusting skin infections, and lots of shots of nude Fred as he takes his bath.

CARING FOR YOUR TOYS
Centron Corp. for Young America Films, 1954, 10 minutes

Bobby and Sally and little Phil Thompson's toys are lost in a pile of junk. While they're whining for Mom to clean up their room, it dawns on Bobby that "taking the responsibility for taking care of his own things was part of his job; his share in making family life happy." So the kids clean up their own room—not because they've been told to, but because they *want* to. Mom tries to help, but the kids shoo her away. "Why don't you go on with your work. We'd like to do this!" Mom agrees. "When you're grown-up enough to be a good citizen, you should be given your chance."

"When toys aren't taken care of, they aren't much good at all."

The kids build a new set of shelves out of bricks and scrap lumber. By the time Dad comes home, everything is orderly. The narrator explains, "By taking care of your toys you can enjoy that good feeling you have when you know you are being a good citizen in your family. Yes sir-ree!"

THE CAUTIOUS TWINS
Pyramid Films for Los Angeles County Sheriff's Department, 1960, 7 minutes

This cartoon follows the adventures of Doreen and Dan, two goggle-eyed Nordic tots who are constantly being approached by men with bad intentions. Seven different "bad" strangers hit on them within three minutes; no wonder they're so cautious. One would think their equally  Nordic mom would take the hint and keep them indoors, but the two youngsters are forever sallying forth into their strange cartoon city, apparently populated only by themselves and perverts. "Bad people may try bad things," cautions the narrator, who speaks in rhyming couplets accompanied by roller rink organ music. "Come and see my pet," offers one of the strangers, but before anything interesting can happen, Doreen and Dan heed the narrator's advice and "scream loudly."

CHEATING
Centron Corp. for Young America Films, 1952, 12 minutes

A young teen boy, John Taylor, sits silently in a darkened hallway. A relentless grandfather clock ticks away the passing seconds. "Why haven't they called?" John anxiously wonders. Then the phone rings and John gets terrible news. He's been voted out of his post as student council representative because he *cheated* on a test.

Flashbacks show how it all happened. The nagging  narrator-as-conscience harps relentlessly on naughty John, telling him he's been "caught in a trap of his own making" and mocking him with lines such as "Yessir, you felt pretty pleased with yourself." In this unforgiving universe, John's classmates shun him as soon as they discover the truth. "So you were caught, John," the narrator says with satisfaction. "You were exposed in front of the class." And all because he didn't want to study algebra.

CHOOSING FOR HAPPINESS
Affiliated Film Producers for McGraw-Hill Book Co., 1950, 13 minutes

Mary is the level-headed narrator of this film, which was shot on the campus of Stephens College in Columbia, Missouri. Her headstrong college chum Eve is "attractive and full of life"—at least in Mary's opinion—but always appears on film as if she were suffering from intestinal gas. Mary is "amazed" that Eve isn't engaged by now, and a series of flashbacks show why.

Eve has gone through a handful of recent college boyfriends, all of whom fail to measure up to her blunt criteria: "Is he right for me?" Considering the guys that Eve picks—an odd mix of jocks and geeks—failure isn't difficult to fathom. In one scene, Eve sits on the ground, idly making a heart out of pebbles, while annoying boyfriend Arthur ("the Brain") diagrams the equation for the area of a circle. Their dialogue is priceless:

ARTHUR: "You're different from other girls."
EVE: "That's what you think."
ARTHUR: "You're smarter. Almost like a man."
EVE: "Oh, no, I'm very much the woman."
ARTHUR: "I don't think of you that way at all."
EVE: "You think math is exciting. But you really ought to get yourself straightened out."
ARTHUR: "You don't think there's anything wrong with me?"
EVE: "Aw, forget it. I've gotta go now."

Obstinate Eve obviously needs some help picking a potential lifemate. With the help of Mary she learns that "You can't make over a man like you do a room." But she still ends up without a boyfriend.

Choosing for Happiness was based on a textbook by Henry A. Bowman, who taught, not surprisingly, at Stephens College. It was directed by Willard Van Dyke, who directed progressive documentaries in the 1930s.

CHOOSING YOUR MARRIAGE PARTNER
Coronet Instructional Films, 1952, 15 minutes

This film features some of the oldest college kids you'll ever see. Angst-ridden Joe has to decide who he wants to marry: the sophisticated Ann ("I've outgrown church") or hometown sweetheart Elsie. Guess which one he picks? Joe's roommate Harvey narrates.

CINDY GOES TO A PARTY
Centron Corp. for Young America Films, 1955, 9 minutes

Cindy, a twelve-year-old tomboy, is hurt when she learns she hasn't been invited to a neighborhood birthday party. She goes to bed, but suddenly her teenaged fairy godmother appears and takes her to the party anyway.

Wearing a frilly party dress, no longer a tomboy, Cindy relishes her acceptance by the group. This new state of affairs is guaranteed since every time the invisible fairy godmother waves her magic wand, party etiquette rules appear on the walls, courtesy of Centron's optical printer. "Don't break things," reads one. "Leave on time," another.

Little Cindy is no actress, but she shines in comparison to her slack-jawed companion, Dennis, whose oversized shirt looks like a mumu that appears to be swallowing his abnormally small head. Cindy wakes up at the end and discovers it was all a dream—but she still gets to go to the party.

CITIZENSHIP AND YOU
Coronet Instructional Films, 1959, 13 minutes

Larry's homework assignment for civics class: make a list of the qualities that comprise a "good citizen." His dad pokes his nose into things and the two are soon recalling many examples of good citizenship from their own lives. "I thought these were just things to write down for an assignment," Larry says, shaking his head in wonder. "You know, I've been practicing good citizenship all along!"

CLOTHES AND YOU: LINE AND PROPORTION
Coronet Instructional Films, 1954, 10 minutes

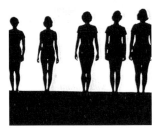

C

This girls-only film opens at the annual Central High fashion show, where a parade of plumpish 1954 coeds model their school dresses and prom gowns for each other. "Fashions change, but not the basic principles of line and proportion," says the woman narrator, ostensibly the home ec teacher in this film. "Getting to know the lines and shapes of our bodies is the beginning of learning to choose clothes that are right for us."

Cloaked in a mantle of education and serious study, *Clothes and You* analyzes "the five general body types" of high school girls, discusses the visual impact of pleats and belt widths, and shows how to choose handbags "in keeping with your size." It's all part of "getting to know yourself," the narrator explains, as the film reduces that lofty goal to a discussion of sweater and skirt ensembles.

CONTROL YOUR EMOTIONS
Coronet Instructional Films, 1950, 13 minutes

A preemptive strike against a generation of uncontrolled, emotional teenagers, *Control Your Emotions* is hosted by an unnamed expert wearing a white lab coat. He sits behind a desk while moving around blocks labeled RAGE, FEAR, and LOVE and a big cardboard disk (well rounded) titled PERSONALITY. He also repeatedly interrupts the story of Jeff

Moore, the film's protagonist, with psychobabble such as, "Your emotions can be your own greatest enemy," and "Severe emotional stress often decreases efficiency." Jeff, who has dark circles under his eyes that make him look like a heroin addict, supposedly has a hard time controlling his emotions.

But the only examples shown are of him losing his temper. Other emotions—sexual desire, for example—are tactfully left unmentioned, although the lab coat guy cautions that repeated emotional outbursts "might lead to a permanently warped personality." By the end of the film Jeff has learned that he's happiest when reason triumphs over feeling, and he joins the gang at a marshmallow roast.

THE COOL HOT ROD
Sid Davis Productions, 1953, 26 minutes

Phil, a pencil-necked "greaser" with hair that looks like a small animal died on his head, arrives in a new town. He intends to educate this "town full of sleepwalkers," where even the teens are "prime squares" who drive "like rich old ladies," on the fine points of living

recklessly. However, his plans are cut short on his first day, when he's hauled into School Court and sentenced to Traffic School.

Phil is perplexed at first, but the new kids soon set him straight. "They weren't behind the times, I was!" Phil concedes. He joins a new kind of hot rod club whose members need clean driving records and have to pass a driving test, and whose rods have to pass a safety inspection. The cars are raced on "a good, safe drag strip" and the kids are all smiling and happy. In this town, hot rodding is all about cars, not teenage rebellion.

Sid Davis shows remarkable restraint in this film. Although its stars are juvenile delinquents, only one teen dies horribly (he tries to outrun a freight train).

The Cool Hot Rod won the Trend Publications Award as "the film that most honestly and accurately depicted the true story of the hot rod hobby." Trend Publications published *Hot Rod* magazine and apparently bankrolled this film.

CRASH RESEARCH
Ford Motor Co., 1955, 10 minutes

This Ford-sponsored film unwittingly gives a good idea how dangerous cars really were in the 1950s.

In 1956, in a radical attempt to position itself in the marketplace, Ford became the first American car company to offer seat belts as an option. This film was apparently made to promote that effort. It concentrates on "a spectacular, exciting part of our job"—crashing cars together—as it shows Ford engineers striving to achieve "a new concept: safely packaged passengers."

Ford's attempt to sell seat belts failed; the public bought Chevys with high-powered engines instead. Seat belts didn't become standard equipment in American cars until 1964.

DANCE, LITTLE CHILDREN
Centron Corp. for Kansas State Board of Health, 1961, 20 minutes

Lynne Corwin is a lovely girl from the poor side of Oakdale. She falls under the spell of boorish Hal Grover, the boy with "the biggest allowance in town." Lynne's mom makes her a party dress—sexy, black velvet, Audrey Hepburnesque—because the Corwins are too

poor to buy one from the store. "Imagine me!" Lynne tells Mom after her date. "Dancing at the country club with Hal Grover! They even had a combo!" But she has tears in her eyes, and the narrator solemnly intones, "The final cost of the dress has not been counted. The price that Lynne Corwin must pay will be a high one!"

Welcome to the diseased world of *Dance, Little Children*, a film that proves that teenagers in the early sixties really did have premarital sex. In fact, the film reports, Oakdale is suffering an outbreak of syphilis among its frisky teens, "fifty or more." It was bound to happen, the narrator sighs, since today's teenagers live in a society that promotes "a worship of sex appeal." Tom-tom drums bop furiously during a montage of titillating lingerie and perfume ads, paperback book covers (*Les Girls; The Wild Party*), and covers of *Daring Romance* and *Battle Station* magazines. "Who is to blame if they respond to what an anxiety-ridden world seems to be telling them?"

Now comes the "frenzy to experience" scene. As murky shots show teens halfheartedly twisting to a jukebox, the narrator becomes overwhelmed with passion. "Dance faster, little children!" he cries. "The lyrics in the shadowy room...suggest something more human than most of the headlines around the spinning globe! Faster! Faster! Race to live while you may!" An anemic surf-rock band sings:

> *Dance little children, don't be shy*
> *There's a girl for every guy*
> *Dance little children, don't be grim*
> *There's a her for every him...*

...and this apparently drives the kids into a sexual frenzy.

Back to the story of Lynne and Hal. A flashback sequence shows Hal and a couple of his loser friends cruising the streets of the big city in Hal's red convertible, looking for "amusement." They pick up a blonde floozy wearing checked stretch pants, and the chain of "blundering blindly into infection" begins. Back to the present in Oakdale, Lynne's mom brings her daughter in for a checkup. She thinks Lynne has the three-day measles, but Dr. Sam has other ideas. "Lynne Corwin?" he asks himself, wrestling with what he suspects is her real problem. "It couldn't be!"

Dr. Sam breaks the bad news to the Corwins. The town enlists the aid of John Camp, "a field representative from the venereal disease program," who smokes a pipe. It quickly becomes apparent that dozens of Oakdale teens have been screwing around and, of course, contracting horrible diseases. John Camp and the town doctors interview them, break the news to disbelieving parents, shoot up everyone with penicillin—and say not a word about condoms or safe sex.

Happily, Lynne's infection is detected early, and thus she's spared "the final tragedy of latent, untreated syphilis." But lest the viewer think that she'll get away scot-free after indulging in premarital nooky, the narrator sets it straight: "Lynne Corwin will be cured of the physical disease, although she may never be free of its emotional consequences."

THE DANGEROUS STRANGER
Sid Davis Productions, 1950, 10 minutes

This was Sid Davis's first safety film. "You've seen in the newspapers about things that happened to other little boys and girls, haven't you?" asks a motorcycle cop as he strides across a busy school yard. "You know, how they went away with strangers, and their mothers and fathers never saw them again? I know you wouldn't want to do that to your folks."

The officer has many stories to tell the kids: of a little girl who accepts a ride from a stranger and "nobody ever saw her again"; of Jimmy, a "wise guy" who "thinks he knows everything" and goes off with a man who offers him a pocketknife; of another girl kidnapped while hitchhiking; and of yet another who was almost dragged away by a man who offered her candy. With flat, shadowless camera work, Sid Davis has the uncanny ability to make even child abduction look unexciting.

"The kids who get in trouble with strangers are those who forget what they've been told," the officer concludes. "And the ones who think they *know more* than their parents and teachers."

All the perverts in this film wear sport jackets.

DATE ETIQUETTE
Coronet Instructional Films, 1952, 10 minutes

Danny Johnson is taking Alice out on their first date. These two are even more wooden than Caroline and Wally from *Are You Popular?*, and though the narrator encourages them to "be natural," they spend so much time obeying date etiquette that they don't appear to have much fun.

The standard Coronet first-date rituals are observed: Danny meets Alice's parents, Alice wears a new dress ("a fellow wants a girl to look nice when he takes her out"), and all four agree on a coming-home time. Danny walks on the curbside and holds doors open, Alice acts demure and subservient. "When money is involved on a date, a girl shouldn't watch to see how much is spent," the narrator cautions. "Fellows like that kind of politeness." Danny and Alice have an awkward moment when they run out of things to say, but the narrator suggests that "asking a girl to talk about herself is a pretty sure way to keep a conversation going."

As Danny stands with Alice on her moonlit front porch—even though she's confided that her trusting parents "are probably already asleep"—the date ends without a goodnight kiss. "Neither one really expects it," the narrator says cheerfully. Danny shakes Alice's hand and buoyantly strides off into the night.

A DATE FOR DINNER
Douglas Productions for Kimberly-Clark Co., 1960, 13 minutes

This production tries to pass itself off as a dating film, but it's actually an exercise in product placement for Kimberly-Clark paper products, which lurk in nearly every shot.

Linda Taylor has been asked out to dinner by Eddie Williams, who works as a bag boy at the local supermarket (he's shown on the store's pay phone, standing behind a stack of Kimberly-Clark paper towels). Linda is "scared to death" at the prospect of eating in a restaurant. "It's so complicated!" she sighs. "I just know I'll do everything wrong! And Eddie will never ask me out any place again!"

Happily, Linda convinces her best friend, Kathy, her brother, Jerry, and her Aunt Kate, who owns a "fancy restaurant," to pitch in and stage a trial dinner so that she can feel at ease. Kathy cuts Kleenex tissues into paper flowers for the centerpiece and Linda and Jerry are given paper napkins. "Your escort will give your order to the waitress," Aunt Kate explains. "A well-trained waitress seldom if ever asks the girl a direct question." The best moment of the film is when Linda has to open her purse in her lap; the camera zooms in to an extreme close-up and out pops a box of Kleenex, its brand name thrust into the lens.

A DATE WITH YOUR FAMILY
Simmel-Meservey, 1950, 10 minutes

Simmel-Meservey produced a half-dozen stiff "manners" films in the late 1940s. This was apparently an attempt to apply that mind-set to everyday family life. The result, as film archivist Rick Prelinger has described it, is a "suburban horror story...so contrived, so

controlled and limiting, that it is hard to imagine living, breathing, thinking people producing it."

A Date with Your Family opens in a kitchen. Teenaged "Daughter" is cooking and teenaged "Brother" is sampling the food. "They're getting ready for an important date," the narrator says, "dinner at home with the family."

Unlike most teens, these two treat every dinner at home as though it were "a truly special occasion." This requires Daughter to cook a several-course meal, set the table with fancy silverware and crystal, create an elaborate floral centerpiece, and then change into "something more fes-

tive" to make her "look more charming." The narrator finds this last point worthy of special praise. "The women of this family," he says, "seem to feel that they owe it to the men of the family to look relaxed, rested, and attractive at dinnertime."

Brother is free from cooking chores and only has to wear a sport jacket. But he and "Junior," his kid brother, are obligated to make happy conversation with "Father" when he arrives home from work. "These boys greet their dad," the narrator observes, "as though they are genuinely glad to see him."

A Date with Your Family has no dialogue and no music, so the narrator is free to provide a continuous stream of observations and rules: "The dinner table is no place for discontent." "Pleasant, unemotional conversation helps digestion." "Let Father and Mother guide the conversational trend...after all, *they made all this possible.*" Daughter is forbidden from making "unkind comparisons about your standard of living," Brother from discussing "unpleasant topics such as gruesome sights or sounds." The narrator reminds Brother, "Tell Mother how good the food is. Maybe Sis rates a compliment, too. It makes them want to continue pleasing you."

This ossifying advice is earnestly given, with repeated assurances that this dinner scene really represents "an atmosphere of warmth and gentleness" and "a thoroughly pleasant meal." It is what the world would be like if everybody obeyed social guidance films: well-ordered, stress-free, brain-deadening. The narrator presents the paradox as the film ends: "With your own family you can relax. Be yourself. Just be sure it's your *best* self."

DATING: DO'S AND DON'TS

Coronet Instructional Films, 1949, 13 minutes

This dating "how-to" classic has received more camp accolades than any other, and it deserves it.

The plot is simple. Happy-go-lucky teen Alan Woodruff ("Woody") receives a free ticket for one couple to the upcoming Hi-Teen Carnival. "One couple," Woody reflects. "That means a date! Not like just going around with the crowd!" After much hesitation

(and a pep talk from his girl-savvy older brother), Woody decides to ask Ann Davis to be his date. With her squinty-eyed smile and chipmunk cheeks, Ann (pronounced "Ay-yun" by the actors in this film) is the perfect companion for supernerd Woody.

At crucial moments during the date, the narrator stops the action and presents Woody with several possible options for his actions. The most critical moment, "How Do You Say Goodnight?," is resolved with a heartfelt handclasp. "Thanks so much," says Ann with a toothy grin. "I had *loads* of fun." Woody watches Ann disappear safely behind her front door, then walks jauntily into the night, whistling with satisfaction at a job well done.

Educational Screen praised *Dating: Do's and Don'ts* for its "effective film-story treatment of a very human problem" and believed it "likely to receive a warm reception in school, church, and community."

John Lindsay, who played Woody, actually did have a crush on Jackie Gleason (Ann). He later became a Chicago stockbroker and lived in a house less than a mile from the spot where *Dating: Do's and Don'ts* was filmed.

Dick Creyke, senior producer at Coronet, had no illusions about the merits of this production. "I used to bring it up years later as an example of a stupid film."

A DAY OF THANKSGIVING

Centron Corp. for Young America Films, 1951, 12 minutes

The Johnson family kids—Dick, Susan, Tommy, and baby Janet—are eagerly awaiting their Thanksgiving dinner. But Dad and Mom have some bad news—no turkey! "We've had a lot of expenses this month," Mom explains, but the kids voice their dissatisfaction anyway. "Even the pilgrims had a feast!"

Dad, sensing a good opportunity for a moral lesson, suggests that instead of the family complaining about what they don't have, they should spend time "toting up the common, ordinary blessings that we have to be thankful for." The film moves to the Johnson family Thanksgiving dinner table (sans turkey) with the Johnsons, heads bowed, offering Thanksgiving dinner prayers as a heavenly choir "mmm"s and "umm"s in the background.

Dick reflects that he likes living in a country "where school books are studied instead of burned." Mother is grateful for her washing machine and "hot water out of the tap." Susan is happy "that families are still important in America," and Tommy appreciates the public library and cookies and milk after school. "If I didn't live in a country where there was plenty to go around—goll-leee!" Dad is simply grateful that when someone knocks on his front door, "it's not some political gangster come to drag us off to jail because we believe in freedom!"

Despite its occasional McCarthyesque rhetoric (things weren't going so well for the Free World in 1951), *A Day of Thanksgiving* stands as the best expression of Centron attitude ever put on film: cornball, well intentioned, idealistic, thoroughly sincere.

DAD: "For all these things, we are truly and humbly thankful. Amen."
HEAVENLY CHOIR: "Ahhhhhhh-mennnnnnnn!"

The angelic choral music was written by Centron cofounder Art Wolf.

DEVELOPING FRIENDSHIPS
Coronet Instructional Films, 1950, 11 minutes

High schooler Bob tells how he used to be aloof and a loner—until he met Joe. "It seemed more fun to think my own thoughts," he reflects, which apparently was a bad thing to do in the early 1950s.

Joe, a squint-eyed, perpetually smiling future politician, "likes people," Bob explains. He "wants to be friends with everybody" and is "sincere and real." Joe quickly becomes the leader of a gang of happy teens who are all slavishly devoted to his welfare. With their help, he places first in the statewide Junior Citizenship essay contest—and wins a trip to the state capital for a week. "Actually, we all won," says Bob, exhibiting the team spirit that will make him a fine, faceless corporate drone in the years to come. Joe hops a train to the capital as Bob and the gang wave goodbye, happily being left behind at age seventeen. "Yessir—with friends, it's a great old world!"

Bob played Woody's older brother in *Dating: Do's and Don'ts*. Other members of the gang include Marie (star of *Going Steady?*), Bill (star of *Social Courtesy*), and supergeek Eddie (star of *Why We Respect the Law*).

DEVELOPING YOUR CHARACTER
Coronet Instructional Films, 1950, 11 minutes

Ken Nordine steps out of the Coronet announcer booth to make one of his occasional appearances as on-screen narrator in this slightly skewed production. Three people interact using the film as a kind of teleconference—Mr. Perry in his office, Bill in his room, and Mrs. Carter in her parlor. Mr. Perry expresses his opinion that "job success and good character go hand-in-hand." Mrs. Carter adds that "good character means better group living, as well as better people." Bill, with whom the students are supposed to identify, has nothing interesting to say.

DICK WAKES UP
Frederick K. Rockett Co. for AAA Foundation for Traffic Safety, 1954, 14 minutes

This film, "presented in the interest of public safety," opens as a boy named Dick thoughtlessly runs across a street, against the light, to join his friends in a softball game. "Hey, Dick!"

one of his pals yells. "Look out for that car!" Too late. Dick is run over by a '54 Buick as the camera zooms into its menacing grill, then cuts to a shot of Dick's broken bat lying on the pavement.

A hypno-swirl appears. Melodramatic music fills the soundtrack as Dick wakes up in his hospital bed, sandwiched between two miniature versions of himself. "Judge" (good judgment) and "Imp" (bad impulse) immediately begin yelling at each other in high-pitched, studio-reverb voices and don't stop until the end of the film. Dick accepts this meekly, but anyone else would question whether it was worth the price of survival.

"It didn't work this time, did it, Dick," Judge declares. "You can't be lucky forever." Imp scoffs at such "safety hokum" and tells Judge, "All you're trying to do is take the fun out of life!" Judge counters that Dick could use "a little common sense" while Imp points out that "there's a lot of things you don't think of until too late. After all, what do cars have brakes for?" And on and on it goes for the next fourteen minutes, with Imp and Judge huffing and puffing at each other across a giant hospital room set.

The usual 1950s safety bromides are trotted out: laws exist for "your protection" and violating them shows "bad sportsmanship." By the end of the film Dick naturally decides that Judge is his pal and develops a positive new outlook:

DICK: "Doctor, will I be able to run and play ball again?"
DR. DAVIDSON: "You just better take it easy, son."
DICK: "Oh I will! From now on!"

DINING TOGETHER
Children's Productions, 1947, 10 minutes

Dining Together follows two boys at Thanksgiving dinner as they polish candlestick holders, set the table, change into suits, hold chairs for the ladies, sit up straight, praise their mother's cooking, engage in restrained conversation, and eat soup "without noise." The saccharine narrator cries, "We are *glad* we have good table manners. Good manners make people happy. And good table manners make eating together a happy time."

The tiny rooms where this was filmed appear to be lit with a home-movie floodlight. *Educational Screen* dryly observed that the piano music track "might well be more subdued at several points."

DINNER PARTY
Simmel-Meservey, 1945, 23 minutes

Dinner Party takes place at a dinner table, surrounded by teens wearing suits and uncomfortable-looking dresses. It's divided into two parts: the seventeen-minute *Dinner Party* and the six-minute *Review of "Dinner Party."* Teens were supposed to watch the first film and "see if you can notice right away when someone is incorrect." The second film replays excerpts from the first film and points out when the hapless teens in film #1 are "awkward" and "make errors." Some examples from the twenty-five-page teacher guide:

+ "The housekeeper points out that Betty has incorrectly placed the napkin and butter knife and failed to include water glasses."

+ "Bob starts eating his soup immediately, not waiting until Betty passes the crackers."

+ "Betty finds it difficult to decide just how to manage the salad implements.... Should she butter her vegetable with a knife or fork? Should she serve Bob's cake, or should the housekeeper?"

The robotic narrator rattles off rule after rule in a nonstop, machine-gun monotone—covering everything from relish placement to "zigzag eating"—and advocates removing candles from the birthday cake and attaching them to the platter before blowing them out to avoid "possible germs being blown on the cake."

A letter in the February 1946 issue of *See and Hear* offered this review of *Dinner Party:* "After a few days had elapsed (since showing the film) the librarian reported that the demand for Emily Post and *The Vogue Book on Etiquette* exceeded anything she had ever experienced in her long term of service as a school librarian."

DON'T SMOKE POT
unknown producer, 1968, 15 minutes

The narrator declares that marijuana is a "hallucinogen" and that "potheads believe that serious thought is a drag." George Willis is a serious aspiring drag racer, but then his hippie friends show up in a VW minibus and take him down the road to oblivion.

Bargain-basement groovy music track, an obligatory trip sequence, and lots of "cool" dialogue. The narrator reads his lines in a monotone so expressionless, it sounds as though he's stoned. A very slow film, perhaps deliberately paced to simulate pot intoxication.

DOORWAY TO DEATH
Aetna Casualty & Surety Co. Motion Picture Bureau, 1949, 12 minutes

Two housewives chat over a backyard fence:

#1: "I was awfully sorry to hear it. They were such a lovely, happy family. And she was a good wife and mother."
#2: "And such a good neighbor, too. Everyone will miss her."
#1: "Strange that a fall from a kitchen chair could kill her, isn't it."
#2: "She was making a berry pie one minute, the next minute she was dead."

This film was circulated in schools accompanied by *Doorway to Death* checklists. Kids were supposed to take them home—as does pigtailed little Grace Clark in this film—and use them to perform safety inspections. "Carelessness and indifference set booby traps for every member of the family," the narrator warns. "Safety within your home is *your* responsibility." No gruesome accidents are shown—Aetna must have thought better of it—but the film

does end in a mythical Court of Carelessness, where a stone-faced judge hands down sentences to weeping adults who broke safety rules. "Home should be a safe refuge. Don't allow yours to become a doorway to death!"

DRIVEN TO KILL
Sound Masters for American Transit Association, 1948, 11 minutes

This film is most noteworthy for its penny-dreadful narration by Lowell Thomas, who occasionally appears seated behind a big microphone, reading aloud from a script on the desk in front of him.

Hal Johnson is a safety-conscious family man, an "average American," a "careful, considerate citizen," a "backbone of the nation." "I like his attitude," Lowell admits. Until, that is, Hal gets

"Don't let your car be driven to kill!"

behind the wheel of a car. Then he becomes a "menace" and a "confirmed bumper-chaser" encased in "a hurtling shell of steel." "He doesn't seem to realize that at the speed he is traveling, his car has the same impact as if it were dropped from an eight-story building!"

Hal gets a thrill out of his driving, Lowell remarks, but "that little thrill is going to be purchased dearly one day; purchased at the price of torn, mutilated bodies and a tragic, heartbroken family!" Of course, about eight minutes into the film, that's exactly what happens.

Driven to Kill won the 1948 "Safety Oscar" (theatrical division) from the National Committee on Films for Safety. *Business Screen* estimated that over fifteen million people saw this melodramatic weeper in its first year of release. Especially memorable is its sequence of sorrowful bad drivers, including the pretty girl with the big facial scar and the young couple with missing limbs.

THE DROPOUT
Sid Davis Productions, 1962, 11 minutes

The Dropout is Sid Davis at his most relentless. As a saxophone wails awesome be-bop (this is Sid's grooviest music track) the film introduces Robert, a smiling, clean-cut teen

who's just dropped out of high school. "Your newfound freedom holds the promise you've been waiting for, doesn't it, Robert?" the narrator asks, disapproval dripping from every syllable. "No more educational restrictions. The time to work and make enough to support your pleasures and your car." Like teenagers in many Sid Davis teen films, Robert has made a fatal error—he thinks he can Break The Rules. This film will serve as his river of destiny, carrying him inexorably downstream to his doom.

Robert is optimistic and confident as he sets out on his initial job interviews—but he soon discovers that his town offers only the most humiliating work for someone without a high school diploma. "The answer is always the same," the narrator says as a succession of suit-wearing men shake their heads. " 'Sorry, son, but we require more education.' " Robert, not yet realizing that he's trapped in a Sid Davis universe, visits an employment agency. After

a "battery of tests and consultations" the experts assign Robert his classification: "common laborer."

"Now you feel adrift," the narrator hammers away. "You're on the outside looking in." Robert gives in and takes a busboy job at the hamburger stand where he used to hang out. He even has to serve fries and Cokes to his upwardly mobile classmates who stayed in school! His dad continually yells at him to get out of bed.

His girlfriend leaves him. "The vision of your future starts to crumble," the narrator says with satisfaction.

Robert quits his job. He develops an "attitude"—very dangerous in a Sid Davis film. He spends his time "wandering aimlessly in the less-desirable sections of town." He wears a ripped T-shirt and leather jacket. And he makes "new friends" who hang out at the pool hall and smoke cigarettes. "They have one thing in common," the narrator points out. "They're 'beat.' They don't seem to care."

The film ends as Robert apathetically watches one of his new buddies being dragged out of the pool hall by the police. "As you watch him being cuffed, your mind races," the narrator says. "Can you continue the way you're going and stay out of trouble? You *wish you knew*." Zoom in on the eight ball. Fade to black.

DRUG ABUSE: THE CHEMICAL TOMB

Alan Kishbaugh for Film Distributors International, 1969, 19 minutes

Degenerate bongos bop and sitars twang as a group of hippies dances in a room, barefoot, painting swirly patterns on the floor with spray cans, smoking pot. "This is the now generation," the narrator declares. "They feel disenchanted with the world around them. They are a part of the wave of the future."

This film tries very hard to come across as hip and open-minded. The narrator worries that a generation on

drugs may jeopardize its chance to create "a meaningful, less materialistic society." He acknowledges that "drugs have been used as a principal means of rebellion against authority" and that "drugs are not the proper tools with which to change a society that somehow hasn't fulfilled all its promise." Yet the visuals show nothing but barefoot hippies, acne-scarred drug dealers in sunglasses, and a girl who rolls her eyes while having hallucinations of airplanes, marching bands, and an erupting volcano.

A guy in a suit, the medical director of the Los Angeles District Attorney's Youth Advisory Council, cautions about the "psychic dependence" of drug users and reveals that "smoking typical pot usually produces mind-altering or hallucinogenic experiences. In high dosage it parallels LSD."

"Is the gamble of drug exploration worth this?" the narrator asks as handcuffed suburban teens are led down a driveway to a squad car parked at the curb. "A criminal record is never an asset. It can mean the end of a fine future."

Yet there is hope. "Many of today's young people are 'turning on' to a world that needs more involvement," the narrator says, as a fresh-scrubbed candystriper feeds a traction patient through a straw. "A nation in turmoil needs the newness of its young!"

DRUG ADDICTION

Encyclopaedia Britannica Films for Juvenile Protection Association of Chicago & Wieboldt Foundation, 1951, 22 minutes

Drug Addiction chronicles the decline and fall of Marty DeMalone, a "good boy" who becomes a junkie. Marty's experimentation begins with marijuana, which produces "profound mental and emotional disturbances." As evidence, the film shows him laughing like a maniac, drinking Pepsi from broken bottles, cutting his mouth to shreds. "He was determined to be one of the gang if it killed him."

"Thoughtless curiosity can lead to a lifetime of pain and torment!"

Marty is too far gone to care. He goes straight to "H," which he buys from Louie, a local dealer who keeps his stash in the base of a lamp. Marty spirals downward from snorting to mainlining, steals some cans of tunafish, loses his job,

and is shunned by girls. "It didn't matter. Nothing mattered but the ever-present craving for the drug." When he steals money from his own mother, it's clear Marty is near the end.

Marty is finally caught shoplifting an iron, sent to a very pleasant-looking drug rehab hospital, where he cuts down dead corn stalks and plays checkers and baseball, and, happily, reforms.

Educational Screen observed, "Even though the life of the young addict is shown to be completely unpleasant, the producers of the film have been careful to avoid showing details of drug administration or paraphernalia used, which might encourage experimentation."

The street pushers in this film have bad complexions and wear dark turtlenecks.

DRUGS AND THE NERVOUS SYSTEM
Churchill Films, 1972, 18 minutes

Although this purports to be an educational film, it's really old-style alarmist mental hygiene. It came along late in the game, but because it was made for kids, it has that one-sided slant that no longer worked for teens.

It opens educationally enough, with five minutes of close-ups of a kid in bed sweating with a fever. The narrator exclaims, "Many young children have eaten several sweetened aspirin tablets thinking they were candy—and died!" From then on the film is all moody, dark, crude animation of outline people, firing brain synapses, and blobby optical effects—which, although this film doesn't acknowledge it, came out of the 1960s psychedelic *drug* movement.

Eerie strings in a minor key fill the music track. The narrator has nothing good to say about any illegal drug, and their effects are described as so universally unpleasant that kids who watched this film would have had to wonder why so many people were taking them. Drug users—no matter what drug—are in it for "kicks," the narrator asserts, although he saves his strongest condemnations for users of marijuana and LSD. "A brain under the influence of marijuana distorts space and time." As for those who take acid: "Some people believe they can fly. Some people believe they are God." To demonstrate this, the film cuts to a shot of two teenaged lovebirds walking down a sidewalk. Suddenly the boy runs, laughing, onto the busy highway and commands the cars to stop! You can guess what happens.

As the film ends, the narrator rhetorically asks what kind of kids use drugs. "Would you guess that they are strong—or weak? Would they be responsible? Mature for their age? Might they have problems getting along in the world? What do you think?"

DUCK AND COVER
Archer Productions for Federal Civil Defense Administration, 1951, 10 minutes

> *There was a turtle by the name of Bert*
> *And Bert the turtle was very alert*
> *When danger threatened him he never got hurt*
> *He knew just what to dooooo . . .*
> *He'd duck! And cov-er . . .*

This little civil defense gem was rescued from obscurity by the 1982 documentary *The Atomic Café*. It presents Bert, a cartoon turtle and "a very, very careful fellow," as a role model for its preteen audience. "Always remember," the narrator warns, "the flash from an atomic bomb can come at any time!" If it comes during class, kids are supposed to *duck* under their desks and *cover* the backs of their necks with their hands.

If it comes outside of class, well, that's when this film shifts into overdrive. A series of bland, everyday scenes ensues—a family picnic, a kid riding a bike, a boy and girl walking down a street. A blinding flash from behind the camera sends the actors into a frenzy. The boy and girl col-

lapse against a wall. The kid falls off his bike and rolls into a bridge abutment. ("Attaboy, Tony!") The dad at the picnic yanks a newspaper over his head while Mom and the kids toss their food into the air and hide under the blanket. "We must be ready every day, all the time, to do the right thing if the atomic bomb explodes." Just like Bert the turtle!

What happens after kids duck and cover? The film doesn't go into that. *Duck and Cover* leaves its human role

models lying where they fall, like corpses, with only this vague instruction: "Stay covered until the danger is over." It's advice that would be hard to follow when overpressure had burst people's lungs, or the heat wave had set their clothes on fire, or the blast wave had hurled them through the air or buried them under debris. But when you think about it, a turtle hiding in its shell wouldn't survive a nuclear attack either.

EARNING MONEY WHILE GOING TO SCHOOL
Coronet Instructional Films, 1950, 12 minutes

High schooler Bill Drake wants to buy a typewriter, so he takes a part-time job in a bookstore. "A bookstore," he gripes. "Boy...I get enough of books all day long." However, Bill quickly learns to enjoy his work, which pleases the narrator of this film. "He was learning to get along with people, just as he would all through his life. And he was seeing what it means to play a useful role in the community."

Unfortunately, Bill also realizes that he won't have much time to study and do homework. Dutiful student that he is, Bill decides to quit. Then, in an ending that's contrived even by Coronet standards, he suddenly realizes that his job will actually help him with his studies. "I'll bet I could learn a lot of my literature work just keeping my eyes and ears open around here! I'll stay on this job!"

This film makes the important concession that Bill, by working, must "turn down chances for fun." "But," the narrator quickly adds, "whenever he did take time to play, Bill enjoyed himself all the more."

EMOTIONAL HEALTH
Audio Productions for McGraw-Hill Book Co., 1947, 20 minutes

A college freshman sits in a doctor's office, complaining of pains in his chest, nervousness, and a fast pulse. The doctor finds nothing wrong with him. "There must be something!" the young man insists. "This can't all be my imagination!" The doctor explains, "You can have pains in your chest even if there's nothing *organically* wrong," and recommends that the young man see a psychiatrist. "A psychiatrist?" he cries. "Gee, doc, I'm not crazy!"

Films like this and *What's on Your Mind* reflect the brief vogue that psychiatry enjoyed in the years immediately following World War II. Here, the doctor reassures the panicky young man that he's merely "emotionally upset." "That sort of thing bothered a lot of men during the war," he explains. "Next to the common cold, emotional upsets are our most common illnesses. Now we're treating them like illnesses."

Most of this film takes place in either the doctor's or the psychiatrist's office, as the young man overcomes his "warped reasoning" and learns that his chest pains are the result of insecurity, fear of failure, and guilt. Happily, after several months of therapy, he is completely cured. "I have a date!" he announces as he leaves his final session. "That's *real* progress!" the psychiatrist chortles, and the film ends with the well-adjusted young man sipping Coke with a buxom blonde.

EMOTIONAL MATURITY
Crawley Films for McGraw-Hill Book Co., 1957, 19 minutes

This depressing Crawley film introduces teenager Dave, who has his share of problems: his dad doesn't respect him, his mom treats him like a baby, he can't afford a car, his girl-

friend leaves him because he "acts like a kid." In most guidance films Dave would have been given a chance to straighten up and fly right. But here, he's doomed.

Dave decides to vent his frustrations inappropriately by slashing the car tires of his girlfriend's new beau. He's immediately caught and humiliated. "How did Dave get in a situation like this?" the narrator asks as Mom, Dad, and the ex-girlfriend trample every last shred of Dave's self-respect. The answer: "Dave was emotionally unstable."

A merciless film, painful to watch.

EXCHANGING GREETINGS AND INTRODUCTIONS
Centron Corp. for Young America Films, 1960, 11 minutes

Social guidance filmmakers were still trying to ram rules and regulations down the throats of American kids in 1960. This film isn't all that different in content from *How Do You Do* (1946), except that it applies its stuffy rules to children instead of teenagers.

"You will be admired if you master the simple skills of exchanging greetings and introductions," the narrator declares, as dozens of kids introduce themselves to one another, to parents, to teachers, teachers to parents, parents to still more kids, etc. "Greetings and introductions will always play an important part in your life." The children seem unconvinced.

EXERCISE AND HEALTH
Coronet Instructional Films, 1949, 10 minutes

Ernie, Jean, and Hal are three teens with problems. Ernie is in "a run-down condition"; Jean is "shy and withdrawn"; Hal is "tense and irritable." Luckily, all three join the Acrobatics Club at school, get into shape, and learn about the benefits of teamwork and "the right kind of exercise." Now Ernie, Jean, and Hal "make friends easier" and have "outlets for their emotional tensions."

FACING REALITY
Knickerbocker Productions for McGraw-Hill Book Co., 1954, 11 minutes

The screen fills with a teenaged girl, a face on the front and back of her head. The narrator explains that she represents one of the "escape mechanisms" employed when people "refuse to face reality." Next, Michael Squires is introduced, a teen who is "pinwheeling through life" and "darting away from reality through the escape hatches of his emotional being." Michael wants to be a writer and gains attention by being a "negativist" and not facing "the hard realities of life." This will not do. Happily, by the end of the film, Michael recognizes the error of his ways, and when he utters his final line, "I guess I haven't been making good sense," it's clear he's well on the way to embracing the status quo.

FAMILY LIFE
Coronet Instructional Films, 1949, 11 minutes

The Miller family is in a rut. Everyone is angry with everyone else. Could they be experiencing the first signs of generational friction or discovering that individuals in families often hold different views? Nah—it's just bad management! Mom decides to take the initiative and "work out a system for living together in harmony." From now on the family will be run "like a business," with weekly family counsel meetings in which everyone's responsibilities will be clearly outlined. This approach strikes the other Millers as terrific—"Say, Mom, you're swell!"—and everyone ends up cheerful and content.

FAREWELL TO CHILDHOOD

Herbert Kerkow for National Association for Mental Health, Inc., 1951, 23 minutes

"Progressive" guidance films often featured perfect teachers as fonts of wisdom. The one here, Mrs. Soams, is so perfect, she doesn't even need to be at school. Her advice is dispensed over cookies and milk in her cozy parlor.

The recipient of her wisdom is Susan Stuart, a fifteen-year-old played, it appears, by a twenty-five-year-old trying to act ten years younger. She screams lines such as, "I might as well be *dead* for all anyone cares!"

Susan's mom gets so jealous of the attention that Susan showers on Mrs. Soams that she heads over to her house to confront her. Mrs. Soams never loses her cool. She graciously pours tea and, perfect teacher that she is, almost immediately has Susan's mom begging for advice. "I know it's a difficult period," Mrs. Soams coos. "But never was there a time when Susan needed you more. Make her your friend!" And mom does.

FATAL SECONDS

The Aetna Casualty & Surety Co. Motion Picture Bureau, 1948, 10 minutes

Jim Wright sits in an overstuffed chair, clad in a houserobe, fidgiting with a cane, staring groggily into the camera. "I'm very much alone now. Yes, very much alone ..."

A flashback sequence shows why. The Wright family—Jim, Mary, and little Bob—are driving over to Clarksville to have Sunday dinner with Aunt Grace. "Jim was a good driver for years, careful and safe," the narrator says. But on that steep hill near the Ashford place, Jim thought he could pass a car in front of him that was moving too slow. It would only take a few seconds ...

"Twenty-four hours a day violent death stalks the open road!"

The action freezes, and the film whisks ahead in time to Jim, Mary, and little Bob arriving at Aunt Grace's, and then enjoying a lovely meal. "Yes, this is how it *might* have been," the narrator says, as the hands on a clock suddenly spin backward. "Once the fatal second strikes, you can't go back!"

Whoops, it's back to the steep hill again. A farm truck comes from the other direction. Jim frantically spins the wheel. Too late!!! The screen goes black. "Bob was killed instantly. With a bad skull fracture, Mary lived but a few minutes. No, they didn't get to Aunt Grace's. They never will again."

"Life is a one-way street. You can't retrace your steps. What's done is done!"

FIRE! PATTY LEARNS WHAT TO DO
Frith Films, 1951, 17 minutes

One of many distinctive films made by Emily Benton Frith, featuring the voice of "commentator" Don McNamara. In this one, Captain Clemens of the fire department teaches Patty Garman how to "chaperone your match" and demonstrates safety techniques by setting fire to a doll on the end of a stick. The bulk of this film takes place in flashback, as Patty relives footage from "the terrible Chatsworth fire," while Don explains that such fires are to be expected "after an earthquake or an atomic bomb."

FITNESS IS A FAMILY AFFAIR
unknown producer for National Film Board of Canada, 1949, 15 minutes

F

Educational Screen described this film well:

> The beginning scenes of the film show children using the street as their unsafe and only playground. Next it shows Ed Logan arriving home in a vile mood. The entire Logan family appear preoccupied with their own interests. They eat supper and spend the evening as very lonely individuals. Mrs. Logan has absolutely no companionship from her husband, since he spends the evening "snoozing."
>
> Ed Logan's neighbor, in contrast, arrives home in a jolly mood and further endears himself to his family by taking special note of each of them in a pleasing way. Supper is strictly a family affair. They enjoy it together and share its responsibilities. A picture of one of their family picnics shows them sharing this fun with a guest.
>
> The success of a basement rumpus room leads the teen-agers to consider a neighborhood center. Ed Logan is approached on the subject of using his garage for this purpose. Strangely enough, he accepts the proposition, and as the project develops he becomes very much interested in it. A film on recreational centers seen by the group provides many practical and excellent ideas. The men's woodworking and the women's needlework transform the drab garage into an attractive recreational center.
>
> The film ends by showing the backyard nursery that the parents developed after having developed and enjoyed first the neighborhood center. Pictures of happy people seem to indicate that the neighborhood projects contribute to the neighborhood friendliness and happiness.

FOCUS ON JUNIOR ACHIEVEMENT: LEARNING BY DOING
unknown producer, 1961, 9 minutes

This film chronicles, in newsreel fashion, several months of activities at the Battle Creek, Michigan, chapter of Junior Achievement, as it tries to help high schoolers "come to a better understanding of our economic way of life."

Junior Achievement, from the looks of this film, sponsored school yearlong projects in which a select group of carefully screened, sensibly dressed teens managed an imaginary company with the goal of earning a profit. "As a new company is founded," the narrator explains, "there is born a new and greater respect for the free enterprise system."

In truth, Junior Achievement more closely resembles Girl Scouts selling cookies door-to-door than anything in the real business world. White, middle-aged men in suits are seen in nearly every shot, apparently running the show (well, actually, that *is* very much like the real business world) despite the narrator's assurances that the teens "make their own decisions, solve their own problems." With no participation from the Achievers (and a music track of overly upbeat flutes, strings, and horns), a name is chosen for their company—DoorMatCo—as well as the products it will sell—ugly doormats and tiny wooden stools. "The manufacture of doormats provides DoorMatCo with the same diversification that industrial giants have."

Much of Junior Achievement's efforts appear to be aimed at learning sales techniques. The kids go door-to-door in boy-girl teams, sample doormats and stools in hand, through the flat, harshly lit, wintertime suburbs of Battle Creek. While some young people in 1961 were joining the Peace Corps or risking their necks to end racial discrimination in the South, those in this film were learning "ways of overcoming sales resistance" and that "sales commissions reward persistent effort." The boys do all the talking while the girls stand aside and fill out the order forms.

The film ends as DoorMatCo liquidates itself, having made a net profit of $262.50. "But no cash dividend," the narrator explains, "can truly reflect the riches the Achiever carries away. The better understanding, the deeper appreciation of the economic way of life that made America great, the faith in themselves and their country—these are the priceless possessions they carry forward into the future!"

FRIENDSHIP BEGINS AT HOME
Coronet Instructional Films, 1949, 15 minutes

Barry is a teenager who doesn't appreciate his family. "Everybody's always picking on me," he says as he decides to bail out of his family's annual two-week fishing trip. "I'd rather stay here with my friends." "Don't you consider your family your friends?" asks kid sister Diana. "How can a guy be friends with his family?" Barry snaps. But Dad is willing

to accommodate Barry and the family departs. "We're going away to have *fun*," Dad declares.

Barry's first few hours of freedom are glorious, but he quickly discovers that his "friends" aren't as dependable as his family. George won't invite him over for dinner; Barry eats canned beans and soup for two weeks. Heartthrob Lorraine gets sick and cancels her party. The rest of Barry's friends are either away, working, or on vacation—with their families, no doubt. Barry ponders the meaning of it all in a continual monologue of internal sentence fragments as wistful strings fill the soundtrack and the camera dollies in for close-ups on his face. He affects these moments of deep thought by suddenly raising his head, narrowing his eyes, and looking up and off-camera at a forty-five-degree angle. "Why haven't any of my friends called? Not much fun spending the day alone. Nobody to do things with. What are friends for, anyway?"

Barry discovers that freedom can't match the "thoughtfulness" of his family. "I never before listened to an—empty house," he reflects. Double-exposure images appear of his family doing thoughtful things that Barry had, until now, not appreciated. Mom brings ice cream, Diana offers to take his suit to the cleaners, and kid brother Dick begs him to play checkers. "Boy," Barry cries, "how I'd like to play checkers with you right now!"

"They're swell people!" Barry declares, the scales falling from his eyes. "All of them! They do the kinds of things you expect of your friends! *Friends!* That's it!!!"

Barry is a changed young man. His family returns to find him scrubbing the kitchen floor. "You know, Mother, you never really appreciate your family until they're not around." He's bought Dick a new tennis racket, and he takes Diana to a dance when her date backs out. "Wow! Is that my sister? Well, no wonder all those fellows telephoned while you were away!"

FUN OF BEING THOUGHTFUL
Coronet Instructional Films, 1950, 10 minutes

"Everywhere you go, people talk about thoughtfulness."

Jane Proctor is a happy teen who—unlike Barry in *Friendship Begins at Home*—is slavishly devoted to her "fine, thoughtful family." Spouting lines such as "It'd be the thoughtful thing to do," and "That's what makes thoughtfulness worthwhile!" Jane tidies her room, fixes dinner for the family, and fixes her geeky brother Eddie up with a date. Her thoughtfulness pays off as the film ends—"A new dress!!!"—and the Proctor family basks in the sunshine of family togetherness.

Goggle-eyed Jane later starred in *Making Your Own Decisions*. Supergeek Eddie appeared in *Developing Friendships*. With cameos by Sue (*How to Say No*), Bill (*How Do You Know It's Love*), and the Coronet candy machine (*Benefits of Looking Ahead*).

FUN OF MAKING FRIENDS
Coronet Instructional Films, 1950, 11 minutes

Joey is a glum little kid who would rather sit home and play with a rubber stamp than get out and join the great fraternity of 1950s democratic togetherness. "Maybe mother knows how to make friends," the sugary-sweet woman narrator of this film suggests. Mother certainly does. "Smile and talk to people. Find good things in people. Tell them the good things. Do this all the time." Joey is encouraged to grin, wave, and to put this new happy-face attitude to work in school. "Look! Barney and Betty are smiling right back!" the narrator exclaims. "And the teacher, too! Boy—it's fun to make friends!" And later, when the school day ends: "Look! Betty and Barney are waiting to walk home with Joey! Going home isn't going to be lonely this time!"

GANG BOY
Arthur Swerdloff for Sid Davis Productions, 1954, 27 minutes

Danny is the nineteen-year-old leader of an unnamed band of Chicanos in "Mex town," somewhere near Los Angeles. Their rivals are the Pepper Tree Gang, Anglo toughs who oppose them for no reason other than that seems to be what gangs do.

Danny's introspective musings provide most of the film's narration. As a kid, he plays in junkyards and muddy, unpaved streets lined with shacks. He explains that his gang gradually formed as a way to fight against "the angry world." Danny is a thoughtful, intelligent leader even though he's a delinquent and is keenly aware that he's failed to fit in to society. "We never grew up," he reflects. "Instead we merged ourselves like animals into a herd and became a gang."

Run-ins with the Pepper Tree Gang produce a couple of fistfights and one overturned car, but the police worry that it will escalate into something more bloody. Under Danny's

leadership the Chicanos decide to get more involved in the community and throw a dance, but it seems as if it will only provide the spark for more violence, since the Pepper Tree Gang is expected to break it up.

Luckily, a police officer suggests that the two gangs "try to settle things in a democratic way." They have a truce meeting and decide that members of both gangs be allowed to attend the dance. Soon the Chicanos, now a "club" and no longer a gang, have built a ballpark for younger kids, donated time and money to the March of Dimes, and held a canned-food drive for needy families in their community. "A small beginning, perhaps," says the narrator. "But it is at least a beautiful straw in the breath of a prayer that is gradually being fulfilled." Danny is more blunt. "If you want something better out of life than a gang, you've gotta start somewhere."

GETTING ALONG WITH PARENTS
Encyclopaedia Britannica Films, 1954, 14 minutes

A group of teens makes plans to go dancing at The Blue Room after the junior prom. Jane thinks it's "the dreamiest idea yet," but all the kids acknowledge that they face a major obstacle: parents. "They just don't understand," whines one kid. "They treat us like babies," gripes another. "Don't they understand the younger generation at all?" asks a third.

The camera cuts to a suburban train station where two dads are having their own gripe session. "I don't know what young people are thinking of these days," one says. "No discipline. No consideration. No sense of the value of money." The other dad agrees. "Everything seems so old-fashioned to them. No sense of responsibility. They get too much freedom."

"Could it be that teenagers are hard to live with, too?" the narrator wryly asks.

That evening, each of the teens has to break the news of their plan to go to The Blue Room to their folks. Betty Anderson, who wears a hypnotic, epileptic seizure–inducing striped blouse, puts her request in a positive light. "Everyone's gonna die of envy!" she exclaims. Mom falls for this approach ("The Blue Room? That's that swanky place with the name band and the floor show!"), but stick-in-the-mud Dad does not and vetoes Betty's plans. "Father!" she wails, "I've gotta go where the crowd goes!"

Betty needn't worry, since none of the other teens has had any luck with their parents either. Things look pretty bleak until Jane's folks suddenly offer a suggestion. "Couldn't *we* make it special?" they ask. "Could you leave it to a group of us? Trust us to make it a special party?"

Suddenly, a xylophone pounds out a telegraph beat on the soundtrack. Staccato strings and clarinets speed the tempo as a series of optical wipes show parents excitedly calling each other on the phone. Next thing you know, it's prom night and, *voilá!*, a party has been prepared in the rec room of Jane's split-level home. Mardis gras masks dangle from the ceiling on mobiles and a big sign reads: WELCOME: THE COMMITTEE OF MOMS AND DADS.

"Hey!" says one of the formerly blue teens as he enters. "This suits me fine!"

GIRLS BEWARE
Sid Davis Productions, 1961, 10 minutes

Peppy cocktail lounge music plays as a woman police officer recounts several stories of "careless" girls being killed, gang-raped, and impregnated by sinister men and sex-mad older boys. "The most difficult part of my job is bringing bad news to parents," she remarks matter-of-factly. "You can never find the right words to tell a mother her daughter has been murdered."

"It is often the things that are done without thinking that get young people into trouble."

Judy meets her death at the hands of a baby-sitting client. Sally is flattered by the attention of two older boys but ends up weeping in her mother's lap, forever haunted by what happened to her at Lookout Peak. Mary foolishly dates a jobless, gum-chewing jarhead who hangs out at the twenty-three-cent hamburger stand, complies with his "desires" (underneath a park tree), and then discovers that she's in trouble. "She had to tell her parents," the police officer says. "But now it was too late for advice."

For all its gloom and doom, this film never shows anything bad happening, just the tragic results—a hallmark of low-low-budget filmmaking. It ends with a vintage Sid Davis conclusion: "Trying to move too quickly into the world of grown-ups with a young person's face often causes heartache and disaster."

GLENN WAKES UP
Centron Corp. for Young America Films, 1950, 10 minutes

Glenn is a brooding, unhappy little boy who walks around with his face downturned and his hands in his pockets. "Everybody's against me," he whines. The narrator agrees: "No one wanted him to have any fun." Of course, Glenn's idea of fun—throwing rocks at a cat in a tree, for example—is not shared by other members of his community.

After eating a pint of ice cream and half a jar of pickles, Glenn is magically visited in his bedroom by "Mr. X," an old man in a windbreaker who

looks like he was dragged out of a hardware store. Mr. X tells Glenn that he needs to become "a good citizen," which involves "brushing your teeth every morning," "accepting the decisions of the majority," and "being kind to people less fortunate than ourselves." (Cut to a scene of Glenn helping a clubfooted kid pick up some dropped school books while other kids laugh.) "If you want people to like you, you have to *make* them like you," says Mr. X, who then vanishes into air as a slide whistle toots.

Glenn decides to follow Mr. X's advice (and, one would hope, improve his diet). The next morning he apologizes to the lady with the cat (she gives him a cookie) and, the narrator points out, feels "happier than he had in a long, long time."

This was Centron's first social guidance film.

GOING STEADY?

Coronet Instructional Films, 1951, 10 minutes

Unhappy-looking teens Jeff and Marie are woeful because they've let their relationship "drift" into what others perceive as "going steady." Is that what they want? "The question

is not answered for them; it is not answered for you," warns a title card as this film begins.

Going Steady? has no guiding narrator, a risky innovation for its time. Instead, Jeff and Marie's self-examining, angst-ridden monologues amply fill the soundtrack and give the impression that going steady is about as much fun as an abscessed tooth:

MARIE: "I'd rather go out with Jeff—but I wish the others wouldn't ignore me so!"

JEFF: "Am I going steady? What does that mean? How did I get into this anyway?"

MARIE'S MOM: "I hope Jeff doesn't feel that he has the right to—take liberties."

MARIE: "Oh, Mother!"

Social guidance films always discouraged teens from "drifting" into steady relationships, apparently so the kids wouldn't "drift" into early marriage (or sex). Thankfully, Jeff and Marie become aware of their dangerous lassitude and leave this film smiling, uncommitted, and significantly further away from uncontrollable urges.

GOOD GROOMING FOR GIRLS

Coronet Instructional Films, 1956, 11 minutes

This is narrated by a nameless, dowdy girl whose hair looks like it was styled with an egg-beater. Her friend is the lovely Rosemary, a part-time teen fashion model who always looks "so confident and smooth and well put together." "Everyone likes Rosemary!" the dowdy girl exclaims. "Wish I could be more like her."

As luck would have it, Rosemary invites the frump to a sleepover, which allows this film to show "all the things Rosemary does to be so . . . so good to look at." Plain girl quickly learns that her outer apparel is important. "When styles change, conservative clothes will stay in good taste." Her underwear is important too. "Knowing they're clean and mended adds to your confidence and poise." She sees the benefits of hair brushing—"Rosemary brushes up and out from the hair line, just like we learned at school"—of nail polish— "Choose one that's not too bright"—and of proper posture—"A good foundation usually helps. Even for girls our age." By the end of the film, the once-gawky geek girl is trim-tailored, has a home-permanent, resembles a 1950s secretary, and couldn't be happier. She concludes, "Knowing you're neat and clean all over, inside and out, lets you forget about yourself and enjoy other people. That's the real secret of popularity!"

THE GOOD LOSER

Centron Corp. for Young America Films, 1953, 13 minutes

Teenaged Ray Medford is a "swell guy" who wins at everything. Then he kindly coaches Marilyn Jackson for a school speaking contest that he's already entered—and she beats him! Ray is resentful; Marilyn is demure and humble. "Gosh, Ray . . . I don't know why they picked me." Mr. Murray, the debate coach, offers advice and blinks a lot. "Does being a good winner make it hard to be a good loser?"

According to Gene Hardtarfer, who played Ray, *The Good Loser* lost its chance to win a film award because Gene didn't wear a tie in the speaking contest scenes. "I came from a poor family. I didn't own a tie."

GOOD SPORTSMANSHIP
Coronet Instructional Films, 1950, 10 minutes

Another film that confuses communal action with conformity—a popular conflation in 1950s social guidance films. This one introduces preteens Joe and Bill as they learn to "think of what's best for the group." Even if, as the narrator explains, things don't work out the way you'd like, "it's more pleasant just to take what happens." And if you don't put up a fuss, "everyone will like you better."

G

GOOD TABLE MANNERS
Coronet Instructional Films, 1951, 10 minutes

Teenaged Chuck has bad table manners and an ugly sweater. He's invited to a supper party at the house of a neighborhood girl but dismisses the idea. "Who wants to go to a supper party?" he asks himself. "You do, Chuck!" answers a booming voice coming from the invitation. It's another Chuck—Chuck-of-the-future—a young man of twenty-one!

"People judge many things about you just by the way you eat."

Chuck-of-the-future, with less acting ability (but the same sweater) than Chuck-of-the-present, makes himself comfortable on the couch. He's upset that his younger self is so unsociable and knows it's because of his sloppy eating habits. "You may not care about table manners now," he says, "but when you grow up to be me, *then* you'll care!" Chuck-of-the-present is leery, but Chuck-of-the-future is persistent, teaches him how to "park a fork" and countless other details of table etiquette, and by the end of the film young Chuck is wearing a suit, pulling out a chair for a girl at the supper party, and liking it.

Chuck-of-the-present never made another Coronet film, opting instead to star in the Chicago TV series *Piano Pals*. Leather-lunged "Dad" never made another film, period; he got the part because he was director Ted Peshak's neighbor. The sweater made appearances in many Coronet films, including *Choosing Books to Read* and *Shy Guy*.

GOSSIP
Sid Davis Productions, 1953, 10 minutes

Despite its potential for gloom and doom this film is surprisingly upbeat, especially for a Sid Davis production. It tells the story of Jean Gage, a "wonderful girl" whose life is nearly destroyed by gossip. Jack Monroe, "the most popular boy in school" (and Marion High's "resident Casanova"), takes Jean out on a date to see *Jungle Girl* and then insists on a goodnight smooch in his convertible. Jack was "confident that no girl could resist him," the narrator

comments. "His popularity had gone to his head." Jean gives Jack a well-deserved slap and storms off, wounding Jack's manly pride. "He'd have to get even," the narrator says matter-of-factly.

The next morning, Jack begins spinning wild tales of his romantic evening with Jean. Marion High's gossips latch on to the juicy news and spread it around. "By the end of the day, the deed was done," the narrator intones. "Jean's reputation was ruined." Why everyone so readily believes "Casanova" Jack instead of "wonderful" Jean is not explained.

Blissfully ignorant, Jean is unaware that her world is crumbling until she is blackballed by the Girls Club. "They didn't want her kind of girl in their club." Jean of course is in tears by this point. She makes the wise move of confiding her problem to an adult (the school principal), Jack is forced to publicly recant his story, and just as quickly as everyone condemned Jean, everyone instantly loves her again.

THE GOSSIP
Centron Corp. for Young America Films, 1955, 14 minutes

Another gossip film with a lead character named Jean. This Jean is altruistic, warm-hearted, and nominated for Pep Club president. But Laura, her best friend, torpedoes her nomination—because she believes the falsehoods being spread by evil Frieda, the school gossip. It turns out that Jean was actually doing nice things for other people (including Laura) that were misinterpreted, but the damage has already been done. The presidency goes to another girl, and Laura is left to stare into the camera and ask that maddening Centron question: "What do *you* think?"

There's almost as much suffering and heartbreak in this bleak film as in *Social Acceptability*. Frieda, who also starred in *The Outsider* and *The Snob*, has a tongue like an icepick.

THE GRIPER
Centron Corp. for Young America Films, 1954, 13 minutes

George Foster is a malcontent teen. In contrast, George's only friend is perky Betty Ann, a terminally chipper cheerleader whose first words on waking up are, "Oh, what a beautiful morning!"

The Griper moves through a typical school day for George, using his ghostlike, double-exposure conscience—a triumph of Centron postproduction—to show how George's "sour-apple" attitude infects even the normally right-thinking teens around him. "I sure don't see how he gets any fun out of life," says one. "His griping always seems to ruin things for everyone else," adds another. Betty Ann smiles bravely and tries to help George see the happy side of life, but the other kids aren't encouraged, only confused. "Why do

you suppose a swell girl like Betty'd go out of her way to be nice to a wet blanket like George?"

Finally even Betty Ann can't take any more. "Oh, George, why don't you relax?" she cries in frustration. "Why do you keep trying to impress everyone with how *stupid* you think everything is?" A look of horror flashes across her face as she realizes that she, too, has become a Griper. Betty Ann flees in shame, and George is left to contemplate his next move. His conscience turns to the camera and asks, "Does George remind you of anyone *you* know?"

GROWING GIRLS
Film Producers Guild for Educational Foundation for Visual Aids, 1949, 13 minutes

This British film about menstruation received wide circulation in the United States. Its protagonist, Mary, is a thirteen-year-old who wears a necktie, vest, blazer, beret, and rides a bicycle with a wicker basket between its handlebars—not exactly the typical American girl.

The first half of the film presents the usual airbrushed, minimally animated diagrams and drawings of the uterus, ovaries, eggs, and sperm. The second half deals exclusively with menstruation and shows many shots of Mary buying her sanitary napkins in plain brown wrappers. "Only soluble pads, without decorous wrapping, may be put down the lavi'try pan," the narrator instructs. She also recommends that soiled pads be used as fuel in the kitchen stove.

"And so, with comfortable pads to wear and good health rules to follow, the monthly period needn't be so very inconvenient."

H: THE STORY OF A TEEN-AGE DRUG ADDICT
Larry Frisch for Young America Films, 1951, 22 minutes

Bill Daniels is a good teen, full of positive intentions and youthful optimism. But he leads a dismal, boring life, and when his girl stands him up for a date, he is encouraged by drug pusher Roy to "get hep, man," and go to a party at "the pad." The pad is the apartment of "Moose," a place where coed hepcats smoke pot, lie on the floor, and play saxophones and guitars. When a scuffle erupts between Bill and one of the partiers, Moose admires the way Bill punches him and decides to turn him into a professional fighter and heroin addict. Bill, who talks like an android, quickly becomes a junkie—but then he decides to quit and recovers almost as quickly, and the film abruptly ends.

A credit at the film's conclusion reads: "Enacted by a cast of nonprofessionals." It shows.

HABIT PATTERNS
Knickerbocker Productions for McGraw-Hill Book Co., 1954, 14 minutes

This grueling film—part of the *Psychology for Living* series—combines the paranoia of *Cheating* with the bleak trauma of *The Gossip*. It opens with Barbara, a teenager, standing behind the closed door of her bedroom, weeping pitifully. "It's a little late for tears, isn't it?" asks the brutally unforgiving woman narrator.

Barbara has had a bad day—and she deserves to cry, because she's habitually sloppy and unorganized. The film travels back in time to show how Barbara's day became a nightmare. Barbara is invited to an important after-school party at Ann Tolliver's house, but the day of the party she discovers she hasn't anything clean to wear, so she puts on a sweater with a huge stain smack on her chest that she unsuccessfully tries to conceal with a little scarf tied around her neck. At the party, Barbara's poor grooming and inept attempts to converse with other girls send her straight to Social Hell. As Barbara's world collapses around her, the narrator cattily comments on "how easy it is not to be invited again," and "how quickly you can be left out of the crowd." "People are going to talk," she adds. When they do, "our faults are more discussed."

Returning to the present, Barbara is still weeping and appears on the verge of a nervous breakdown. Thankfully, she pulls herself together, and as the music swells, she vows to become prettier, cleaner, and never again the subject of films such as this. Relentless.

HEALTH: FOOD AND NUTRITION
Charles Cahill and Associates, 1967, 11 minutes

Most of this film takes place inside an Alpha Beta supermarket, as a well-tailored mom and her two kids learn that "picking out your food is an important job." Chockfull of odd information such as "yellow vegetables have vitamins in them that help you feel calm and cheerful," the film also features a weird segment introducing "Mr. Protein," a felt-board character with a T-bone steak for his face.

> **"The more different foods you like, the more fun you'll have at mealtime!"**

HEALTH: YOUR CLEANLINESS
Centron Corp. for Young America Films, 1953, 12 minutes

Among other things, this film teaches children that "if your nails are usually dirty, others may get the wrong impression of you." It places as much emphasis on creating a good first impression as on health. "Your cleanliness makes you more attractive to other people. Is your cleanliness giving the picture you want it to give?" But do nine-year-olds really care?

HEALTH: YOUR POSTURE
Centron Corp. for Young America Films, 1953, 11 minutes

Adrelene, an attractive young girl, is at a party where she is not having a good time. The narrator explains that Adrelene "usually sits all alone, slumped in her chair in the corner,"

and that "for some reason, she doesn't fit into the picture," but she doesn't know why. "What is it that creates this unfavorable impression the others have of her?"

Now the fun begins. Adrelene goes home and admires herself in her full-length bedroom mirror. Mirror-image Adrelene puts her thumbs in her ears and wiggles her fingers. "You listen to me for a change!" she yells at Adrelene. "I'm tired of helping you pretend! I can't show you how you really look because when you're around me you put on an act! Do you want to see how you *really* look?" The mirror-image Adrelene gives a demonstration of Adrelene's slouch; it's not pretty.

"Yes, Adrelene, the mirror may have gone crazy, but for the first time it's telling you the truth," the narrator tells her. "Your posture is your problem. What are you going to do about it?"

"I'll tell you what I'm going to do," Adrelene yells back, pointing at the mirror. "I'm going to have good posture! You just wait and see, hmmph!" Her reflection watches Adrelene storm out of the room and smiles. "Attagirl, Adrelene!"

Dull health information follows as Dr. Martin gives a lecture in Adrelene's science class about "stretched muscles" and unsupported "vital organs." But this doesn't last very long and as the film ends Adrelene has achieved good posture, increased her popularity, and gotten "the last laugh" at her cheeky mirror image.

HEALTHY FEET
Coronet Instructional Films, 1958, 11 minutes

A film for foot fetishists. Teen hunk Tom has strong, healthy feet, and the camera pays close attention as he dries between his toes ("even a healthy foot can have fungi") and slips into his argyles and cordovans. "Pointed toenails could tear his socks and cause discomfort. Tom doesn't want that to happen." Some disgusting close-ups of blisters, corns, and ingrown toenails.

HELPING JOHNNY REMEMBER
Portafilms, 1956, 11 minutes

This entire film—which is about social behavior, not memory—is shot on an empty, echoey set with a black backdrop. Johnny is a jug-eared little brat whose five friends won't play with him (they're building what looks like a miniature city block out of cardboard boxes and construction paper) because he is "selfish" and "always yelling." An omniscient, invisible narrator is apparently standing right behind the camera, and the children are not shy about complaining to him about Johnny's behavior. "He said all our ideas were corny," says one. "He wouldn't let anybody else use the blue paint," whines another. "Gee whiz, what a creep!" adds a third.

The narrator behind the camera beckons Johnny in (just his arm is visible) from the edge of the black void and draws two cartoon faces on a conveniently placed blackboard: Smiley and Sulky. "If you want other children to like to play with you, you'll have to be a Smiley, not a Sulky," he explains. He tells Johnny that "learning to be considerate of others is like learning to tie your shoes" and instructs him to put on "a happy, considerate-of-others face." Johnny vows to try, but what if he slips up? The children suggest tapping their temples—"giving him the signal"—whenever Johnny begins to act rudely, thus helping him remember to be a good team player.

"If Johnny keeps trying hard," the narrator says, "it won't be long before he'll be nice all the time!"

HELPING THE CHILD TO ACCEPT THE DO'S
Encyclopaedia Britannica Films, 1948, 10 minutes

Educational Screen gave this film an interesting review:

> Actual pictures of young children from the age of three to five being urged by their mothers to shake hands, to eat with clean hands, and to use socially accepted table manners indicate that much emphasis is placed upon the child's conforming to the adults' ideas of social behavior. Other photographs of children being guided around puddles, being urged to wear their clothing in the conventional manner, and being put to bed at a regular and early time show that some of the emphasis is placed upon developing acceptable patterns of behavior which will be conducive to the child's well-being and comfortable personal living.

The next sequence shows a small boy and girl combing their hair and thus beginning to accept the masculine and feminine do's. The little girl enjoys playing with her doll while the little boy delights in boxing with his dad. Both children are next shown in the kitchen helping Mother by wiping the dishes. The commentary here points out that the do's for boys and girls are changing just as the roles of men and women in our present society are changing.

The last sequence shows that the ultimate goal is to teach boys and girls to play and work together, to settle their differences in a friendly manner, to give and take.

HIGH SCHOOL: YOUR CHALLENGE
Coronet Instructional Films, 1952, 11 minutes

It's yearbook day. Johnny Corry, a dropout, is very sad as he comes by school to pick up his copy and looks at his happy classmates. "Once they drop out, they rarely come back," comments Mr. Hamlen, a teacher, as Johnny slinks off into oblivion. But for every Johnny there's a Mac Wilson, a graduating senior with foresight and a positive outlook, who understands that high school is "a wonderful place" where you get the "skills you need for living" and where you "learn to live with people."

"Boy," Mac says to himself as he stares at the school's honor roll plaque. "If you just stop to think about all the things you can get out of high school, you begin to see how really lucky you are to be there!"

HIGHWAYS OF AGONY
Highway Safety Films, Inc., 1969, 11 minutes

Under the title frame, a shredded shoe lies in the foreground, an eighteen-wheeler in the background, and an unidentifiable pile of human meat between. Just another highway safety gore film, courtesy of the drivers of northwestern Ohio, most of whom were no longer alive to appreciate it. "On the highway, the penalty for failure to obey is often instant death."

This film, as well as every other one made by Highway Safety Films, Inc. (formerly Safety Enterprises, Inc.), is reality-based entertainment ahead of its time, with a bloody splatter of anarchy. The technique is consistent: as one of a dozen reenactments is shown, the somber narrator sets up the accident that's about to occur—focusing especially on any children and pregnant women involved. The film then cuts to footage of real accident scenes filmed by Highway Safety Films' network of freelance cameramen with police scanners. "It's safe to say that he was dead before the collision dust settled on the street," the narrator grimly remarks as men with crowbars pry a bloody corpse out of a car. "An autopsy revealed enough physical injury to kill three people."

HOLIDAY FROM RULES
Portafilms, 1958, 11 minutes

An omniscient narrator with magical powers grants the wishes of four bratty kids by teleporting them to a tropical island where there are no rules. The "island" consists of a minimalist set with black backdrops and 2-D cardboard rocks and palm trees. As in *Lord of the Flies*—which this film suspiciously resembles—the little children quickly become dirty, hungry, and physically battered, and their anarchist Eden falls apart.

Holiday from Rules conflates happiness and conformity (as do many films from the 1950s), but after the kids have been slapped around a little, they're more than willing to see things the narrator's way. "If we're going to have any fun, we've got to make some rules!"

THE HOME ECONOMICS STORY
Iowa State College, 1951, 25 minutes

In the years following World War II professional schools discouraged female enrollment. Women who wanted to pursue a higher education were instead encouraged to major in "home economics." Colleges in Ohio, Iowa, New York, and probably many other states

recruited high school girls through promotional films for their Home Economics departments. These films take the odd position that women's second-place status can be learned properly only on a college campus. A lot of folks bought into the idea that gadget-laden postwar homes required college-trained housewives.

As this film opens, Mom and Dad have an important decision to make. Would it be "worth the sacrifice" to send their daydreaming daughter Kay to college? You bet it would, the narrator explains, so Kay can prepare herself for a "wonderful future" by majoring in home economics. Career choices range from "tea-room manager" to "home life," and the dumbed-down courses include physics (with a toaster and electric mixer as lab equipment) and applied chemistry (where the girls learn the proper way to make cream of tomato soup). Kay masters the curriculum with minimal effort and probably found herself a good husband after graduation.

HOMEWORK: STUDYING ON YOUR OWN
Coronet Instructional Films, 1953, 10 minutes

Teenager Chuck Davis hosts an on-camera discussion with several friends about "problems of homework." The teens show their problems through home movies that they've made, shown as films-within-this-film on a clunky 16mm projector. Unfortunately they don't look like amateur movies; they're just typical scripted scenes that would show up in any other Coronet film. The kids have already solved their problems (through "scheduling" and coming up with "plans"), so there's no tension, confusion, or angst. "The further you go in your studies, the more you have to study on your own. That's homework!"

How these overworked kids had the time to make movies isn't clear.

THE HOUSE I LIVE IN
Frank Ross Productions for Anti-Defamation League of B'nai Brith, 1945, 11 minutes

"America's most popular educational film...not only something new in entertainment, but something extraordinary as a force for good...your students will be just as enthusiastic over the lesson it teaches as they are about Frank Sinatra, its star" (advertisement).

In 1943 race riots in Los Angeles, Detroit, and New York left forty dead. This film was made to stop further bloodshed. It was also made to boost the public image of Frank

Sinatra, who had refused to entertain troops during the war and instead stayed home and made millions playing sold-out concerts to teenyboppers.

It opens as Frank, who's in a recording session, ducks into a back alley between songs for a smoke. A gang of little white kids enters, chasing another little white kid. "What's he got, smallpox or somethin'?" Frank asks. "We don't like his religion," one of the toughs replies. (No mention of race in this race-relations film.) "You must be a bunch of those Nazi werewolves I been reading about," Frank chuckles. "Mister," one of the more intelligent kids asks, "are you screwy?" "Not me," Frank replies. "I'm an American."

Frank tells the little monsters that America was built on guts, know-how, and most important, melting-pot teamwork. "You guys remember Pearl Harbor?" Frank asks. "Those Japs socked us so it looked like we could never do anything about it. But a couple of days later something very important happened." Right—President Roosevelt approved the order sending all Japanese-Americans on the West Coast into internment camps. Perhaps that's why the gang in this film isn't shown chasing a Japanese kid; there weren't any in Hollywood.

Frank has just about run out of chummy things to say, so he launches into the film's theme song, a "song of democratic thought" written by Earl Robinson and Lewis Allan:

> *The house I live in, a plot of earth, a street,*
> *The grocer and the butcher and the people that I meet...*
> *The "howdy" and the handshake, the air of feeling free,*
> *And the right to speak my mind out, that's America to me!*

Frank instructs the kids to "use your good American heads" and warns them not to be "dopes" or "first-class fatheads." *America the Beautiful* plays softly and the kids depart, the tormented and the tormentors now buddies.

HOW BANKS SERVE
Murphy-Lillis for American Bankers Association, 1950, 10 minutes

The Miller family sits around the dining room table exchanging after-dinner pleasantries. As the subject turns to money, kid brother Joe casually remarks, "I don't see how I'm ever going to make much use of a bank." Uh-oh. The conversation immediately devolves into a lecture about loans, savings, and checking accounts for the remainder of the film, with Mom, Dad, and Sis taking turns setting Joe straight.

Older sister Susan, in particular, is a positive role model. Susan "has learned the secret of successful saving and knows that saving is the surest way to build security and get the things she wants." Which, in Susan's case, includes a fur coat. Considering she takes home $38 from work every week, buying that coat is going to take a helluva lot longer than this film cares to reveal.

Film credits note, "The United States currency in this picture was filmed by special permission of the Secretary of the Treasury."

HOW BILLY KEEPS CLEAN
Coronet Instructional Films, 1951, 10 minutes

Billy is a normal dirty kid at school or play, but when he gets home he turns into an obsessively clean child. He washes everywhere. "No monkey business!" cautions the narrator.

Along with the usual dry-between-your-toes and change-your-underwear patter, this film has a memorable scene in which germs are depicted as a big, sticky X that gets passed from kid to kid in a touch football game—a concept that was improved upon by Audio Productions in their classic *Sniffles and Sneezes*.

As the film ends, Billy is going out to play, but his friend Jerry has to stay inside because he's sick in bed. How did this happen? He "didn't wash," explains the narrator. Billy shrugs nonchalantly and heads out anyway, no doubt to find some cleaner friends.

HOW DO YOU DO
unknown producer for Young America Films, 1946, 13 minutes

Peggy is a teenager with a pronounced lisp. She sits in an overstuffed chair, sometimes talking directly to the camera, sometimes talking to the narrator, who is apparently standing stage left, just off camera.

Through a flashback, Peggy remembers the day she and her friend Ann were sipping Cokes at the soda shop when "smooth" Frank Norton (who walks like he has a two-by-four down the back of his suit jacket) arrived with "kind of sloppy" Bill Phillips. Peggy wanted to introduce the two boys to Ann but didn't know how. "I wish I weren't so vague about such things," Peggy sighs, recalling the moment. "I felt so adolescent!" Right then and there she decided "it was high time to get the whole matter of introductions straight so I would never have to think twice about them again!"

The narrator provides cheerful encouragement ("We're all apt to make a boner now and then") and explains who to introduce to whom, when to offer hands, when to stand and sit, and to say not "*How* do you do" or "How do *you* do" but "How do you *do*."

Peggy, who lives in a universe where all boys wear suits and all girls wear pleated skirts, couldn't be happier. "It's more fun to meet people when you're at ease!" she says. "All's well that begins well!" adds the narrator.

HOW DO YOU KNOW IT'S LOVE?
Coronet Instructional Films, 1950, 12 minutes

"The title of this film," explains the accompanying teacher's guide, "is a question all boys and girls must face—usually under circumstances that make clear thinking difficult."

Young Nora thinks she's in love with equally young Jack. Mom isn't so sure (dads were rarely consulted in love films) and tells her daughter that true love is "more settled." After Nora receives some general advice (borrowed almost word for word from *Are You Ready for Marriage?*), she and Jack go on a double date with Jack's older brother and his

fiancée. Nora decides to compare the older couple's "mature love" to the feelings between herself and Jack. Self-centered Jack fails the test, Nora realizes she isn't really in love, and common sense triumphs. Everyone goes home happy (and chaste) in the end, with Jack and Nora exchanging an affectionate handshake on her front porch.

JACK: "How about going roller skating next Friday night?"
NORA: "Oh, Jack, that's a wonderful idea. That's the kind of fun I like!"

HOW FRIENDLY ARE YOU?
Coronet Instructional Films, 1951, 10 minutes

Dick York stars as Phil, who teaches younger brother Ray the fine art of being friendly. "Some boys feel that 'being friendly' is synonymous with being a sissy," reads this film's description in the Coronet catalog. "Ray corrects his social errors and begins to try harder to make people like him."

HOW HONEST ARE YOU?
Coronet Instructional Films, 1950, 13 minutes

Did basketball star Bob really steal money out of Ben's locker? Since this is a Coronet film, he probably didn't, but the characters have to find out the truth for themselves.

Lots of deep self-examination and debates as to what was and wasn't seen interplay with the camera. The acting is actually pretty good and there's even a plot twist, when Rose confesses her reason for ratting to the coach about Bob. "I can just see it," she says, her eyes glazed, as the camera dollies in for a close-up. "You'll get Bob off the team and Terry will become the regular center. My Terry. He'll be the star of the team. And I'll be sitting on top of the world!"

A tight little film and a good example of Coronet's social guidance style at its peak.

HOW MUCH AFFECTION?
Crawley Films for McGraw-Hill Book Co., 1957, 20 minutes

Another depressing Crawley film. Teenaged Laurie (who looks about twenty-five) comes home from a date in tears because boyfriend Jeff has just tried to steer her into "wrong behavior." "Oh, Mother, I don't know what to think," she cries. "I'm so mixed up!" Mother is surprisingly cool and composed, considering that her daughter was nearly a date-rape victim. "Your physical urges fight against your reason," she coos. "In the height of emotion it's not always easy to think things through."

Jeff and Laurie obviously need to learn a few of life's painful lessons, which they do from Laurie's friend Eileen, whose physical urges obviously knocked her reason for a loop. She had to leave school as a result (and get married, of course) while her boyfriend, who wanted to be a lawyer, now has to work in a steel mill. They are a very sad couple—as are all people in Crawley films who make incorrect decisions.

Jeff and Laurie, now more mature, reasonable, and perhaps a little numb, come back to Laurie's house from a date. They find a note from Laurie's parents explaining that they won't be home for at least several hours. Jeff and Laurie stare deeply into each other's eyes. Will they succumb to temptation and suffer the inevitable tragic consequences?

HOW QUIET HELPS AT SCHOOL
Coronet Instructional Films, 1953, 10 minutes

This film takes a tour of a typical boisterous grade school classroom. "You couldn't be proud to be part of such a noisy room, could you?" asks the narrator. Next comes a visit to the classroom of Miss Bradley, a place where all sound has been banished. Miss Bradley explains that keeping a classroom this quiet is good because it's "like an office," and that "knowing when to be quiet is a part of growing up." Bobby, a cheerful geek, provides demonstrations of quiet behavior around an elaborate tabletop model farm, and the narrator ends the film rhetorically asking, "This is a good room, isn't it?"

HOW TO BE WELL GROOMED
Coronet Instructional Films, 1948, 10 minutes

The grooming rituals of teenaged brother and sister Don and Sue are explored in excruciating detail. Both are incredibly neat. Their evenings seem to be devoted exclusively to ironing outfits, sewing on loose buttons, and polishing shoes.

A man and woman narration team do their best to cast Don and Sue's behavior in a positive light: "Both Don and Sue look like the kind of people you'd like to know, don't they?" The narrators also point out specifics: "Sue avoids red nail polish, since it would call attention to her stubby hands." They emphasize the virtues of early bedtime, a hearty breakfast, and "easy

"All through the day others are looking at you."

does it" when it comes to lipstick. They also encourage bland attire, urging Sue to wear "appropriate" blouses and steering Don away from loud sport shirts. "Your success depends a great deal on how you look."

Don and Sue have what must be the world's smallest closets, which makes their extensive wardrobes all the more amazing.

HOW TO DEVELOP INTEREST
Coronet Instructional Films, 1950, 10 minutes

For understandable reasons, average teenager Cliff Williams can't seem to develop a passion for botany. His perpetually smiling dad reminds him of "the development of hybrid corn that yields twice as much per acre," but Cliff still isn't convinced. However, by the end of this film, he does concede that "it's fun to collect leaves."

HOW TO KEEP A JOB
Coronet Instructional Films, 1949, 11 minutes

Ed is a teen seeking employment. His interviewer, Mr. Wiley, is a little leery of Ed, since the brash teen has the audacity to criticize a previous employer during the job interview. "Nobody thinks very much of a man who talks against the company he works for," Mr. Wiley says. However, Ed "might really amount to something," so Mr. Wiley tells him the story of identical twins Bob and Walter Anderson, who worked in the shipping room.

Through the miracle of split-screen cinematography a single actor plays the dual roles. Bob is presentable and conscientious and gets a promotion, while identical twin Walter is sloppy and ungrateful and gets the boot. Hmmm...which one of the twins most resembles Ed?

Ed is humbled and promises to be a good company man from now on.

HOW TO LOSE WHAT WE HAVE (IN OUR HANDS, PART 3)
Wilding Picture Productions for American Economic Foundation, 1950, 12 minutes

This is a kind of businessman's *Red Nightmare*. It opens as average Americans Tom and Midge watch a presidential debate on TV. (This is the future, of course.) "We've already amended the Constitution dozens of times," smirks the portly, obviously evil candidate.

"Let's throw it away for a Master Plan run by a Master State!" The thinner, tousle-haired good-guy candidate is appalled. "We have free choice," he cries. "We're free to try and make a profit." The well-fed fellow traveler, however, promises "full employment and full security" and adds, "We're already on our way."

Tom and Midge's friends fall for the soothing commie line. "I'm tired of being kicked around!" says one. "I think it sounds wonderful!" adds another. "Full security! Why shouldn't the government take care of us?" Tom and Midge, well-intentioned, misinformed fools that they are, hesitantly agree.

Now comes the montage of screaming headlines: BANK ACCOUNTS FROZEN; MARKETS SUSPENDED; LABOR FORCE TO BE REDISTRIBUTED; a capitalist's worst nightmare. Tom and Midge discover that life is a bad dream for them, too, as a Master State

truck arrives to forcibly relocate them to another part of the country. "But I like my job!" Tom protests. "Sorry," smirks a government agent in an ominous large hat. The truck driver agrees: "Whatta you yappin' about? You voted for it."

How can Americans avoid the horrible fate of Tom and Midge? The narrator sums it up: "We all want to live in a better world. We all want to have more!" But, he concludes, "Nobody in his or her right mind would willingly sacrifice freedom for the iron discipline of a regimented state." Shots of Red Square and Stalin clarify what he means. "Where government is not limited, no man is free!"

HOW TO SAY NO
Coronet Instructional Films, 1951, 10 minutes

Much more than just a laundry list of negatives, this classic Coronet film ponders a surprisingly delicate question: "How can you say no and still keep your friends?"

A group of clean-cut teens talks directly to the camera as the film flashes back to situations in which they felt they had to say no: drinking beer with the boys after football practice; smoking cigarettes with the girls at a pajama party; and the ever-popular "petting." While the examples may be cornball, they help pinpoint the moment when "fitting in" became something to discourage, not encourage—a cruel dilemma for social guidance filmmakers. Not even the kids in this film seem satisfied with the clumsy "bag of tricks" they use to walk the line between teen popularity and adult morality. As Marty (the non–beer drinker) moans, "I don't want them to think I'm a drip!"

H

HUMAN BEGINNINGS
Medical Arts Productions for E. C. Brown Trust Fund, 1950, 23 minutes

This highly atypical film from 1950 was "designed to promote the emotional well-being of young children through satisfying activities and discussion with understanding adults,"

according to its title crawl. The children are six years old, the discussion is about childbirth, and that's what makes this film so odd.

For the first ten minutes a class of screeching six-year-olds shares their unusual theories of childbirth with a teacher as they draw pictures of babies in the womb. Then the film leaves the classroom to tell the story of Tommy Johnson, his open-minded parents, and his new baby sister. Mom and Dad even allow six-year-old Tommy to participate in naming the baby—"After all, she belongs to you as much as to mother and me!"—and in bathing and feeding her. They also take delight in explaining every detail of childbirth to their boy, reading out of a book titled *Human Growth*, written by the same doctor who worked as consultant for this film. "The baby comes out of this opening, called the vagina."

This is probably the only sex ed film made before 1968 with close-ups of breast feeding, and it's certainly the only one ever made for six-year-olds. Kids from the private Walt Whitman School in Manhattan were used as actors.

THE IMPORTANCE OF GOALS
Audio Productions for McGraw-Hill Book Co., 1951, 18 minutes

Little Tommy is a bright thirteen-year-old but a lackluster student because his teacher fails to recognize what motivates him. It turns out that what he wants to be is a school-crossing guard.

There's much progressive ballyhoo here about the student as a person, about how learning must be tied to "a feeling of worth," and about how "learning situations" must be crafted to fit each kid's personal needs. "Why can't school," the narrator asks, "be more

165

like life?" That's a valid point, but a film like this makes it understandable why the kids of Tommy's generation grew up to be the most self-absorbed adults in American history.

In the end, the teacher realizes the error of his old-fashioned ways and adjusts to fit Tommy's needs. Tommy—now highly motivated—gets his white sash belt and a shiny badge. "No, there's nothing wrong with *this* boy!"

IMPROVE YOUR SPELLING
Coronet Instructional Films, 1948, 11 minutes

You have to give Coronet credit for turning a dull subject into a mildly entertaining film. Young Tom Stafford has been ordered by his teacher to write a report for the school paper, but it'll be rejected if there's even one word misspelled—and Tom is a lousy speller. Happily, an omniscient, invisible narrator with magical powers (Mike Wallace) barges into Tom's universe and teaches him five debatably useful spelling rules. Wallace is occasionally cruel—"You'd never see *that* report in a newspaper!"—but plucky Tom, who blithely accepts the existence of this invisible narrator, can handle his brand of tough love. As the film ends, Tom is chosen the "personal reporter" for his class and proudly holds aloft his custom-made dictionary.

IMPROVE YOUR STUDY HABITS
Coronet Instructional Films, 1961, 11 minutes

"Let's not fool ourselves. Study habits are important." So begins the public confession of Ron, a would-be member of the varsity football team who's been cut because his grades weren't good enough. Ron has written a description of his misery as a school essay assignment, and his teacher thinks it's so important that she forces him to stand in front of the class and read it aloud.

Ron explains that in order to improve his grades he first needed to improve his study habits. "Of course, I didn't become a scholar overnight," he allows, as the film shows scenes of Ron and his study buddy, Bert, poring over books in the library and having cookies and milk in Ron's kitchen. "A short break keeps us from getting too restless and gives us a pickup." Ron would rather look at the girls in his class than his books, but Bert keeps him on the straight and narrow path. The result? "Once you get the hang of it, studying can be interesting."

THE INNOCENT PARTY
Centron Corp. for Kansas State Board of Health, 1959, 11 minutes

This VD film is actually an antipremarital sex film, but all VD films before the 1970s were antipremarital sex films.

Don and Nicky, two high school boys, are in the city one night, and they pick up two brunette floozies who smoke cigarettes and wear too much eye makeup. They all have sex. The very next night, Don—apparently driven mad by his newly unleashed urges (or could it be the film's cool jazz combo music track?)—goes parking with his virtuous girlfriend, Betty. He has sex with her, too!

166

Nothing good can come of all this jiggity-jig, and Don is soon confiding to Nicky that he's got "some sort of sore... down *there*." Nicky brushes it aside. "It's probably just a pimple or somethin'. The same thing happened to me and it cleared up all by itself!" Nevertheless, Don visits the school doctor. He finds out he has syphilis.

Don's in a bind. Although the doc tells him that syphilis is a deadly disease that "may cripple you, blind you, destroy your brain," Don won't tell him about Betty. The doctor suspects a coverup. "If you're lying to 'protect' a girl, just consider what it might cost her." He shows Don helpful visual aids: pictures of women with tongue sores and hideous facial warts, and a photo of a baby without a nose. "If you're the young man I think you are, you'll bring that girl in to see me!"

Don eventually does, of course, although it must have been difficult, since Betty refuses to look him in the face. She has syphilis, too. "You took a risk by doing something that society condemns," the doctor tells her. "Perhaps you didn't realize some of the penalties involved."

Happily, the two former lovebirds have had their infections detected early. "We've caught this thing in time," the doctor tells them. "You're both going to be all right."

"You may be right, doctor," Betty replies, her eyes moist with tears. "But right now I'd rather be *dead*."

The actors who play Don and Betty spend most of this film with their heads downcast, looking miserable.

IS THIS LOVE?
Crawley Films for McGraw-Hill Book Co., 1957, 14 minutes

Yet another depressing Crawley film. Peg, who is "impulsive and emotional," falls for cleft-chinned football star Joe. They want to get married, but everybody else in this film knows that that would be a *big mistake*. Peg's college roommate, Liz, tries to explain the complexities of marriage. Peg shrugs it off. "That theoretical stuff gives me a pain." Peg's parents aren't any help. Not only do they disapprove of Joe, but they dismiss Peg's disapproval of their disapproval as "just a touch of hysterics."

In the end, Peg and Joe elope. Although this film mercifully overlooks the gruesome details, it's clear their troubles are only beginning.

IT'S ALL IN KNOWING HOW!
Chicago Film Studios for National Dairy Council, 1954, 13 minutes

Teenager Bob Troy is having a bad day. His girlfriend thinks he's dull, he's out of "pep" on the gridiron, and he's "fed up" with life in general. His coach, Mr. Farrell, knows the reason and sets Bob straight by telling him to get more sleep and eat the right foods. Since this film was sponsored by the National Dairy Council, those "right foods" include three pats of butter and a quart and a half of milk a day. Bob and his girlfriend make a nutrition chart,  restructure his diet, and resurrect his bowling game (and love life). "How easy and pleasant it is to eat intelligently."

IT'S UP TO YOU
Vocational Films, 1969, 11 minutes

This film was designed to give its teen audience a real head trip, man. It's obvious this is a groovy film the moment it opens with a shot of a door with the words GUIDANCE COUN-SELOR on it. The door swings open, revealing a sunlit field on the other side—and beyond it sits a Maharishi Maheesh Yogi look-alike! Far out!

There's no unseen "authority figure" narrator to tell the story of this film, but the end-less musings of pimple-faced protagonist Barry Martin more than fill the dead air. Barry is pissed off; his parents have "really messed things up" because they want him to get a job. "It's not as bad as when they told you to get a haircut," his unnamed buddy remarks, but Barry's revolutionary spirit is bummed. "I can't see why I have to put up with this society," he says. "If I could only change it." Barry's friend nods in agreement. "It's enough to make a guy crack up. You wind up doing what everybody else wants you to do instead of what you want to do. I'd rather do nothing at all than end up like that." Right on!

Unfortunately for rebels like Barry, the people who made this film weren't about to let their protagonist reach the closing credits with such an unwholesome attitude. Barry reaches a turning point when he halfheartedly visits his school guidance counselor, who resembles a balding, bloated toad instead of a yogi, and emerges with a completely differ-ent point of view! Barry's friend is understandably skeptical. "Go to school, get a job, play the game," he says. "Sounds like the same old establishment line to me." But Barry sticks to his new guns. "It's not as simple as that," he replies, almost wistfully. "You only sell out when you start letting them do your thinking for you. As long as you do your own thinking, you sell out to nobody." It doesn't occur to Barry that someone put that idea in his head.

Lots of spontaneous interjections such as "outtasight!" and "man!" lend credibility to this film's characters. *It's Up to You* was filmed on location in happening Park Ridge, Illi-nois, with occasional arty shots of downtown traffic and out-of-focus close-ups of chain-link fences. David Amaral's Hammond organ soundtrack sounds like it was lifted from old Zombies singles.

IT'S UP TO YOU!
Harvest Films for Wise Owl Club, National Society for the Prevention of Blindness, 1959, 11 minutes

The first real-life gore on America's civilian classroom screens appeared in 1959: Dick Wayman made *Signal 30* in Ohio and Leo Trachtenberg made *It's Up To You!* in New Jer-sey. This film was targeted at shop classes of teenagers who were apparently immune to (or bored with) standard safety films. They remembered this one. It wasn't made to impress film festival judges; it was made to make its audiences throw up. It still does.

A narrator with a sneer in his voice introduces Eddie Briggs, "an average Joe in an average-sized plant." Eddie is reckless; his biggest concern in life is to get home as early as possible so he can watch TV. But, the narrator continues, "on this day, in a single moment of carelessness, Eddie's luck ran out on him." A grinding wheel shoots a piece of metal into his eye. Eddie grabs his face, doubled over in pain. "So, instead of going home today, Eddie Briggs is going to the hospital. And we're going with him. Maybe by sharing Eddie's experience, you'll learn a valuable lesson."

Eddie is wheeled into the emergency room (still clutching his face), and the narrator explains, "What you're going to see is routine. Routine, that is, if you're an eye doctor or a surgeon." What follows is four relentless minutes of bloody, gruesome, revolting eye surgery footage, all shot in extreme close-up.

"Taking a piece of metal out of an eye that has been punctured is no easy matter," the narrator says. "By the way, Eddie hasn't been given any anesthetic at all up to now."

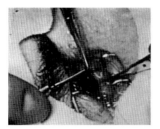

The narrator explains that the surgery will use a "special magnet" to locate the metal in Eddie's eye. "If you watch closely you can actually see the eye bulging when the magnet is directly over the piece of metal." It does. "But the piece of metal is off to one side of where it punctured the eye. No luck. Our friend Eddie is in trouble."

The next few minutes on screen are gut wrenching. "Now Eddie is given a local anesthetic and the surgery gets under way. First, an incision is made with a surgical knife. As the operation continues, the incision has to be enlarged with surgical scissors. Keep in mind that Eddie will be conscious throughout the entire operation. The surgeon again probes for the metal. Now, watch the tip of that magnet. There. There it is. In a way, Eddie is lucky—if you can call this lucky. If Eddie had glass in his eye, or wood, or aluminum, the magnet would have been useless."

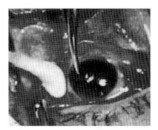

Eddie emerges from the hospital unscathed, with no scars, not even an eyepatch, which is amazing—and strangely disappointing—considering what this film has just put the viewer through. "If Eddie could talk to each of you personally, he'd say that the responsibility of protecting your eyesight lies entirely with you," the narrator says. "No amount of compensation could ever pay for the pain and suffering he went through."

Translation: Workman's comp? Don't be ridiculous. It was all *your* fault.

J. P. Goeller is given special credit for the gruesome eye-surgery cinematography.

IT'S WONDERFUL BEING A GIRL
Audio Productions for Personal Products Corp. [Modess], revised edition 1966, 22 minutes

This film follows the trials and tribulations of spunky twelve-year-old Libby as she learns about the menstrual cycle. "I don't know if I'll like it," she protests, but her liberated mom scoffs at such unprogressive thoughts. "You said you couldn't wait to grow up,"

Mom reminds her and quickly introduces Libby to the wonders of Modess sanitary napkins. "See this blue polyethylene on the side? That's a special moisture-proof shield!" Soon it's "Guess what, Mom?" when Libby has her first period, but with her newfound knowledge and her Modess sanitary napkins, she can still go roller skating with the gang.

"You *can* have fun while you're menstruating!"

JAYCEE TEEN AGE ROAD-E-O
Potomac Films for U.S. Junior Chamber of Commerce, 1957, 15 minutes

The Road-E-O has to be the most dull-looking activity involving cars ever committed to film, a test of parallel parking and weaving at a snail's pace through a barrel course in a parking lot. The producers saw what they had to work with and wisely spent most of their time on the plot. Clean-cut Bob of Centerville climbs the Road-E-O ladder to the national championships. Sandy, the town "rod," learns that it's better to prove driving prowess on an adult-approved Teen Age Road-E-O skill course than on Centerville's public streets. It's pure fantasy, of course, and has little to do with highway safety and everything to do with instilling respect for authority.

Bob loses his chance to win the nationals when he forgets to honk his horn after completing his parking test. It's one of the Road-E-O's most stupid rules, but obeying rules is what matters, not good driving.

JOAN AVOIDS A COLD

Coronet Instructional Films, revised edition 1964, 11 minutes

Joan, a little girl, is a Typhoid Mary to her dance class. One by one, Joan's little friends fall victim to Joan's cold, until all that's left is an empty room with an abandoned record player. Not even the teacher was spared. But Joan learns from this sad episode! From now on she will heed the advice of the narrator of this film and will remember "not to be too cold or too warm when you're outdoors" and that "having your own towel helps you stay well." Even Joan's mom and dad join in the fun by boiling all their dishes for twenty minutes and spitting into the toilet after they gargle. "Everyone in the family is working together!" the narrator cheers, and the next cold pestilence passes harmlessly over their home. "Joan avoided a cold. Good for Joan."

JOHNNY LEARNS HIS MANNERS

Milton Salzburg, revised edition 1968, 18 minutes

> *If you eat like a pig, you're a pig (oink! oink!)*
> *Better be neat, or they'll treat you like a pig (oink! oink!)*
> *So be neat when you eat, when you walk and when you talk*
> *And then when you're all grown up and biiiiiiiig...*
> *You will never ever be a pig, pig, pig.*

Johnny is a little brat who slurps his food and doesn't hang up his clothes. Good Self (an angel) warns Johnny that if he doesn't change, he'll turn into a pig. Bad Self (a devil) scoffs and says that tidiness is for sissies, and Johnny is inclined to agree. Although Johnny's bad manners eventually alienate him from his friends and even his dog, and even though he gradually does physically turn into a pig-boy, he doesn't change his ways until his mom sits him down in front of a TV and turns on the Overduplicated NASA Footage Channel. "See how smartly and neatly they're dressed?" she says, as they watch bleached film of astronauts in space suits. "If the space explorers of the United States can keep clean and neat, you should be able to also!"

Bob Holt performs every voice in this cheaply animated cartoon, and Eliot Daniel provides the opening song and minimalist piano soundtrack.

JUNIOR PROM

Simmel-Meservey, 1946, 21 minutes

Junior Prom follows the glacial progress of Jerry and Margaret (the smart couple) and Frank and Helen (the silly couple) as they double-date at a surprisingly highbrow junior prom. It trots out so many rules to remember that the kids hardly have any time for fun. That was probably the point.

Consideration and "correctness" in dating is stressed, as well as an endless list of details, details, details. The narrator even cautions Frank to wear a tie with a "quiet pattern" and urges him to avoid socks that clash. "Allow the ladies to be more colorful."

According to the trade ads for *Junior Prom,* it presented "a high-standard pattern of positive behavior" and was "contributing to the cultural development of young people." It was also reportedly "directed by qualified authorities in educational techniques and motion picture dramatics," but given the performances of Frank and Helen, that's debatable.

Junior Prom ends happily for all, with a scenario used as a template by the dozens of classroom dating films that followed: "Since Jerry and Margaret have been dating for some time, a goodnight kiss is considered proper. But Frank very wisely merely offers his hand to Helen."

KEEP OFF THE GRASS
Sid Davis Productions, 1970, 22 minutes

This film represents the work of an older, more mature Sid Davis, who at last created an understanding dad and did not kill off the characters he didn't like.

While vacuuming, Mom discovers a joint in her teenaged son's room.

"Oh, Tom, how could you?" she wails.

"Mother!" Tom snorts. "It's only grass! I'm not a dope fiend!"

Tom's dad sits him down for a lecture. "You think we're stupid...but does that make your generation so all-fired smart?" He tells Tom that pot smoking produces "an uncontrollable feeling of hilarity" and that "prolonged use may result in a loss of ambition...because of the induced 'couldn't-care-less' attitude." Pot may not be addictive, Dad admits, but it is "habituating." "There's no cold turkey for that!" he adds.

Tom isn't convinced and insists that grass "expands your mind." Dad, although still concerned that "every time you blow a marijuana cigarette, you take a chance on blowing your future," liberally allows Tom to go out and find the "truth" about marijuana from the people who should know—Tom's teenaged friends.

Tom seeks guidance from Mac, who insists that pot is merely "a groovy way of relaxing." Mac takes Tom to a poolside pot party, then to a head shop "psychedelicatessen," then to Waco, an artist. Waco used to paint "imaginative, creative posters," but he now draws junk—pot has ruined his mind! "Turn on! Tune out of the rat race and its square problems!" Waco cries.

Tom, in his neatly pressed chinos, cardigan sweater, and button-down shirt, is continually nagged by flashbacks of his dad's lecture. He's also out of place in this drug-addled universe, and the nodding stoners he meets are oblivious to him—as they are to everything else.

Tom meets several friendly cops with good posture who, after being harassed by a group of sloppy weedheads, gladly tell him more facts. Pot produces an "ersatz maturity" and a "wholesale abandonment of goals and ambitions." "Not every pot smoker goes on to heroin, of course. A personality factor is undoubtedly largely responsible for that step. Very likely the same personality factor which turned the user on to pot!" What about the hypocrisy of liquor-drinking adults telling kids not to smoke pot? "The daily drink may not

 be the best thing in the world, but a man who takes a drink after his day is done has worked! He has achieved! Not so the teenaged user. He deliberately seeks to cop out. He uses his grass as a mental crutch because he fears to stand on his own!"

His head reeling from all this new information, Tom wanders into a dark alley—and is mugged by dangerous, desperate potheads! Even worse, the next day he sees his

friend Mac selling a joint to a tousle-haired little boy. "He's just a kid!" Tom protests, but Mac just laughs. "If he's old enough to have a buck, he's old enough to blow pot. Easy money, man!"

Tom doesn't need to see any more; now he knows the straight dope on dope. "Will it turn you on? Or turn on you?"

KITTY CLEANS UP
Key Productions for Young America Films, 1949, 10 minutes

Helen, Kitty's youthful owner, wakes as this film begins. She is very excited. "Today's the pet show!" she cries as she drags peacefully snoozing Kitty—a full-grown tabby with the patience of a saint—out of a basket and into the mael-  strom of her world.

"Kitty and I do many things alike," Helen announces. To prove this, the film spends the next several minutes showing topless Helen rubbing herself with a washrag at the bathroom sink while the camera repeatedly cross-cuts to Kitty, sitting on the toilet, licking herself. "This is the way I wash my arms, wash my arms, wash my arms," Helen sings, part of a continuous stream of mindless chatter. "Don't forget those dirty paws! That's a good kitty! I'm going to be proud of you today!" Helen—speaks—every—

 word—very—slowly in a voice *so* cute that one suspects that the dubbed voice of Helen is actually an adult attempting to sound like a six-year-old. Helen eventually drags Kitty to school and the pet show. Kitty is uncrated into a sea of groping, jelly-stained hands, clutching her from every direction. It's plain that the poor cat only wants to get away, but Helen is oblivious to it. "I was so proud when Kitty won the prize!"

The film ends on a close-up of Helen, smiling gap-toothed into the camera, squeezing Kitty tightly to her scrawny chest. Kitty, who has had quite enough, struggles to break free.

LAST DATE
Wilding Picture Productions for Lumbermen's Mutual Casualty Co., 1950, 15 minutes

This classic safety film coined the word "Teen-a-cide"—which thankfully never caught on— and was the first to specifically brand teenagers as reckless breeders of highway mayhem.

Dick York stars as Nick, a maladjusted thrill-jockey who always drives with the pedal to the metal. Jeanne Dawson, who narrates the film in flashback, blows off sensible suitor Larry Gray because she finds Nick's suicidal behavior exciting. That turns out to be a bad move, as Nick promptly drives himself and Jeanne head-on into another car. Everybody dies except Jeanne, who suffers an appropriate fate for girls who think they're so smart: her pretty face is destroyed! "It would have been better if I had died in the hospital," she laments with her back to the camera as somber organ music fills the soundtrack. "I've had my last date!" She walks over to her familiar makeup mirror and smashes it with a hairbrush.

Last Date was a big deal. It had a gala premiere in Palm Springs with a network television broadcast of the ceremonies and won awards from the National Committee on Films for Safety and the American Public Relations Association. Palm Springs premiere guest William "Hopalong Cassidy" Boyd said, "I'm convinced that *Last Date* will cut down Teen-a-cide." Bob Hope called the film "a wonderful lesson for boys and girls."

Wilding, the film's producer, got into the spirit of things by parking wrecked cars in front of theaters where *Last Date* was shown.

THE LAST PROM
Gene McPherson, 1972, 24 minutes

Speaking of wrecked cars, this film opens with one—parked in front of a high school. "Was it a pretty face that made this gaping jagged hole in the windshield?" the narrator asks. "Whose body came crashing against this steering wheel, twisting it with fear-crazed hands?"

The film goes back in time to find out. Senior Bill Donovan, "basically a good boy," takes sophomore Sandy Clark to the prom in his newly purchased car. "The roads are filled with 'Bill Donovans,'" the narrator explains. "Good boys but *bad* drivers." Bill and Sandy decide to slip away from the prom in Bill's car—"to seek just one more thrill"—and end up crashing into a tree. "With the stirrings of consciousness come the screams of the maimed, the moans of the dying."

The people who made *The Last Prom* also appear to have gone back in time—to produce it. The kids' preppy clothes and short hairstyles, the prom's crepe paper decorations and big band music, even Bill's car—a '59 Chevy convertible—date from two decades before it was made. Its only concession to modernity is gore—in the form of long close-ups of Sandy's face, liberally dribbled with Karo Syrup.

"Sandy Clark is wearing her formal gown today. She wears an orchid corsage. But few will realize this—for the lid of the casket was not opened. It was best that way." The creepy, discordant "ahhhing" and "ohhhing" on the soundtrack was provided by the Anderson, Ohio, High School Vocal Ensemble.

LAW AND SOCIAL CONTROLS
Coronet Instructional Films, 1949, 10 minutes

The gang at the Teen Canteen can't decide if they should close their soda fountain at 10:30 or 11 P.M. Adult advisors guide them to the correct decision—guess which it is.

Coronet believed an issue even this trivial warranted the efforts of three teens, two adults (one a lawyer), and a formal meeting to resolve. Jack MacGregor is the lone hold-out for later hours, but the lawyer, Mr. Parks, sets him straight. "The town could pass a law which would *compel* you to close at ten-thirty. Or ten. Or even nine." Jack is dumbfounded—

"Aren't *we* part of the community?" he protests—but Mr. Parks speaks for "the community as a whole" and that's that.

"And so," the narrator announces approvingly, "Jack is learning about social control!"

LET THE LIGHT SHINE THROUGH
Cooperative Extension Service, Montana State University, 1965, 14 minutes

East Helena, Montana, a town that appears to have been dropped into the middle of nowhere, has had a "nuclear protection area" built into its new high school. An incredibly wooden school principal wearing a skinny necktie is proud of it and introduces some teens who are happy to give a tour: ten-inch-thick concrete ceilings, baffled entrances ("because of the scattering effect of radiation"), a well, a generator, bathrooms. It's a big concrete basement that supposedly can hold everyone in town—although how much dignity they'd have after a day or two together is questionable. The teens use it as a rifle range and to play Ping-Pong. "We're quite optimistic about the whole thing," says the principal. He points to the shelter windows currently sealed with cinderblocks and says, "When the time comes that this world of ours will accept faith, trust, and brotherly love, we'll pull these blocks out and let the light shine through."

> **"When a town does all it can to ensure the public safety, then we are answering the challenge to keep our nation strong. And reaffirming our faith in the dignity of man."**

L LET'S BE CLEAN AND NEAT
Coronet Instructional Films, 1957, 11 minutes

A woman narrator explains that "part of the fun of growing up is having your very own toilet articles." With her as a guide, this film follows a day in the life of Bobby, Jane, and their parents, a family of unnaturally spick-and-span people. Dad, who works as a garage mechanic, shows up for dinner wearing a seersucker suit. "He comes home looking so clean, you'd never guess his work sometimes gets him quite greasy." Jane is praised for her "well-trained" hair, which, the narrator cautions, should be washed only once a week, and then only with a tablespoon of soap. "Too much soap would be hard to rinse out."

The high point of the film comes after Bobby's bath, when he's faced with the odious task of tidying up. Poof! A cheap tinfoil crown appears atop his head as he commands his mother to do his cleaning. Thankfully, the narrator is on hand to nip such fantasies in the bud. "Your mother is no serving girl, my boy. And you, Bobby, are not the King of Sheba. So quit dreaming."

LET'S BE GOOD CITIZENS...
John F. Criswell for Gateway Productions, 1953–54, 10 minutes

In the mid-1950s, John F. Criswell produced what he called the *Primary Citizenship* series of social guidance films. They featured Jack and Susan Lewis, who lived on Elm Street in Grovedale. Most of these films were nothing more than a series of disconnected vignettes of positive behavior—cleaning up after playtime, being friendly, etc.—that the soothing, sing-song narrator would conclude with: "[insert positive behavior here] is an important part of being a good citizen." The concluding remark was repeated up to a dozen times in some of the films, inducing a trancelike state when all seven are viewed consecutively.

Let's Be Good Citizens at Home (1953) has Jack and Susan taking turns in the bathroom and sharing household chores; Mom rewards them with beanbags and a custard pie.

174

In *Let's Be Good Citizens at Play* (1953) the Elm Street softball team goes to church to keep their star player company while he attends altar boy class. And *Let's Be Good Citizens at School* (1953) has several odd scenes in which kids burst into energetic hand waving for no apparent reason.

Let's Be Good Citizens at the Library (1954) defines good citizenship as returning books on time and not defacing them with crayons or dirty fingers. *Let's Be Good Citizens in Our Neighborhood* (1953) is the only social guidance film that includes scenes of a Jewish family's Sabbath dinner rituals. *Let's Be Good Citizens in Our Town* (1954) stresses helping others and keeping picnic tables tidy. And, finally, *Let's Be Good Citizens When Visiting* (1954) follows Jack and Susan to Uncle Bill's farm, where they remember to use the doormat and ask permission before crossing the cow pasture.

LET'S BE SAFE AT HOME
Portafilms, 1948, 11 minutes

This has the nasty bite of a Sid Davis film, but it's credited to William H. Murray. Little kids fall down stairs, electrocute themselves, and shoot each other with guns as the unsympathetic narrator declares that "courteous people seldom get hurt; selfish people often do." The film tries to make the violence palatable by stopping the action, superimposing ghostlike double-exposure children over the real kids, and then having them suffer the

accidents. "We won't see anyone really get hurt," says the narrator, "but watch!" There are fun special effects when Steve and Dick are electrocuted and George blasts Bobby.

LET'S GIVE A TEA
Simmel-Meservey, 1946, 22 minutes

The Tea Committee of the Teen Times Club has to arrange a mother-daughter tea for its members. "The girls are fearful," the narrator confides. Not only are they "afraid of not knowing what is proper," some of them actually dismiss teas as "involved and stuffy." Those girls, it turns out, are correct—but the folks at Simmel-Meservey seem unaware of it. This film would have been considered involved and stuffy anywhere outside of a Park Avenue brownstone or a Grosse Pointe manor.

The narrator rattles off the rules and regulations: "Jewelry should not be overdone." "Hats are worn only by the guests." Gloves should be removed "unobtrusively, without interfering with a conversation." Thanks to this grueling attention to detail the Teen Times tea comes off delightfully, complete with mothers wearing odd-shaped hats and gargantuan corsages, and four teen girls in ballroom gowns playing violins. "It is all very simple and really quite enjoyable when one learns how."

Teas were such a complex subject that *Let's Give a Tea* was released with two five-minute satellite films: *Arranging the Tea Table* and *Arranging the Buffet Supper.*

LET'S MAKE A MEAL IN 20 MINUTES
Simmel-Meservey for American Gas Association, 1950, 4 minutes

Sally Gasco is an energetic teen who is "rapidly learning homemaking" and who already knows "the basic techniques of good kitchen behavior." As a result of the hectic pace and tight schedule imposed by her 1950 teen lifestyle, she must prepare dinner for her family in only twenty minutes. Thankfully, she has the assistance of "modern frozen foods," thanks to Mother's "intelligent marketing," that she can cook on her "modern gas range," thanks to the American Gas Association. *Voilà!* In only twenty minutes her corned beef hash and baked pudding meal is complete. "She wasn't in too much of a hurry, though— and you should never be—to wash her hands thoroughly."

Simmel-Meservey also produced *A Date with Your Family* in 1950, which endorsed a slow-motion, prewar approach to dinner.

LET'S PLAY SAFE
Portafilms, 1947, 10 minutes

"Our student safety council normally handles at least five safety violations per week. Since showing *Let's Play Safe* to all classes they have reported only one safety violation in four weeks"—principal's testimonial.

Educational Screen wrote that in this film "animated characters show the possible consequences of unsafe attitudes at play." Giddy Goose is hit by a swing, Foolish Fish leaves "a treacherous pool of water" on the ground after he squirts water from the drinking fountain, Pushy Pig falls off of the slide ladder.

Portafilms, in an early example of cross-media marketing, gave teachers decals of the animal victims to place at "danger points" around their schools.

LET'S SHARE WITH OTHERS
Coronet Instructional Films, 1950, 11 minutes

Young Jimmy Blake has a lemonade stand he wants to run by himself, even though the narrator notes that "when we share things there is often more for everybody." Sure enough, Jimmy's off-the-job responsibilities start cutting into his lemonade sales and he realizes that the way to success is through group effort. Jimmy calls in his friends and soon "everyone is having fun."

This is an excellent look at the 1950s mind-set that equated fun with profit, "sharing" with a business, and group action with popularity. "Learn to share with others. You'll like it. Your friends will like you too!"

LET'S THINK AND BE SAFE
Portafilms, 1957, 10 minutes

Remember the inane head-tapping signal in *Helping Johnny Remember?* Portafilms does that one better in this film, as Miss Jensen asks her elementary school class to "put on your thinking caps" whenever they find themselves in dubious safety situations. Each of the children mechanically obeys, one by one donning an invisible, imaginary cap.

"Isn't it too late to think of safety after someone gets hurt?" the narrator asks. In response, the eight-year-olds stare, zombielike, into space, lightly caressing their crew cuts and curls—i.e., those invisible thinking caps. Then the camera rushes into several of the

kids' faces, going wildly out of focus, to serve as the transitional device leading into a paper-cutout universe. Here, blob-faced late-fifties' cartoon representations of the children repeatedly injure each other through carelessness. It's all great fun; multicolored stars wink on and off above the victims' heads. Buck-toothed George's injury is the best: as he pokes a crayon into his ear his cartoon double's eyes change into bull's-eyes while an alarm rings and his face turns green, matching the color of the crayon.

The film ends with a "Class Safety Meeting" in which each child professes his or her concerns in front of all the others. It's supposed to come across as very democratic, although it looks more like something out of the Cultural Revolution.

"When we think of being safe, we won't get hurt," Miss Jensen concludes. The narrator cheerily adds, "We won't get hurt at our school as long as we all wear our thinking caps!"

LIVE AND LEARN
Sid Davis Productions, 1951, 12 minutes

This is Sid Davis's most darkly entertaining film, guaranteed to cause nightmares for any kid. It's nothing more than a series of vignettes of horrible things happening to audacious children who "did first and thought last." The calm, malevolent narrator sounds like O'Brien from *1984*—"You youngsters can save yourselves a lot of pain if you just stop and think"—as a boy burns his face off, a girl (played by Davis's daughter, Jill) impales herself on a pair of scissors, and other children have their eyes shot out, fall off cliffs, or are run over by cars. Every accident is followed by a scene of a doctor laboriously wrapping an injured child's limb or torso or face in gauze, which gives the narrator another chance to grind some indignity and horror into the audience. "Is it worth this, boys and girls? Suppose this were *you*."

The film ends on a patriotic note, with a shot of a waving American flag and a reminder that youngsters "are the America of tomorrow." Those who survive, anyway.

THE LOADED GUN
Jam Handy Organization for General Tire & Rubber Co., 1958, 8 minutes

Scary horns moan and timpani drums rumble. Two little boys wearing cowboy hats pull a Colt .45 out of a dresser drawer; one points it at the other. Thankfully, Frank Blair (listed in the credits as "noted news commentator") wanders onto the minimalist set and yanks the gun out of the boy's hands an instant before it fires. "'I didn't know the gun was loaded,'" Frank sighs, his voice full of sorrow. "How many times have you heard that expression? How many heartbreaking tragedies do you think it has caused?"

This might sound like a noble public service spot about handgun safety, but in fact it's a sleazy advertisement disguised as a fear film for General Tire's new Dual 90 with "squeegee action." Frank Blair ambles up to a freestanding display of 8 x 10 glossies of car wrecks and completes his analogy: "In each of these cases, somebody didn't know 'it was loaded.' In each case the defect that sent these people to a mindless, screaming death... was *tire* failure!"

A scene follows showing a woman and a little girl dying after a tire blowout (the woman's car weaves a full quarter mile across a grassy median before slamming into an oncoming car), and then another of a woman who's almost run down as she tries to change a flat. To bring the mood up, the film cuts to a happy woman swinging blissfully on a Dual 90 suspended from a cartoon tree. Next comes the superscientific "burst test" in which General Tire scientists in white lab coats, carrying clipboards and stopwatches, pump air into tires lying in a field until they explode.

"Let those tires fail," Frank concludes, "and the car you drive instantly becomes the deadliest weapon devised by man! Don't *you* pull the trigger!"

LSD-25
David W. Parker for Professional Arts, Inc., 1967, 25 minutes

A man in a corduroy jacket stands in a dark doorway. This is the "traveler," a nasal narrator explains. "A traveler who just bought a ticket for a very special kind of trip. The cost? A few dollars—and his mind! Courtesy of LSD-twenty-five."

The narrator knows his subject well because he is, in fact, a tab of LSD. This film will tell his story. But first it cuts to teens gyrating in an underlit nightclub while a bad rock band sings the *LSD-25* theme:

> *Drown, drown, out of your mind*
> *You think you're seeing things, I know you're blind*
> *A million bright colors explode in your head*
> *Today you're just high, tomorrow you're dead.*

LSD-25 imitates cinéma vérité and television documentary techniques to mask its bias. Handheld cameras show teens "rapping" about how easy it is to get acid—"I can get it anywhere from four blocks to ten blocks from my house in twenty minutes"—but the teens are actors, the dialogue is scripted. Militant anti-LSD views—also fake—are shown to make this film's position seem valid in contrast; these include a matron who asserts that kids who take LSD "paint themselves green and yellow" and repeated shots of three guys in furry robes who supposedly are using LSD to start a place called Acid City.

"The head of a pin could hold enough of me to send a roomful of people out of their minds!" LSD cries at one point. "I'm like a depth charge in the mind!" As proof of this, the camera cuts to a teen babbling madly about his drug experience. "I couldn't see anything except *colors* and I thought this was supposed to be reality but it wasn't! It wasn't anything except *things* that weren't *objects!*"

"Drop a cap of me, man, and drop out!" LSD says mockingly as another teen, this one wearing a button-down shirt, screams, "Help me! Oh God, help me!" and rolls on the floor. Then, as bloody footage of accident scenes appear, LSD confides, "The ultimate destination with me can be the morgue."

LSD sighs; too many "oddballs" are giving it a bad name (the Acid City trio reappears). But worst of all are the "really promising kids" who use LSD. "There's no known way to get your fingerprints out of the police files once they're in there. And that's not much help when it comes to getting a job or getting into college or launching a career."

LUNCHROOM MANNERS
Coronet Instructional Films, 1960, 10 minutes

This strange and entertaining film has probably been seen by more people than any other Coronet production, thanks to its inclusion in Pee Wee Herman's 1981 HBO special. It

stars Phil, a squint-eyed, slow-moving child who licks his lips frequently, and Mr. Bungle, a hand puppet with big blue eyes, a toothy smile, messy white hair, and a red stocking cap with a big bell on the end of it.

Phil watches a classroom puppet show in which ill-mannered Mr. Bungle demonstrates bad manners in the lunchroom. Then Phil goes off to lunch himself. But "Phil didn't want to be like Mr. Bungle," the narrator cautions, so Phil first makes a pit stop in the boys' room, pumps about a gallon of soap out of a dispenser to wash his hands, and spends the rest of his time in front of a mirror pretending to comb his hair, which is of a length usually associated with Marine boot camp.

Now it's on to the lunchroom. The narrator is full of praise for the "good food" on the serving line as Phil pushes his tray along. He helps himself to a humongous slab of chocolate cake—it dwarfs the plate—but the narrator reminds him that "only a Mr. Bungle would eat his dessert before he had finished the rest of his lunch."

Although Phil's face remains blank during this film, the narrator is certain that he will never forget the lessons he learned from the puppet show that morning. "Phil and his friends wouldn't like to have a Mr. Bungle at their table. Then lunchtime wouldn't be as much fun as it is!"

MAINTAINING CLASSROOM DISCIPLINE
Caravel Films for McGraw-Hill Book Co., 1947, 14 minutes

This teacher-training film could have been the inspiration for *The Blackboard Jungle*. It begins by introducing the classroom of Mr. Grimes, "where a teacher and the students are not working in harmony." That's an understatement. Mr. Grimes's boorish pupils have turned his class into Anarchy 101, but the narrator explains that the kids' bad behavior is actually Mr. Grimes's fault. He's an "old sourpuss" who hates "confusion and disorder" and has created "undesirable learning situations." Mr. Grimes punishes some of the little monsters, but the narrator asks, "Aren't you covering up a symptom of your own deficiency?" Happily, by the end of the film Mr. Grimes learns progressive teaching methods and becomes a quick-witted, respected pal to the kids. The kids rally around him almost instantaneously. "That Grimes is a good egg."

MAKE YOUR HOME SAFE
Centron Corp. for Young America Films, 1957, 11 minutes

This stultifying film means to teach that people who live safely are "thoughtful, skillful, and careful." As an example, the film shows a nameless family that lives in the shadow of the Lawrence, Kansas, water tower. They are sloppy and careless, and full of "aches and scars" as a result. Then Jack, a tubby boy, adopts a "grown-up viewpoint," and the family's house quickly becomes a "safe and happy place to live." "No more running and dashing," the narrator remarks. "And whenever possible, they use blunt tools."

MANNERS AT SCHOOL
John F. Criswell for Gateway Productions, 1956, 10 minutes

This manners film stresses politeness as a ticket to popularity. It was made for elementary school kids, creating an odd world, like the one in *Exchanging Greetings and Introductions*, full of intensely well mannered children.

"Most of our lives are lived with other people. Living would not be much fun at all if we had to be alone!"

The narrator contends, "You want to be well liked, and happy, too," and then presents a list of manners advice to achieve that goal: "If we mind our own business, people will like us better." "We should try to find out what it is that we like best in other people, and then make ourselves liked by acting the same way."

"Bless you, Susie Ann!" the narrator says to a girl who sneezes. "Using your handkerchief instead of spraying the class is good manners."

MANNERS IN PUBLIC
Centron Corp. for McGraw-Hill Book Co., 1958, 11 minutes

Barbara is a new girl in her housing development who wants to make friends with next-door-neighbor Jane. But Barbara has a terrible handicap: bad manners. She's rude to her mom, yells out the bus window, talks during movies. Jane wonders why Barbara doesn't "know better" and tries to excuse her actions because she is "new and excited." But Jane soon realizes that Barbara is a mannerless "ninny" and refuses to play with her. Barbara hears Jane voicing her opinion through an open window and staggers off-camera, weeping into her hands. "The truth hurts," the narrator says. "But it's lucky you found out!"

Barbara runs to the library, checks out a book from a shelf labeled "manners," and learns good rules of behavior. The narrator is pleased. "You're on your way to a happier life!"

MANNERS IN SCHOOL
Centron Corp. for McGraw-Hill Book Co., 1958, 11 minutes

Larry Carson is a bratty school kid and an awful child actor. Miss Rand, his teacher, makes him stay after class to clean the blackboard. Instead, he draws a stick figure man with a big head—"Chalky"—and it comes to life! For some never-explained reason, Chalky, who talks like a cartoon Martian, wants to help Larry develop better manners and become a "regular guy." Scowling Larry

just wants to erase the annoying creature. "I'm gonna wipe you out!" he cries, lunging toward the blackboard, but silver-tongued Chalky soon has the arrogant youngster eating out of his two-dimensional hands. "I guess I have been pretty bad," Larry finally admits, and by the end of the film he's abandoned his bratty ways and cleaned the board to a jet black spotlessness.

TEACHER (*surprised*): "Larry, you've done an excellent job on the chalkboard."
LARRY: "Thank you, Miss Rand!"

MARIJUANA
Avanti Films, 1968, 34 minutes

This film is narrated by cultural icon Sonny Bono, which provides some indication of its credibility. Sonny, who looks and sounds as if he were stoned, announces that this film will present the facts "and only the facts." He then proceeds to explain that people who smoke marijuana "run the risk of an unpredictable and unpleasant bummer." This is demonstrated by a pot smoker who stares at his

180

reflection in a mirror—until his face is replaced by a rubber monster mask! He's "tripped out," Sonny explains, which is just the same as being an alcoholic "square and unhip adult."

Sonny's flat, nasal monotone drones on and on, explaining that the reason marijuana has not been legalized is because "there are too many unstable people in America" who would end up as "nonfunctioning weedheads." Even with all its absurdity, *Marijuana* tries very hard to be earnest and credible—although Sonny gives every indication of having no idea he was even working on this film.

MEALTIME MANNERS AND HEALTH
Coronet Instructional Films, 1957, 10 minutes

The odd premise of this film is that the more courteous you are at the dinner table, the healthier you'll be. To prove this point, *Mealtime Manners and Health* introduces Phil, a teen with a flattop haircut and no appetite. Why? Because Phil is "all wrapped up in his own thoughts." Dad notices the problem and tells Phil he lacks the right "mental condition" while eating. But Phil doesn't change his ways until he sees a TV program in which rabbits are poked and given electric shocks, demonstrating that upset animals don't have good appetites. The power of the visual image strikes home; Phil doesn't want to end up like one of those doomed bunnies! Now he goes "out of his way to try to make mealtime pleasant for the members of his family" and learns that "it can be relaxing to help with the dishes."

At the end of the film Phil is rewarded for his improved attitude by being invited to host a Parents' Dinner. "Yes, Phil, people do notice good manners!"

MEASURE OF A MAN
Wetzel O. Whitaker for Brigham Young University, 1962, 22 minutes

M

It would be too much to expect the Mormons not to get involved in mental hygiene films for teenagers.

Mike Miller is a square-jawed young man who enjoys raiding the cookie jar and shooting hoops in his driveway. But his friends are not so clean-cut—specifically Hal and Blaine, two boys with bad reputations and a red 1955 Chevy convertible. The three go to Bob's Big Boy drive-in for root beers, then the evening turns into a test of wills to see which of the boys is a "chicken" or a "powder puff."

Mike goes along with Hal and Blaine to pick up a trio of "wild girls." Then Hal drives to Eagle City to buy some beer. Mike is upset but acts cool. "How's a guy get involved in a crazy deal like this?" he asks himself as he sits in the Chevy's backseat with Sue, a beer in hand. Sue, with her Sandra Dee bubble-fronted bouffant, is just as uncomfortable as Mike—and she won't show her true feelings either. "Beer! Ugh! I can't think of anything worse!" she tells herself. "But I don't want this cute guy to think I'm...oh, whatever am I gonna do?"

A title card suddenly appears on the screen: WHAT WOULD YOU DO? But, unlike Centron films, this film isn't ending here. Instead, the action resumes, and Mike tells Sue that he's not going to drink his beer. Sue is overjoyed, and the rest of the gang is so swayed by his manly stand that they don't drink their beers either. The film ends as cheerful, relieved Mike and Sue stand at a pay phone, calling their moms to let them know they're safe and on the way home.

This film has no narration; instead, the scriptwriters wrote anguished voice-over self-examinations for each main character, giving the actors many opportunities to bite their lips and arch their eyebrows.

MECHANIZED DEATH
Safety Enterprises, Inc., 1961, 28 minutes

Although *Signal 30* and *Wheels of Tragedy* have their fans, this is probably director Dick Wayman's most purely artless gore film. "These are the sounds of excruciating agony," the

narrator says as a woman lies in a smashed car, hacking up blood. "This is not a dream, not a nightmare. This is real."

For the next half hour numerous similar scenes of honest-to-goodness roadside carnage unfold: a family is crushed by a truck, a mom is killed in a head-on collision, a girl is hurled to her death after her car is hit by a train. Two bland narrators barely vary their voices beyond a monotone as the endless procession of bloody-faced, limp corpses passes on the screen. "This boy thought he was pretty sharp," says one narrator, as a jean-clad body is dragged from under a wrecked car. "It seems, however, he had too flippant an attitude. Sure, he knew the area real well. But not that well."

There's no filmmaking style here; no plot, no drama, no clever editing. Just grainy handheld footage of accident scenes and incessant, droning, judgmental narration. "Speed is a relative matter. How will your relatives feel if you speed and kill?"

MEN OF TOMORROW
Mode-Art Productions for Weirton Steel Co. and American Legion, Dept. of West Virginia, 1962, 27 minutes

In West Virginia, 350 seventeen-year-old "future leaders" (the West Virginia American Legion Mountaineer Boys' Club) are selected by adults, bussed to a retreat, and then brainwashed into accepting the political processes of their elders. The boys get to run a make-believe nation, elect a "governor" and "supreme court," and play baseball.

The campaign rally for the two gubernatorial candidates is this film's most frightening moment. What's being depicted really *is* politics—a mindless, yelling mass of meatheads who draw no distinction between government for the people and a frat party. And this is a fraternity—No Gurlz Allowed.

> *Mennnnnnn of tomorrrrrrrow,*
> *A group of all-American boyyyyyyyz!*

MIKE MAKES HIS MARK
Agrafilms for National Educational Association, 1955, 28 minutes

Mike is a leather-jacket-wearing teen who "just wouldn't go along." He starts fights, grumbles, and—on the first day his new school opens—leaves a big pencil mark on its front door. "The first black mark against our school," the principal says, scowling. He orders that the mark be left as it is until the vandal can be hunted down.

Mike, meanwhile, wants to quit school and become a TV repairman. But his counselor and homeroom teacher—after consulting Mike's massive "cumulative record" dossier—decide that he should instead play kettle drums in the school band. Mike is understandably leery of this advice, but he comes around when he realizes that he can't read his TV repairman tube tester instruction manual. He also confesses his crime, and the pencil mark is removed. "Mike had begun to show the mark of a man!"

182

MIND YOUR MANNERS!
Coronet Instructional Films, 1953, 11 minutes

Woody from *Dating: Do's and Don'ts* made his final screen appearance in this film as Jack Connors, an unfailingly polite high schooler. The film contains no teen turmoil and requires no decision making on the part of its characters. Jack is a one-dimensional role model, picking lint off his sister's dress, asking about a classmate's tonsil operation, helping a girl who's dropped her school books. "That makes Jack rate high with her!" the narrator cheers. Perhaps more to the point, the film ends with a series of close-ups of pleased adults who smile and think kind thoughts of Jack and his equally polite friends. "There's a pleasant, well-mannered group of young people," an old lady reflects. "Not like *some*."

MISSING WITNESS
Sid Davis Productions, 1958, 10 minutes

Tony is an average teen whose Ford Fairlane is plowed into by a Caddy. A guy in a cowboy hat sees the accident and knows that it wasn't Tony's fault, but he drives away. Even worse, the Caddy's driver suffers a serious concussion—and everyone thinks Tony is to blame! "I knew just what they were thinking," Tony groans as the camera pans over a crowd of skeptical onlookers. "Another hot rodder. Another wild teenaged driver. They're all alike!"

Even though he knows that teenaged drivers are "looked upon with blanket suspicion," Tony decides to enlist the aid of his high school's car clubs to track down the missing witness. "Let's show the adults in our community that we can drive as carefully, intelligently, and responsibly as they!"

Tony admits that the teen crowd does have some "yo-yo drivers," but all of his friends display "courtesy," "obvious earnestness," and "careful driving practices" as they track down the errant witness. When the cowboy is finally found, Tony comments that "he simply hadn't wanted to get involved," and that his attitude was "typical of the irresponsible citizen." As the film ends, Tony is happily cleared of all charges and remarks that "it pays always to drive with care and courtesy in every way."

Missing Witness was shot almost entirely outdoors, flat and lifeless, in Arcadia, California. It seems more like the Arcadia police department's dream of how teenagers should behave than anything approaching reality.

MOLLY GROWS UP
Medical Arts Productions for Personal Products Corp. [Modess], 1953, 16 minutes

For many years this was *the* film that girls got to see in health class while boys went out and played kickball. Molly, played by actress Betsy Hawkins, who is much too old to be in pigtails, is a perky bundle of energy as she anxiously awaits her first period, a happy sign—at least in her mind—that she'll soon be dating and going to dances in sweeping 1950s prom dresses.

It's easy to see that this film's long list of M.D. and Ph.D. advisors told the producers to make it deliver a "positive" message, with the result that everyone in the cast is golly-gee-whiz excited about menstruation: Molly, Sis, Mother, even Father. The only one who seems blasé about it is Miss Jensen, the school nurse, who has to point to the same cutaway drawing of the uterus and sperm that seems to appear in every sex ed film, regardless of decade or gender. As usual, there's no mention of how those pesky sperm get into that uterus in the first place.

Overall, *Molly Grows Up* is not a bad effort for its time. Miss Jensen cautions menstruating girls against square dancing, advocates changing sanitary napkins five or six times a day (note the sponsor of this film), and recommends that while menstruating, "pay more attention to your hair and nails, and wear your prettiest dress. In other words, be your most attractive self."

MOMENT OF DECISION!
Sid Davis Productions, 1961, 10 minutes

Teen pseudohoods Robert, John, Paul, and Bill come across a 1960 Pontiac Catalina convertible with its keys in the ignition. Each has to make a decision whether or not to take a joy ride. The narrator cautions: "You may yet learn to make wise decisions before it's too late." Paul is the only one who heeds the advice.

If real criminals hesitated as long as Robert, John, Paul, and Bill, no car would ever be stolen.

MONKEY ON THE BACK
Grant McLean & Julian Biggs for National Film Board of Canada, 1956, 29 minutes

Dick Smith is a middle-aged white guy with a broken-down face. He lives in a city where it's always gray and cold. He's also "a confused, harried human being"—and a heroin addict. His wife and kids leave him, he loses his umpteenth factory job, he steals whenever he can, he gets thrown in jail repeatedly. Finally he OD's and dies.

Monkey on the Back is from the So What? school of drug films, which took the position that drug users were beyond salvation and that the only reason to make drug films was to show nonusers the horrible fates of those who transgressed.

"This true story is not a pleasant one. It's not for very young eyes and ears."

Lots of frisky flutes and xylophones play on the discordant music track, noticeable because this arty film often has long gaps between dialogue. Dick's "agony of withdrawal" is unequaled for sweating and twitching.

MORE DATES FOR KAY
Coronet Instructional Films, 1952, 10 minutes

In most Coronet films dating is portrayed as a gentle activity, with protagonists varying between shy and sweet, perhaps a little confused, but always endearing. This Coronet film is different. It's designed specifically for girls, and its role model is Kay Stratten, a plain-looking woman who's supposed to be a high schooler. The narrator exclaims, "Kay's an amazing girl!" and it's soon apparent why.

The only thing Kay values is boyfriends. She hunts them with a riveting, relentless intensity, throwing herself at every male she meets: in a school hallway, in a classroom, at the soda shop. Her small talk is calculated to ferret out

184

each boy's interests, which she then instantly embraces as her own: food, sports, dogs. She feigns helplessness at her locker to meet one boy and calls up another on the phone to help her with her Latin homework, which she's obviously already completed. In each instance the tactic fails to land a date, and in each the camera dwells on Kay to show her annoyance and frustration. But Kay "never lets anything get the best of her," the narrator insists as Kay volunteers to be chairman of the Clean-Up Committee for a big school party. "I'll do it!" she yells to the two boys who are hand-

ing out assignments. "Somebody has to clean up after a party! I'll be glad to!" "Hey," whispers one boy to the other. "Put me on that committee, too, pal."

The narrator tries to put a positive spin on all this by noting that Kay is actually demonstrating "friendliness" and "helpfulness." But her forced smiles and hungry eyes project no sincerity. Every friendship she forges is in pursuit of landing a date. Without a man dangling at her side, life is not worth living for Kay. Apparently, the girls who watched this film were supposed to feel the same way. "Well? Do you get the picture?"

More Dates for Kay—along with *Shy Guy* and *How to Say No*—was recommended by *Educational Screen* as a film for church youth meetings.

Lots of close-ups and extreme close-ups on faces, which is unusual for a Coronet film (or any educational film), and which makes this production all the more creepy and disturbing.

MOTHER MACK'S PUPPIES FIND HAPPY HOMES
Frith Films, 1953, 11 minutes

This is one of eighty-five wobbly films produced by Emily Benton Frith, many of which star Patty Garman (her niece), all of which look as if they were shot with a home-movie camera and are narrated by Don McNamara, who never uses any contractions.

Mother Mack is a Scottish terrier who gives birth to seven puppies. Her owners, youthful Doug and Don Dowell, decide to keep the littlest puppy and give the other six away. As the soundtrack echoes with a maddening cacophony of puppy barks and kitten mews (there are cats in this film too), the puppies are distributed to a rainbow coalition of families: one goes to a Hispanic American, another to an African American, another to an Asian American, etc. The implied message is that all races and nationalities are equal—at least when it comes to puppy love—which makes this film unique for its intolerant time.

There's a prequel to this film, *Mother Mack Trains Her Seven Puppies*, and a sequel, *The Littlest Puppy Grows Up*, both of which were used as metaphors for other social concerns of Emily Benton Frith.

MOTHER TAKES A HOLIDAY
Jam Handy Organization for Whirlpool Corp., 1953, 29 minutes

This film equates women's liberation with the arrival of modern electric household appliances, which isn't surprising considering its sponsor.

185

Teenaged Marilyn is writing a paper on the emancipation of women with two of her chums. Her thesis: the ultimate embodiment of women's freedom is her family's Whirlpool washer and dryer. "That's the kind of emancipation *any* woman can understand!" Her envious girlfriends agree and conspire with Marilyn to trick their doofus dads into buying new washers and dryers for their homes.

The girls take their moms away for a weekend so the dads can indulge themselves in an all-day cribbage game and experience the wonder of Marilyn's mom's "complete home laundry." The plot is interrupted by an extended visit to the Whirlpool manufacturing plant, where Marilyn's washing machine—"a clean-lined, simply designed, purely functional beauty"—is being assembled. With such overpowering stimuli the meek dads come around pretty quickly.

MR. B NATURAL
Kling Film Enterprises for C. G. Conn Ltd., 1957, 27 minutes

C. G. Conn, a manufacturer of musical instruments, sponsored this film—and what a film it is. Mr. B Natural is an elflike character played by a middle-aged woman named Betty Luster, who was probably a summer-stock Peter Pan. As Mr. B Natural, she wears a powder blue Robin Hood cap and blazer covered with musical notes and delivers every line as if it were punctuated with three exclamation marks. Mr. B Natural represents "the spirit of

fun in music" and has come to earth to help twelve-year-old Buzz Turner discover that being in a school band (stocked with Conn musical instruments) can be "fun, fun, fun!!!"

Buzz certainly needs help. He's a shy bookworm who wants to get to know Jeanie, "the cutest girl in school," but lacks any skills to help him "fit in with the gang." Then Mr. B Natural appears in his bedroom and tells him he can be popular by joining the school band. "Wait'll you see the kicks you get out of it, Buzz! The glamour of the uniform! The thrill of traveling for band competition! Just like being a member of a football team!!!"

Buzz swallows Mr. B Natural's argument, and several minutes later he's playing lead trumpet at a romantic school dance, with Jeanie looking on admiringly.

This strange film has many unreal moments, but nothing tops Betty Luster for pure, inescapable insanity. She is a shrieking, grimacing menace, squealing lines such as "A clarinet's not just a clarinet, it's a happy smile!!!"

NAME UNKNOWN
Sid Davis Productions, 1951, 10 minutes

Prune-faced juvenile court judge McKesson sits behind a desk. Across from him sits young Edie Adams, flanked by her parents, tears in her eyes. "Just another case," the judge grunts, utterly unmoved.

Judge McKesson says that Edie "tried to prove she had nerve—ran off with a stranger who promised to marry her. And here she is in my chambers. A delinquent!" As he makes clear time and again, the judge has no compassion for ungrateful young people who won't "listen to their parents' good sense or follow the rules."

"Teenagers can be such suckers!" he snorts. "And for what? A kick? Or a fling? A thrill? You think you're smart enough to get away with it!"

Several vignettes follow of "normal average kids"—all girls—who have their lives "ruined in a few hours or even in minutes." A teenaged girl is raped by a gun-wielding pervert in a suit with a hanky in the breast pocket, but, after all, she and her boyfriend had the audacity to park on a dark road, "just looking for trouble." Next, a younger girl named Mary Hanson is allowed by her permissive mother to place a classified ad soliciting baby-sitting work. "You think it's silly to worry, don't you, Mrs. Hanson?" the judge clucks. "After all, what could happen to Mary on a baby-sitting job?" The soundtrack fills with ominous stock music as the clock strikes half-past midnight. "And now, Mrs. Hanson, it *is* time to worry. But I'm afraid it's too late to do any good."

A screaming Sid Davis newspaper headline appears—BABY SITTER SLAIN BY UNKNOWN ASSAILANT—and the film immediately whisks to the next tale of woe, that of Ethel Ryan, "one of the nicest girls in her school." Ethel, unfortunately, thinks she's "too sophisticated for boys her own age." When two older men pull up in a convertible, the soundtrack hopping with jazzy trumpets, Ethel tries to persuade her girlfriend to go on a double date. Her friend refuses, but since Ethel's mom "never forbids her daughter anything," Ethel decides "she certainly isn't going to give up a good time" and goes by herself. "I wish that were all there was to it," the judge sighs. "But life is not quite that simple. When one breaks the rules, we pay for it."

Another screaming headline appears—SCHOOL GIRL FOUND UNCONSCIOUS IN HILLS—and the judge goes ballistic. "Go ahead!" he dares his unseen audience. "Have a good laugh!" Ethel struggles with the men in the car and the judge crows, "Here's something *really* funny!"

The film ends back in Judge McKesson's chambers as he sentences poor Edie, who by now is weeping into her hands, to three months in a detention home. "Plenty of time to think about whether a few minutes of showing off or feeling sharp is worth a lifetime of regrets!"

NARCOTICS: PIT OF DESPAIR

Mel Marshall, 1967, 29 minutes

It's a crowded field, but this may well be the stupidest drug film ever produced.

Ominous bongos fill the soundtrack as the film introduces John, a sandy-haired, snaggle-toothed high school senior who drives a snazzy British sports car, is a star on the

track team, and has a cute girlfriend. He also has a friend named Pete, a smug-looking, bearded hipster who wears a turtleneck with a zipper front. Pete is a drug pusher. For reasons never explained, Pete decides to invest a great deal of time and money getting John into his clutches. John, who would rather pursue "kicks" than finish his homework, is an easy mark.

Pete invites John to a party. Badass Hammond organ music and dizzying handheld camera work signal that drugs are somewhere near. John is introduced to Helen, "the hip

187

chick of the gang," who flutters her false eyelashes, thrusts her large breasts forward, and lures John into the garage, where "the grasshoppers" are "really blasting." "Take a trip from Squaresville," the narrator crows as the gang passes a joint. "Get with the countdown. Shake this square world and blast off for Kicksville."

John does exactly that (grinning like an idiot after only one puff), immediately becomes "psychologically dependent" on pot, and almost as quickly starts mainlining heroin. His girlfriend, sports car, and track team are abandoned. John steals his mother's silverware for money to buy drugs, and the unsympathetic narrator lays it on thick. "At first it seemed like such harmless fun. It was hip to go along with the gang. But where's the gang *now*?" (And where were his parents?) "Too late he realizes that by joining to belong, he's more alone than ever."

Poor John, who was only employing the fitting-in skills he learned from years of watching social guidance films, is left screaming in withdrawal agony on a dirty mattress in a garage. The cops bust in and the narrator somberly remarks that John will have "a police record to haunt him as long as he lives." Then—amazingly—a ray of hope appears amid all the gloom and doom. John is sent to a hospital where he'll receive "the very best treatment modern science can give."

But a happy ending just wouldn't seem right in a nasty film like this. The ominous bongo music returns as John, just released, walks down the street near the garage where he was arrested. "I wonder if Pete is out of prison yet," he thinks. "Won't do any harm to just stop by and say hello...." A title appears over a shot of a spitting cobra: THERE IS NO END.

NEVER A BRIDE
Wetzel O. Whitaker for Brigham Young University, 1969, 21 minutes

Laura Allen has big, false eyelashes, is eighteen years old, and very seriously wants to get married. It's not surprising, since this is a Mormon film. "Do you realize that by fall I may be the only old maid in the neighborhood?"

Laura is spending the summer at her aunt Jean's dude ranch in the mountains. "This is the kind of place you dream about," she sighs. "Stars and crickets—and the right man comes along. Oh, it all fits in!" Plain but cheerful Elaine wonders why Laura isn't "worried about being the right kind of wife," but such thoughts bounce off Laura's preoccupied noggin. She doesn't even make her own bed, a bad sign for any future Mormon bride.

Aunt Jean and Elaine leave the ranch for a few days. Laura decides to use this time to steal the affections of Neal, Elaine's handsome boyfriend. A montage of them having fun ensues, including a shot of the two singing *Old MacDonald* in Neal's pickup truck. Laura is convinced that Neal is gonna pop the question when Aunt Jean and Elaine return—and he does. To Elaine! Neal tells Laura that his dad taught him to "look for a happy woman" and adds, "Elaine's a hard worker. I'd sure hate to come home to a dirty house every night!"

Laura sees the wisdom in this attitude and promises Aunt Jean that she'll change her ways (or at least her sheets). "I'm gonna try really hard not to worry so much about finding the right person as *being* the right person!" she announces. "Then maybe I'll be able to make someone else happy!"

NONE FOR THE ROAD
Centron Corp. for Young America Films, 1957, 15 minutes

None for the Road chronicles a weekend evening of three teenaged boys: a heavy drinker, a moderate drinker, and a nondrinker. Interspersed are scenes of a physiologist who injects alcohol into staggering white rats. Despite the obligatory car crash (suffered, ironically, by the moderate drinker), this is one of the tamer films in the driver safety genre.

OFFICE ETIQUETTE
Encyclopaedia Britannica Films, 1950, 13 minutes

Most high school girls in the 1950s who couldn't go to college and weren't getting married immediately after graduation tried to get office jobs. To improve their chances, educational filmmakers created secretarial social-skill training films. Although they were ennobled

under the vague heading "human relations," it's doubtful many men saw them.

Office Etiquette opens in a typing class that actually does have some boys in it—although they're shown only in soft focus in the back rows. The woman teacher tells her students the purpose of office etiquette is to "get along in the business world." She doesn't say anything about getting *ahead* in it.

The rest of the film shows eighteen-year-old Joan Spencer as she becomes acquainted with her first job. She has lunch with the girls, signs up for the office bowling team, and

learns that if any mistakes are made, they're her fault. The women sit in a big room, eyes downcast toward typewriters and steno pads, while most of the men have private offices and give dictation.

Office Etiquette is most memorable for its "bad office worker" sequence featuring a series of ungrateful clock watchers, candy eaters, and newspaper readers. They are the happiest people in the film.

ON YOUR OWN
Sid Davis Productions, 1961, 10 minutes

Sid Davis really knew how to take a metaphor and beat it into the ground. Cannibalizing lots of free NASA and Soviet space footage, Davis teaches preteen Bob that it's his "duty" and "responsibility" to be "adult and smart" by using "the safety devices" provided for him by his community: sidewalks, crosswalks, traffic signals, etc., "like the astronaut." Perky flutes and elevator Muzak strings fill the soundtrack. The narrator makes the unusual observation that city streets are "like small missiles."

THE OTHER FELLOW'S FEELINGS
Centron Corp. for Young America Films, 1951, 8 minutes

Judy sobs at her desk, her face buried in her hands, and Miss Brown's class is atwitter. "It was Jack," Judy cries, pointing to the boy sitting behind her. "He did it. He's always teasing me!" Jack replies indignantly that it was all Judy's fault and here goes another Centron discussion film.

Judy, it turns out, accidently bumped into Jack several weeks back and dropped a bottle of perfume. "Whoo-ee, Stinky!" Jack cries, and he never lets up. He teases her by  holding his nose, scrawling "You Smell" in her notebook, and taping "Stinky" to her back. Like any good program of torture, these small incidents slowly break Judy until she can't go anywhere without a sing-song refrain of "Stink-y, stink-y" playing in her brain, accompanied by visions of tiny floating, smirking Jack heads. She's losing her mind!

Judy suppresses her rage—until she blurts out, "I stink" instead of "I think" when answering one of Miss Brown's questions. The floodgates open, Judy breaks down in tears, and the film ends where it began, with Judy in tears. "What could have been done?" the narrator asks. "What should have been done? What do *you* think?"

OTHER PEOPLE'S PROPERTY
Centron Corp. for Young America Films, 1951, 11 minutes

Three glum-looking preteens sit in chairs in a school hallway outside a principal's office. The narrator explains, "They're in trouble. Real trouble."

NARRATOR: "You planned this, Frank. It was all your idea. What do you think about your fine idea now?"

FRANK: "Golly, if I had it to do over I'd sure do it different."

NARRATOR: "And you, Jimmy...you really didn't give any thought to how it might turn out, did you? To you it just seemed 'fun.'"

JIMMY: "It was awful funny—for a while. It isn't any fun now, though."

NARRATOR: "You could've stopped it. You knew it was wrong. Then why did you do it?"

DALE: "I knew we shouldn't do it and I tried to tell them. But they said I was just a chicken."

A flashback sequence reveals that the three boys planned to set off a stink bomb in the wastebasket of Mr. Craft, Frank's most despised teacher.

FRANK: "He deserved something. Making me stay in 'cause he caught me throwing paper wads. I wasn't the only one. Made me miss the ballgame, too."

Jimmy goes along, thinking "it would be a whale of a good joke," and Dale, the conscience of the group, is too wimpy to stop it.

Unfortunately, the stink bomb is too powerful (it explodes in a miniature atomic cloud) and everyone thinks the school is on fire. When the three boys survey the damage, "the feeling change[s] from 'fun' to 'fear.' And finally to shame."

The film returns to Frank, Jimmy, and Dale, still waiting for the door of doom to open, trying to shore up their defense.

FRANK: "We're not the only ones. What about those guys drawing pictures in the washroom? What about the time when all those kids broke the windows?"

JIMMY: "Sure! And the carved-up desks in Miss Smith's room. And the library books that were marked up last week. We're not the only ones who've done stuff around here."

DALE: "Gee whiz, you don't think that excuses us, do you? There's no getting around it. What we did was *wrong*."

THE OUTSIDER
Centron Corp. for Young America Films, 1951, 12 minutes

Flat, twangy Kansas accents abound in this production, another that portrays group bonding as an ideal to be striven for. Susan Jane Smith is the protagonist—pretty, but "out of step." "Why is everyone else having such a good time when you're not?" the narrator asks. "What makes you the outsider? The one [*pause*] nobody [*pause*] asks."

Susan Jane really should rethink her priorities, since the kids in the group she desperately wants to join are a bunch of losers. Junior, for example, is a fatso who orders the "super duper special" at the soda shop and keeps referring to the upcoming party at Marcy Clark's as "the big feed." They talk about Susan Jane as "that quiet girl" and "stuck up"— that is, when they talk about her at all. "Aw, forget her!" yawns one kid at the soda shop. "Let's all go over to Lewis's and look at television!"

Susan Jane weeps a lot in this film ("I just don't fit in!"), especially when she overhears two of the girls trashing someone she believes to be herself. However, it turns out they're only slandering an unimportant teacher, and Susan Jane is invited to Marcy's party after all. She vows to "work hard" at making friends. "I'm going to fix up!" she tells her mother excitedly. "I'm going to join in and not hang back! I'm going to be friendly! I'm going to like them and, oh, Mother, do you think that'll make them like me?"

"Well, it's certainly a start, Susan Jane. Yes, I think this may be your chance."

PARENTS ARE PEOPLE TOO
Audio Productions for McGraw-Hill Book Co., 1954, 15 minutes

Unlike *Getting Along with Parents,* this film has no narrative story line. It unfolds in an ideal classroom, populated by courteous, quick-on-the-uptake, articulate teens who are more than willing to share details of their home lives with their equally articulate teacher.

The kids, it turns out, have many bones to pick with their cranky parents. Doris is upset that her dad yelled at her for wearing lipstick. Betty has to endure "cereal nagging" from her mom at breakfast. Tubby Tom complains that his dad—a real bullet head—won't let his older brother take the car out alone. The kids admit that their complaints sound petty but whine, "If they want us to act like adults, why do they still treat us as if we were children?"

191

The very wise teacher, who apparently has nothing else planned for the day, listens closely to his students' griping, reminds them that "pleasant emotions are important to a healthy life," and encourages "understanding on both sides" and "reasonable handling."

"Once you learn that what your parents ask you to do is for your own good," he tells them, "you'll be able to accept it."

PATTERN FOR SMARTNESS
Hartley Productions for Simplicity Pattern Co., 1948, 22 minutes

Johnny and Betty are two adult actors trying very hard to portray high school teens. Johnny is all agog at Betty's new dress and declares that she has "that 'know-how' look." "It's what fellahs like a girl to have, and you have it! Plus!" Betty confesses that she makes all of her clothes from Simplicity patterns—"But your clothes look so…professional!"

Johnny protests—and that dressmaking is an embarrassingly simple thing. "I just let my pattern tell me what to do and it comes out all right."

Next, an eight-foot-high Simplicity pattern packet slowly slides into the center of Betty's room. Girl models emerge from behind it and the giant pattern's voice delivers step-by-step instructions as Betty creates yet another feminine frock. "A good pattern is one of a girl's best friends," the pattern says. "Your pattern catalog is a book of magic—for it turns all who use it into creative artists." "She's a regular boy scout with that knot!" adds the dumb guy narrator.

Betty's dialogue is sprinkled with praise for her home ec classes (Simplicity knew where this film would be shown) as the new dress is completed. Johnny's eyes bulge. "Why don't you and the other girls put on a fashion show to get money for new equipment for the basketball team?" he suggests. "Wonderful, Johnny," Betty replies. "The girls will be crazy about it!"

PERSONAL HYGIENE FOR BOYS
Coronet Instructional Films, 1952, 11 minutes

Two narrators duel in this film: a whiny teenaged boy and a calm, reassuring adult. Larry is the center of attention in his little gang. "Larry's got good looks and everybody likes him," the whiner pouts. "Some guys have all the luck!" The adult voice of authority points out that it isn't luck but "personal health habits" that make Larry so likeable. "Personal habits of body care and hygiene can have a lot to do with popularity and social success."

> **"Personal health habits can have a lot to do with your social success and well-being."**

Larry gets up "bright and early" so that he has plenty of time to shower. "If your hair is healthy you can wash it every day." He also dries carefully between his toes, lines public toilet seats with paper, and eats well-balanced meals. "Larry looks clean and *is* clean," the adult narrator comments. "That's what gives him such an air of self-confidence!" "It sure works for Larry," the whiner concedes. "And all the time I thought it was luck!"

George Tychsen, the scriptwriter, reportedly was a clean fetishist who worked many of his own idiosyncrasies into the screenplay.

THE POLITICAL PROCESS
Vision Associates for McGraw-Hill Book Co., 1970, 11 minutes

Unlike citizenship films of earlier decades such as *Are You a Good Citizen* (1949) or *Public Opinion in Our Democracy* (1950), *The Political Process* does not concern itself with grass-roots movements working to improve local communities. Instead, it shoots straight up to the congressional and presidential levels, where nuts-and-bolts democracy is replaced with an unwieldy, unanswerable "process." It drags teenagers right along with it, trying to convince them that the best way to change the world is to become a faceless cog in the established political machine.

"If the political process in a democracy is to succeed, the young people of the nation must be involved and committed."

"It begins, as always, with the volunteer," the narrator explains. "The citizen who believes that, within a democracy, he can work to bring about the kind of democracy he wants." No wild-eyed activists or boat-rockers in this film, no sir. Instead there is a cavalcade of shots of pimple-faced teens in neckties working the phones, doing their thing within the system to make a difference. "What role can you play in politics?" the narrator asks. An extremely minor one, if this film is any indicator.

POSTURE AND EXERCISE
ERPI Classroom Films, 1941, 12 minutes

James Brill, ERPI's android narrator, drones on about "motor units" and "the tonus reflex." There are lots of shots of perfectly built gymnasts flexing muscles and bounding about, and one weird pseudoexperiment in which a woman's arm is strapped to a table with her index finger tied to a weight on a pulley while her blood supply is slowly cut off.

POSTURE AND PERSONALITY

P

Social Science Films for Hardcastle Film Associates, 1949, 9 minutes

The badgering narrator of this odd film asserts that everyone can develop posture and personality as a succession of teens, their faces chalk white under the intense lighting needed for early color film, become more "alert" and "friendly."

"Poise, radiant health, and a good appearance are of great importance in the adult world," the narrator remarks. "Modern parents give more thought to it than formerly."

"Without poise no one can be truly attractive."

The most enjoyable part of this production is its last few minutes, shot outside a high school football stadium. "Modern teachers of physical education have developed interpretive exercises that can be fun as well as healthful," the narrator explains. "These folks are having fun as well as exercising, and they have their eye on the future!"

And what a future. About a hundred teenaged girls, all wearing black leotards, shorts, and diaphanous, long skirts, strut and bow and wave and salute the sun en masse in a kind of pagan dance as they slowly make their way around a track encircling the football field. At the fifty-yard line a matronly woman stands behind a big pole-mounted microphone, barking orders. Next to her is an upright piano. In front of her sits a giant loudspeaker.

"Good posture will help you enjoy life, not only as an individual, but as a member of the community and as a citizen of America!" the narrator exclaims as the camera pans to an enormous American flag spread across the bleacher benches. "Remember, if you want to have fun, if you want to really enjoy life, practice good posture! Get that balanced feeling!"

POSTURE PALS
Avis Films, 1952, 9 minutes

Miss Martin gives her third-grade class a posture test, which involves standing behind a screen while she traces their silhouettes onto the blackboard. Tommy, Jimmy, Jane, and Mary don't fair very well. Miss Martin suggests that they become "posture pals" and keep an eye on each other. They do so eagerly, pointing out each other's slumping and slouching at the drinking fountain, the blackboard, at their desks, on the playground. By film's end this mutual nagging has improved the four so drastically that they're declared king, queen, prince, and princess of posture and are rewarded with robes, scepters, and cardboard "posture crowns."

PREPARING YOUR BOOK REPORT
Coronet Instructional Films, 1960, 11 minutes

Jim Clark has to prepare an oral book report for Mrs. Norton's class. Since this is a Coronet film, he pays excruciating attention to organization and list making, and after many long minutes, he is ready to test his report on his family. "Of course, his mother and father and sister were happy to listen to his book report," the narrator comments. "They helped Jim remember to stand up straight and to speak distinctly in complete sentences."

Jim gets a good night's sleep and the next day presents his classmates with an oratory that sounds as if it were written by a Coronet screenwriter—which, of course, it was. "Can you imagine what would happen if you turned up at your own funeral, or what it would be like to be lost in a large cave? You can find out by reading this book!" Jim is applauded by both his peers and teacher, and the narrator adds his share of praise. "Mrs. Norton thought it was a fine report! All that preparation had really been worthwhile."

PREVENTING THE SPREAD OF DISEASE
National Motion Pictures Co., 1940, 10 minutes

This strange little film first introduces "poor Barbara," a young bedridden girl who is "miserable with suffering and pain." Suddenly, the screen fills with low-angle shots of troops marching menacingly toward the camera. "Her body is just like a little country that has been invaded by an enemy army!" the narrator cries. "Except its soldiers are the germs of communicable disease!"

"Every step taken to prevent the spread of disease means increased happiness and greater living efficiency for all of us."

Poor Barbara is forgotten at this point, and the film moves on to a series of shots of frozen-faced people who are obviously very uncomfortable in front of a camera. A little girl and boy stand with the words SICK and WELL written on sheets of paper that are pinned to their clothes. A woman with too much eye makeup sneezes and a hand-held pointer edges tentatively into the frame, indicating

194

where the spray of her sneeze traveled. Uncalled-for waltz music plays on the soundtrack. Window screens, cleanliness, and paper cups are praised, and two children run away from a door on which has been posted a sign: SCARLET FEVER.

Not a very coherent film, but fun to watch.

PROBLEMS OF CITY DRIVING
Progressive Pictures, 1949, 10 minutes

"Don't be a line straggler." "Keep in step with the flow of traffic." "Double parking only leads to trouble." The constantly nagging backseat driver of a narrator passes the first part of this film showing what not to do and the latter half appealing to a late 1940s American sense of values. "The strictly 'fair-play' driver never consciously breaks a traffic rule," he proclaims. "He would no more cheat in traffic than he would cheat at games or in sports!"

THE PROCRASTINATOR
Centron Corp. for Young America Films, 1952, 12 minutes

Jean Nelson is the subject of this film, a ditzhead who's more interested in socializing than in get-your-hands-dirty American work. "You fiddle-faddle your time away!" her mother scolds. "It's a wonder to me you ever get anything done!"

Nevertheless, Jean is elected social chairman for her class dance—with predictable results. Pock-faced Jim is a sober voice of caution, but no one listens to him until the night before the dance, when the other kids realize that Jean has accomplished nothing in the past five months. The camera dollies back as Jean is left, head bowed, slumped in a chair, humiliated, while the rest of the class feverishly hangs crepe paper in the gym.

THE PROM: IT'S A PLEASURE!
Jam Handy Organization for Coca-Cola Company, 1961, 17 minutes

This obsessive film shows the elaborate prom preparations of America's Junior Miss 1960, Mary Moore of Missouri, "the nation's ideal high school senior girl." Mary repeatedly insists that proms are fun, but the kids here seem too preoccupied with protocol to notice.

Handsome sports star Dick Carter arranges his date with Mary by phone and thoughtfully chooses a corsage to complement her voluminous taffeta dress, which seems designed to keep all dance partners far, far away. The slow-moving music, the expensive outfits, the rigidity of the dance card system—if ever there was a way to take all the passion out of dancing, this film shows it. There is an element of fairy-tale romance to it all, but can a girl really

enjoy spending the biggest night of her life stiffly moving on a dance floor with a card dangling from her wrist and constricting underwear squeezing her frame?

Mary and Dick end the evening with a courteous exchange of pleasantries on her front porch, but without so much as a handshake. Mary's dress keeps Dick at a safe distance.

195

PUBLIC ENEMY NO. 1
Fred S. Niemann for National Women's Christian Temperance Union, 1951, 21 minutes

Dad is a doctor. His teenaged son, Bill Jr., wears snappy two-tone shoes and drives a woody wagon. As a result of a "college initiation fraternity prank," Bill Jr. is pulled over for erratic driving and fails a sobriety test. An "understanding fellow" of a police officer spares the doctor's son the "unpleasantness" of arrest by calling the doctor to the scene. "Perhaps I'd failed him since his mother passed away," Dad reflects, and he decides to take Bill Jr. and his kid brother Johnny on a hunting or fishing trip—it changes from scene to scene—in the mountains.

For the next twenty minutes nothing in the film bears any relation to its soundtrack. Endless footage over Dad's shoulder is shown while he drives his convertible past trees and deer and sweeping mountain vistas and delivers a nonstop diatribe about the evils of alcohol. Liquor is "obnoxious stuff," Dad declares, and drinking it leads to a "crumbling of mental inhibitions" and "a lessening of potency." "I don't mean to frighten you, boys; I'm just telling you in your own kind of language exactly what happens to the drinker in the long run," says the doctor's voice as he and the boys go fly-fishing, completely indifferent to each other.

Dad doesn't have anything nice to say about people who sell liquor, either. Madison Avenue is "tricking the people" and feeding them "a pack of lies." Liquor stores represent "an industry that virtually peddles misery and death on nearly every street corner in our country," Dad insists. "It literally makes my blood boil when I think what fools we are to allow taverns or dram shops or saloons or whatever you choose to call them in this highly civilized country of ours."

"It seems impossible that anyone would want to drink when this is such a great and wonderful world we live in," the doctor says, having parked his expensive convertible next to his private cabin in the mountains. "Without question, alcohol is our public enemy number one!"

A deaf viewer would have no idea what this film was about. Did the ladies at the Temperance Union feel cheated when they saw what they got for their money? Did Fred Neimann, who's credited with directing and writing this mess, simply take an old travelogue he had in the can and drop some rambling narration on top of it? Indeed, there is a theory of filmmaking that holds that narration should never mimic what's on the screen, but this is ridiculous.

RED NIGHTMARE
The Warner Bros. Co. for U.S. Department of Defense, Information and Education Division, 1962, 29 minutes

It's Hollywood vs. Moscow in this legendary classic shot on the Warner Brothers back lot (under the personal supervision of Jack L. Warner) using resources beyond the wildest dreams of most filmmakers. For pure campy entertainment that nearly everyone can appreciate, *Red Nightmare* is hard to beat. Its continuity is unbelievably bad—the film appears to have been edited from what must have been a much longer original—but the plot is so outlandish that its audiences probably never noticed.

Jerry Donovan is an average working Joe who, according to his wife, "can't think of anything besides bowling and television." This may be all right for a sitcom dad, but it isn't all right by Jack Webb, who keeps walking into scenes like a stone-faced, jug-eared muse. Jerry, Jack remarks, is "prone to take his liberties for granted" and doesn't want to "assume responsibility." Jack has a cure for that. "Let's give Jerry a nightmare," Jack growls. "A real Red nightmare!"

Somehow, Jerry (and everybody he knows) is teleported to "Mid Town, U.S.A.," which in the story is actually a Soviet training facility shrouded in secrecy deep behind the Iron Curtain. Jerry never really seems to understand that a drastic change has taken place, even though all the people around him have become tight-lipped, unemotional robots who call each other "comrade" and who never use any contractions in their speech. Jerry's slim-waisted, buxom daughter leaves home for a collective farm (to free herself from the "lingering bourgeois influences of family life"), his community church is replaced by a People's Museum, and Jerry is eventually sentenced to be shot because he's "an ugly remnant of the diseased bourgeois class." "Someday," Jerry snarls as the pistol is pointed at his head, "there's gonna be enough holes in that Iron Curtain that all of your people will be able to escape to freedom!" Happily, he chooses this moment to wake up in his twin bed and vows to become a more compassionate, dedicated, and loyal American.

"What you have seen is not entirely fiction," Jack Webb remarks, somehow keeping a straight face. "To prevent Communism from consuming the entire free world, there stands but one man. That man is you!"

RESPONSIBILITY
Centron Corp. for Young America Films, 1953, 11 minutes

Lincoln High's student council president election is deadlocked between Hank Evans and Lloyd Smith, as Principal Jim Gordon explains, waving a slip of paper—the tie-breaking vote—at the camera. "How would *you* vote?" he asks, and the film spins back in time to review the candidates.

Principal Gordon points out, "it's the things that come out after you've known a person a while that really tell you about him," although it only takes about five seconds to see which candidate this film is pushing: Lloyd Smith. Hank may be "more popular," but Lloyd is "more responsible." Principal Gordon concedes that Hank has "a way with people." But he also has "an attitude toward his work." (Not to mention a perpetual sneer and hair that looks like it's about to leap off the front of his head.) Irresponsible Hank is by far the most interesting of the two candidates, but Principal Gordon is blind to that harsh political truth as he brands Hank "on the wrong track" and declares that he "needs to mend his ways."

The film ends where it began, with Principal Gordon clutching the tie-breaking vote in his hand. Although the decision is supposedly the viewer's, there's no doubt who Principal Gordon wants to win. "My job is to help boys and girls be the kind of young men and women they'd like to be—capable, educated, and *responsible!*"

RIGHT OR WRONG?
Coronet Instructional Films, 1951, 11 minutes

A gang of preteen toughs breaks some warehouse windows, and the night watchman recognizes one of the punks as youthful Harry Green. He's hauled into the police station and has to decide which is worse: "squealing" on his friends or "hiding lawbreakers." This dark film takes place in the course of a single night and every character agonizes in voiceover as they make moral decisions.

An interesting film; winner of the unexciting Diploma of Participation at the 1952 International Film Festival for Children. Sergeant Kelly at the police station—"It'll be much easier for you if you help us"—played Dick York's weird dad in *Shy Guy.*

ROAD RUNNERS
Wanda Tuchock for Southern California Timing Association, 1952, 13 minutes

Mel is an oily-faced hot rodder with a bad front tooth and a bad attitude about traffic laws. But he cheerfully abandons his rebellious ways when he discovers the Santa Ana drag strip and the Lake El Mirage timing trials. These provide a "safe and constructive outlet," according to the narrator, and help mitigate the "juvenile nuisance problem." "Trophies now instead of traffic tickets! He'll never speed on the highway again!"

SAFE LIVING AT SCHOOL
Coronet Instructional Films, 1948, 10 minutes

Ted and Ruth have been elected to the Junior Safety Council. They apparently have no classes to attend, and they spend their time roaming the halls, appraising the safety fea-

tures of their school. These include drinking fountains with "no sharp parts" that "are safely constructed to reduce the danger of bumping your teeth while drinking." Ted and Ruth devise three "rules for safe living" for all the kids, such as transferring books from the right to left hand whenever the stairway is used, and touching lips only to the water at those very safe drinking fountains.

All the grade schoolers in this film were apparently told not to smile. With his sphinxlike demeanor and wild sport shirt, Ted is more like a department-store mannequin than a human being.

R THE SAFEST WAY
Penn State Motion Picture & Recording Studio, Pennsylvania State College, for Traffic Engineering and Safety Dept., AAA, 1948, 17 minutes

Educational Screen wrote:

> David soon realizes that his habitual route to school is not the safest way, so he decides on another one. When David shows his map to his family, his father agrees to accompany him to school the next morning to check the route. When they reach the school, David's father signs the map, giving his approval to the route, and reminds David that there is a "safest way" to get to other places too, such as church and a movie.
>
> ...an effective method of presenting walking safely to our young population, who must live safely if they are to plan for a safe tomorrow.

SAFETY BEGINS AT HOME
unknown producer for Young America Films, 1945, 10 minutes

Bill—"an average, all-around American boy"—and his younger sisters Frances and Jane learn safety lessons as they decorate their parlor for a party. Or rather, Bill learns them;

Frances and Jane spend most of the film watching passively. At one point Dad arrives with a gift for the party—two crummy electric candles. They're "more safe" than real candles, Dad explains, and they provide an excuse to teach proper respect for outlets and wires. "Bill will help Dad," the narrator instructs. "Frances and Jane will watch."

The narrator in this film takes the odd position that home safety is not only smart, but thrilling. "Don't you think the safe way is the exciting way?" he asks. "Safety at home can be an adventure. And it sure is fun!"

Baby sister Jane is much too old to wear a pinafore and ringlet curls. She skips everywhere she goes, as if this will make her miscasting less obvious.

SAFETY BELT FOR SUSIE

Charles Cahill and Associates, 1962, 11 minutes

The Norwood family consists of the narrator, his wife, and their daughter, Nancy. Nancy has a creepy, life-sized doll, Susie, whom she drags everywhere. Susie gets smashed when the parents plow their 1962 Dodge into a tree. Luckily, the doctor who treats the parents' cuts and scrapes also happens to be an expert on test-crash baby dolls. He repairs Susie, and Mr. and Mrs. Norwood promise to strap both Nancy and her look-alike doll into the backseat whenever they go driving from now on.

This film spends a *lot* of time showing staged test traffic accidents, lovingly filmed in slow motion on an airstrip somewhere near UCLA's Institute of Transportation and Traffic Engineering. As bulky 1950s sedans T-bone each other at forty miles per hour, test baby dolls fly into windshields and camera lenses. Follow-up shots include close-ups of severed doll arms and legs on the pavement. All this is accompanied by dramatic horns and ominous timpani rolls, and sound effects of crashing metal, squealing tires, and crying babies.

SAFETY RULES FOR SCHOOLS

Charles Cahill and Associates, 1966, 10 minutes

Five circus clowns perform acrobatic tumbles in a black void. Then they magically appear in the middle of a busy intersection, and then almost as suddenly in the hallway of a school. A teacher scowls at them and they run away. "Clowns definitely don't belong in school," the narrator explains. "Schools are for children and teachers."

After this promising beginning this film quickly cartwheels downhill, delivering banal safety instructions such as "keep your feet on the floor" and "sharp objects are made to cut things, not people." It does, however, have another sequence of merit, in which real-life school scenes are superimposed with stick-figure drawings of children falling down stairs, sliding off chairs, falling flat on their faces when crowding into a bus, etc., accompanied by snare drum rim shots and cymbal crashes.

"If you're smart, you'll do things the right way," the narrator barks. "Safety is doing things the right way. Don't be a clown at school or anywhere else."

SAFETY THROUGH SEAT BELTS

Charles Cahill and Associates for Institute of Transportation and Traffic Engineering, 1959, 13 minutes

This film purports to give the lowdown on seat-belt safety in family cars—"that most lethal of wheeled wonders"—but its real purpose is to show off the airstrip crash tests conducted by nerdy graduate students at UCLA's Institute of Transportation and Traffic Engineering. A montage of bloody accident-scene photos is accompanied by broad observations ("collisions are inherently dangerous"), but this is quickly brushed aside as the test-crash coverage begins.

> **"The brutal facts about auto mortality are now painfully clear!"**

The crashes are almost poetic, shown in slow motion with sound effects of shrieking metal and shattering glass. It's all presented as very exciting and *very* scientific and is made all the more dramatic by the narrator's insistence that "all human errors must be eliminated!" and that "facts must be checked and double-checked!"

All the victimized cars date from the late 1940s, which makes the usefulness of the data gathered in these tests a little suspect. But as ominous strings crescendo, test dummies fly, and the narrator cries, "the ragged metal carved away a portion of his face!" it all seems very urgent and important.

SAY NO TO STRANGERS!
Irvmar Productions, 1957, 10 minutes

In their classroom, preteen twins Wendy and Jamie learn that "safe behavior is just as important as spelling or arithmetic." It's a good thing, since every time they walk around their neighborhood they encounter people or cars or animals or streets that *seem* perfectly normal—but you never know. When this happens—and it happens frequently—a doorbell sounds and the voice of the children's teacher reminds the kids to move along.

A film with a premise this thin makes for many *l-o-n-g* gaps in the narration, which gives the audience time to appreciate the irrepressibly peppy 101 Strings music track.

SCHOOL RULES: HOW THEY HELP US
Coronet Instructional Films, 1952, 10 minutes

Mr. Taylor, a school principal (and also this film's narrator), spends most of his time micromanaging the incredibly petty problems of his young students. One needs a pass to get gym shoes. Another wants an up staircase made bi-directional. Mr. Taylor takes even more time out of his busy day to explain how exceptions to rules are unfair and inevitably "spoil the game." To prove his point, the film cuts to a fantasy sequence in which a library "Exceptioner," who wears an oversized hat and wields a giant rubber stamp, distributes arbitrary book fines.

Jim Andelin, who plays Mr. Taylor, later went on to star as the band instructor in *Mr. B Natural* and was a successful Hollywood character actor well into the 1990s.

SEDUCTION OF THE INNOCENT
Sid Davis Productions, 1961, 9 minutes

This is one of the wildest fear films ever made. And it's really fast paced, thanks to Sid Davis's compulsion to cram as much plot into as little footage as possible.

Imprisoned in a jail cell, Jeanette, her face covered with sores, writhes in agony. She's a slave, the merciless narrator proclaims, "a slave by choice." Only a couple of months ago she was just another fresh-faced know-it-all teen who wanted to belong to the gang. And what a gang: they ride around in an open convertible, swallowing "reds" with 7-Up! "What can be the harm?" the narrator taunts. "After all, the twentieth century runs on pills. Why not a pill to make you happy?" Jeanette goes along— and within just seconds of film time she's ignoring her schoolwork and swallowing a whole pharmacy: Nembutal, Benzedrine, and "the hypnotics."

It's not enough, of course. "Nerves begin to wear thin. The guilt grows and, as it does, the need for something that will bring more relief." Jeanette's boyfriend pulls what must be the world's skinniest joint out of his sock and the two "toke up" in a parked car. "You feel like you're floating...time slows down...this is called 'tripping,'" the narrator explains, but Jeanette has developed an insatiable thirst for bigger kicks. Within thirty seconds she's at the apartment of Eric, her pusher, and she's mainlining heroin.

Now Jeanette has a $50-a-day habit, and she needs money. Since "her moral fiber has collapsed," she turns to "a life of degradation and crime." She steals from parked cars, becomes a call girl, and then, as her looks decay, ends up a streetwalker. Jeanette is finally caught hooking by the police—on her twentieth birthday—but Sid Davis offers no hope for her, the worst kind of punk teen smart aleck. "Jeanette Michaels, age twenty, white, Caucasian, drug addict," the narrator intones. "Lost to society, she'll continue her hopeless, degrading existence until she escapes in death. Today. Tomorrow. Maybe not for *years*."

SELF-CONSCIOUS GUY
Coronet Instructional Films, 1951, 10 minutes

Marty wants a lead role in the school play but his self-consciousness dooms him to the inferior role of stagehand. He feels, he explains, "as if there was a spotlight on me," and the stagehands at Coronet demonstrate this by shining a spotlight on Marty whenever he has a nervous moment. Cheap, but effective. His life turns around when he discovers that he's more confident than leading man Jack when it comes to Ping-Pong.

SEX HYGIENE
U.S. Signal Corps, 1941, 29 minutes

This film, directed by John Ford, is the one every World War II serviceman saw and remembered for years afterward. It's actually an instructional film titled *Sex Hygiene* inside a wraparound film titled *Sex Hygiene*. Why the Signal Corps nested one film within another is unclear; they must have thought it would be most effective to cut away to reaction shots of servicemen wincing and flinching as they watch the film within the film.

Most of *Sex Hygiene* features a silver-haired army "doctor" played by a man who appears to be a Shakespearean actor. His fifty-kilowatt voice wraps itself around phrases like "sexual act" and "reasonable self-discipline" and he slams his pointer on the desk whenever he's incensed by human stupidity.

Of course, he's incidental to what makes this film memorable—its many graphic close-ups of tongues, lips, and penises oozing with open sores. Even worse is the "prophylaxis treatment" that soldiers were to voluntarily undergo whenever they had sex. Not only did the soldier have to wear a rubber during sex, then surgically scrub his hands, belly, and genitalia immediately after sex, but he had to report to the base hospital where a

201

medical officer would inject a huge syringeful of bichloride of mercury up his willy and then watch while he held the stuff inside (pinch here) for at least five minutes. Every glorious detail is shown, mercifully in black-and-white.

SHARING WORK AT HOME
Coronet Instructional Films, 1949, 11 minutes

The Taylor family—Mom, Dad, Howard, and Martha—live in a messy house. What's worse, they don't seem to care. But Martha has culled some modern ideas from her home economics textbook. The Taylor renaissance is about to begin.

"General housekeeping is made much easier if each person picks up after himself," Martha reads to Howard; he thinks for a moment and responds, "Hey, Sis...maybe we should get organized!" In Coronet films, "get organized" is always an irresistible rallying cry. Soon the smiling Taylors are making neat, handwritten lists for everything. "Here! It's all organized!" cries Howard as he holds aloft yet another list. "That's the idea. Each of us picks up after himself!" echoes Dad.

In less time than it takes to pull a tally sheet out of the Job Jar, the Taylors have become "a far happier and better family" as a result of their new thinking. "This is more than just a story of wallpaper and slipcovers," the narrator says. "It's a story of improvement in the Taylors themselves!"

Lots of over-the-shoulder shots show list writing in action.

THE SHOW-OFF
Centron Corp. for Young America Films, 1954, 12 minutes

Kay Reynolds, a junior at an unnamed high school, sits in an empty classroom and talks directly into the camera. "Our class is in a *terrible* fix. And I thought maybe if I told you about it, you could help us."

It turns out the class has fallen into the clutches of "funny boy" Jim Brewster, a goony greaser with helmet-like hair. "At first, it seemed amusing," Kay confesses, as the film shows Jim deliberately falling off his chair in class, cracking jokes during a school play rehearsal, and tripping a kid at an after-school party. "There was just something in him that made him always want to be a center of attention."

Unfortunately, Jim's "wise-guy behavior" begins to give the whole class a bad rep. "A bunch of smart alecks," one dad brands them. "It makes you wonder about kids nowadays."

Then Jim goes too far. He sneaks into the school one night and hangs a YEA, JUNIORS banner over the entrance. That may not sound like such a bad thing, but this was the 1950s, when anything that even hinted of rebellion was considered threatening. Jim's banner is "an eyesore on the whole school," Kay laments. "Like a badge of dishonor for all the town to see."

The principal calls the junior class officers on the carpet. "This class has put itself in a bad light. I've had several telephone calls from people who want to know what kind of school we're running here! What's behind all this?"

Kay turns to the camera again, sincerely perplexed. "If you were in our shoes, what would *you* do?"

SHY GUY
Coronet Instructional Films, 1947, 15 minutes

Shy Guy was the most successful social guidance film of its time and was the first film for teens that pushed "fitting in," rather than regimented rules of etiquette, as the way to social happiness. It was also the first to show teenagers wrestling with personal difficulties and solving problems themselves—with occasional guidance from wise adults. Both approaches were praised for their progressiveness and "realism" and helped establish Coronet as the premier social guidance film studio.

For all its importance to the educators of 1947, *Shy Guy* is a hoot to watch today. Dick York plays high schooler Phil Norton, a transfer student with no friends. A true geek, he spends all his free time in his basement, building a radio or maybe a record player—it varies from scene to scene. One day his dad, who always wears a three-piece suit, pays him a visit and tells Phil that he's like the oscillator in his radio. "You...have to fit it in with all the other parts."

Phil sees the wisdom in this and begins studying the most popular kids in school. He sees that they're good listeners and always "polite" and "helpful." Finally, at an after-school mixer, Phil publicly offers to help Beezy Barnes (a fellow radio geek), and the gang immediately becomes interested in Phil. "They know he's *alive* now," the narrator (Mike Wallace) explains, as the teen boys and girls, smiling approvingly, crowd around him. The film ends back in Phil's basement as Dad, still in his suit, descends the stairs with a tray of Cokes for Phil and his many new friends.

SITTING RIGHT
Grant, Florey & Williams, 1946, 9 minutes

Educational Screen wrote:

> Opening with a series of brief incidents in which girls are rebuked by their elders for poor posture, the film goes ahead to point out that one's mental attitude is very important and that good posture is fun. It suggests observing movie stars and local girls who seem to be well poised.
>
> The commentator emphasizes the importance of a good mental approach. Each girl must be willing to work on herself day after day, exercising and practicing not only at school but also at home in front of a mirror. After good posture has become automatic, a girl can forget about it and concentrate on having a good time.
>
> Taking advantage of the average girl's desire for something at least approaching Hollywood glamour, it presents effectively a few rules for good posture which are generally shrugged off as just more adult nonsense.

SIX MURDEROUS BELIEFS
Emerson Film Corp. for National Safety Council, 1955, 12 minutes

Atrocious acting and bargain-basement production give this film a shot-in-somebody's-garage look. It's so cheaply made that it never shows the accidents that injure and kill its cast

"Any time you feel lucky, look out for *murder!!!*"

members, instead cutting away to painful grimaces or the horrified reactions of on-lookers. It also compensates with over-the-top narration, ominous tom-tom music, and pencil illustrations of skull-faced Death grinning at calamities caused by arrogant or stupid people.

Jim wrenches his arm in a football game, Sue is run over by a car, Dad mangles his hand in a table saw, Mom is nearly electrocuted by a faulty switch, Marilyn almost drowns after eating junk food, Harry dies when he drives too fast.

Undoubtedly the only film ever made that shows Death wearing a chef's hat, holding a hot dog.

SKILLS BUILD AMERICA
unknown producer for General Motors Corp., 1973, 8 minutes

One of the last school films made the old-fashioned way, filled with bombast, shameless generalizations, and an utter lack of self-doubt. Even the grandiloquent title reflects an attitude more befitting 1948 than 1973.

Skills Build America tells the story of the Vocational Industry Clubs of America (VICA) Skills Olympics, held in the Tulsa, Oklahoma, convention center. VICA is "aimed at helping young people develop respect for the dignity of work." Heroic fanfares and uptempo music swell with optimism as the narrator explains that this "spirited competition" determines "the nation's top performers in vocational and industrial fields." VICA's definition of "vocational" is broad: bricklayers push loaded barrels of wet cement, an electronics nerd pokes a switchboard with a circuit tester, and a dental assistant rubs giant teeth with an oversized toothbrush.

Because General Motors sponsored this film, much attention is paid to the Tomorrow's Auto Mechanics contest. Nervous xylophones tinkle as the camera passes row after row of pimple-faced boys with long sideburns tinkering with disassembled engines and crankshafts. The winners get their pictures taken on an Olympic-style dais, a handshake from G.M. executive John C. Bates, and a tool set.

Perhaps the scariest thing about this film is the spin it puts on the kids. They dress in neckties, cheery red blazers, and straw hats, participate in high school–style elections for their national officers, and jump up and down, applauding wildly, at every opportunity. It's like watching a meeting of the Model United Nations or an Up with People concert, not a bunch of stoners and hoods who spent most of their formative years in a grease pit.

"This is just the beginning," the narrator concludes. "The real value of what occurred here will be felt eventually by the entire country as these young people take their leadership attitudes and pride in their trade to the marketplace. And bring credit to their theme, Skills Build America!"

Lots of close-ups are shown of people hammering nails.

SKIPPER LEARNS A LESSON
Paul Burnford for Sid Davis Productions, 1952, 10 minutes

You've got to give Sid Davis credit: no other educational producer would touch the subject of racial intolerance in 1952.

Still, this is a weird little film. It's shot in a weedy, threadbare neighborhood, "pretty much like yours perhaps," says the narrator. Four children—Mike and Larry (Caucasian), Betty (Asian), and Pete (African American)—are entertaining themselves by digging a trench in a vacant lot.

Susan is a new girl in the neighborhood, and she has a mutt named Skipper. The kids come over to her cinderblock house and invite her to help them dig their trench. "You can have one of our shovels," they offer. Susan is happy to join in the fun—but Skipper refuses. "I won't have anything to do with such funny-looking children," he says, courtesy of the narrator. But Skipper accidentally spills some paint on himself—and then the dogs in the neighborhood attack him! Now *he* looks "funny."

The children work together to give Skipper a bath, and as he soaks he reexamines his attitudes. "Being nice is the only thing that counts. And being nice is something inside. Nothing else really matters."

SNAP OUT OF IT!
Coronet Instructional Films, 1951, 13 minutes

Weird Mr. Edmunds reprises his principal-as-psychologist role from *Act Your Age*. Confused teen Howard Patterson won't show his report card to his parents because he "should've gotten" an A in social studies. Enter Mr. Edmunds. "Sometimes we expect great things," he reflects, leaning back in his chair as Howard looks on. "And when we're severely disappointed, we become emotionally upset." Mr. Edmunds counsels Howard against "expecting too much" and tells him to keep his emotions in balance. "If your emotions are in balance," he explains, "you channel your emotional energy into a direct attack on your problem!" Howard promises to lower his expectations and be more balanced.

SNIFFLES AND SNEEZES
Audio Productions for McGraw-Hill Book Co., 1955, 11 minutes

This creepy film about the common cold has a lot of shots of kids sneezing and coughing. When they talk to each other, visible vapor clouds engulf their hapless friends. There's a

sequence where "tiny particles of saliva and mucus"—made visible as an ominous black smudge—are passed along, unknowingly, from hands to doorknobs to book pages to pencils to dinner plates to *you*. And if that isn't enough to traumatize the kiddies, a scary montage reviews the deadly diseases that can begin as colds: diphtheria, scarlet fever, polio.

Films like this certainly do put things in perspective.

THE SNOB
Centron Corp. for McGraw-Hill Book Co., 1958, 14 minutes

It's a warm Friday evening. While the gang is having fun dancing at Ron's house, Sarah sits next door, laboring over algebra problems, her sweater buttoned to the neck. Sarah doesn't like her neighbors and has a low opinion of "fun" and "having a good time"—a very bad attitude in social guidance films. She tells her parents "there's nobody over there I want to see," and no one at Ron's house—Ron in particular—wants to see her, either. "She wants a special invitation, and if she gets it, it'll be just one more reason for her to think she's better than anybody else," Ron complains.

After much discussion, Ron's mom convinces him that what Sarah really needs is a friend. He invites her to the next party, but Sarah is an uncooperative guest: she sits in the corner, smirks, refuses to dance, and thinks nasty thoughts about the kids who are enjoying themselves. When one of them confronts her as a "snob," she breaks down and runs out into the night, weeping. "They're so mean and hateful!" she cries. "They don't understand anybody who isn't one of *their* gang and who doesn't do all the silly things *they* do!"

Dark, moody, and complex, *The Snob* really gets under your skin. When Sarah's dad asks, "All these people that you don't like—aren't they *happier* than you?" you either want to burst into tears or put your fist through a wall.

Vera Stough, who played Sarah, went on to play supporting roles on Broadway. Harper Barnes, who played Ron, went on to play a syphilis victim in *The Innocent Party.*

SOAPY THE GERM FIGHTER
Avis Films, 1951, 10 minutes

Billy Martin is a dirty kid who's convinced that cleanliness is for "sissies." He's drifting off to sleep in his bed one night when Soapy appears—a guy wearing a cardboard box painted to look like a bar of soap. Soapy is a big, scary-looking block with arms and legs but no head, who continually leans back and forth, wags his finger, taps his chest, and

waves his hands—all completely out of sync with his dialogue on the soundtrack. He also appears not to be wearing any pants.

Soapy teaches Billy "good hand habits" and offers advice such as, "girls should wash their hair at least once every two weeks." He never steps out of the murky darkness of Billy's bedroom, so it's impossible to see just how awful his costume really is. But that doesn't appear to bother Billy, who takes Soapy's advice to heart and becomes "one of the cleanest boys in our town." The film ends with a shot of Billy in a bathtub, soap dripping out of his ear, winking at the camera.

SOCIAL ACCEPTABILITY
Crawley Films for McGraw-Hill Book Co., 1957, 19 minutes

This is possibly the most heart-wrenching social guidance film ever made. Cute, perky, shy Marion desperately wants to be part of the gang. But her drippy parents, her callous friends, and fate combine to make her efforts ultimately futile. "All of us want to get along with other people," the narrator explains. "Lack of social acceptance can leave emotional scars." And how. This film demonstrates that only geeks and maladjusted people shun social accep-

tance—and they soon live to regret it. The ultimate depressing Crawley film.

SOCIAL CLASS IN AMERICA
Knickerbocker Productions for McGraw-Hill Book Co., 1957, 15 minutes

This matter-of-fact film skewers the popular image of the 1950s as a classless society. It follows the lives of three small-town high school buddies: Gil, who is rich and happy; Dave, who is poor and doomed; and Ted, who is middle class and doomed.

Gil is sent to an Ivy League school where he meets "men of his own kind," returns home wearing a bow tie, and is groomed to take over his father's profitable business. Dave gets married, has lots of kids, and winds up working in a gas station. Ted wants to be an artist, but he falls in love with Mary and becomes a white-collar bookkeeper. Mary, however, wants a man with a bigger bank account, so she dumps Ted.

Ted decides to turn lemons into lemonade. He moves to Manhattan to "make something" of himself. After many years of hard work, he lands a painfully dull copywriting job in an advertising agency and gets to play golf with rich men. This is "vertical mobility," the narrator says proudly, "particularly characteristic of the United States." Ted returns home wearing a snappy hat, but Mary has married Gil and both don't really want to have anything to do with him.

SOCIAL COURTESY
Coronet Instructional Films, 1951, 10 minutes

Sourpuss Bill is invited to a party with his girlfriend, Carol, but he believes that social courtesy is old-fashioned. Whoa, just a minute! says the feisty interactive narrator, who sets Bill on a proper course. Bill takes the narrator in stride, as he does being teleported through space and backward in time repeatedly in this bizarre Coronet production.

"Let's take a picture of this situation," says the narrator. A strobe flashes from behind the camera and the scene is transformed into a photo on a wall in the next scene. "You'd better back up and start all over again. Maybe you'd better try to be more *friendly* this time." Bill beckons the invisible narrator closer so that they can talk in private, and the camera obligingly dollies in (its wheels audibly creaking) while the other teens at the party remain utterly oblivious. "You discourage others when they want to be friendly," the narrator scolds. "Come on, Bill. Sit up! That's a chair, not a bed." It's odd that Bill, who is so nasty to his friends, puts up with this invisible nagging narrator.

"Learn from watching others," the narrator concludes. "Be friendly. Thoughtful. You'll get along!" The mom chaperon whispers, "Isn't that the boy who used to be so *rude?*" and Bill is accorded the ultimate symbol of Coronet social guidance success: he's invited to another party. "Those changes made a big difference, didn't they!" he exclaims in wonder, chewing a cracker. "Social courtesy does pay! Thanks!"

SOCIAL-SEX ATTITUDES IN ADOLESCENCE
Crawley Films for McGraw-Hill Book Co., 1953, 24 minutes

This companion film to *Age of Turmoil* is equally as entertaining. It traces the lives of Bob and Mary from childhood to marriage but spends most of its time on the teen years, emphasizing that the kids have "pleasant, natural, and secure" homes and praising their moms, who are never afraid to talk about sex.

Despite the general aura of well-adjusted behavior, there are plenty of awkward moments that allow narrator Lorne Greene to spout psychobabble taken from the book *Adolescent Development.* Lovestruck Mary is in her "hangout stage," when she always has a need to "be more sophisticated than she actually is." Teenaged Bob brags to his pal over the phone ("Elsie...what a doll!"), while his mom cleans his room and finds a crude drawing of Bob and another girl on a couch, naked! "It became apparent that his interest in girls was getting to be more than casual," says Greene, whose sonorous baritone sounds as if it were pronouncing a death sentence on every hapless kid in this film.

Happily, Mary has maintained her virginal purity and Bob has sown his wild oats—with other, less-important girls—by the time they meet. "They knew this time it was for keeps," says Greene as the two lovebirds admire a window display of refrigerators. When they find themselves alone and in each other's arms on a darkened front porch, they refuse to succumb to temptation. Greene tactfully explains, "They wanted their marriage vows to have *real meaning.*" Church bells, rice, tin cans tied to a car bumper, end of film.

THE SOUND OF A STONE

Centron Corp. for Board of Social and Economic Relations of the Methodist Church, 1955, 26 minutes

Henry Jordan is a high school English teacher and devout member of his church. He's young, earnest, devoted to his students and his very pregnant wife, a lifelong resident of Moreland—but he does wear glasses. He's obviously read a lot of books, and you have to keep an eye on people like that.

Mr. Jordan assigns a reading list to his class. It turns out that one of the books is also on a list of subversive communist literature. A whispering campaign begins behind his back. A threatening note is stuck in the front door of his house—"We know your kind." At first blissfully unaware that his life is collapsing around him, Mr. Jordan finally has

his eyes opened at a raucous PTA meeting, where he's branded as "a man who's trying to poison the minds of our children." People that he has known his whole life have turned against him. He tells the angry crowd of neighbors and former friends that the book is just a harmless novel, but no one is interested in what he has to say. "We have all the proof we need right here!" cries Mr. Hughes, ringleader of the witch-hunters, waving the subversive literature list in the air.

However, as the narrator points out, "Who knows what a stone, carelessly thrown, may bring? The rippling waves touch everything, even shores for which they were never intended." It seems that Mr. Jordan's star pupil, Ernie, also happens to be the son of Mr. Hughes. Soon a new whispering campaign begins against Ernie. People begin to detect "creeping communism" in his high school newspaper editorials. "Looks like plenty of this

communist stuff has rubbed off on him," says one. Ernie's suggestion for a teen recreation center smacks of "handouts and socialism."

Mr. Hughes is aghast when he discovers what's happening. "They can't call you a communist—not on any more than that!" he cries. Ernie fixes him with a stare. "Then what are they calling Mr. Jordan a communist for? Have you read the book, Dad? Have you even *read* the book?"

Mr. Hughes does, and at the next school board meeting he stands up and publicly confesses his sins. "I charged Henry Jordan with subversion. I find out now that it was...prompted by ignorance. I've read the book! It is not subversive. *That's* the proof!"

A happy ending? Not on your life. Several weeks pass, and Mr. Jordan, his wife, and their new baby are snug and content in their living room. Then a rock—or maybe a stone—crashes through the window. "Jordan," the attached note reads. "You never fooled *us*. Get out while you can."

STOP DRIVING US CRAZY
Creative Arts Studios for General Board of Temperance of the Methodist Church, 1961, 10 minutes

Undoubtedly the world's only religious–sci-fi–highway safety cartoon. Rusty is a spy from Mars who looks like a big-eyed bug with tiny wheels, but in this early-1960s blob-art uni-

verse he also looks like a car. Lots of geometric shapes bounce around while a jazz quintet honks on the soundtrack. Rusty reports to his bosses that cars are "slaves" to people on earth—"Man, I mean, like, you know, they drive us ca-ray-zee!"—and equates poor driving habits with theologic doctrine. "The right of way is not as important as The Right Way." "Reckless driving is a sin."

Overall this is a hellish mess, but its creators were obviously proud of what they'd done; the credit roll takes up the last minute and a half of this ten-minute film.

THE STORY OF MENSTRUATION
Walt Disney Productions for International Cellucotton Products Co. [Kotex], 1946, 10 minutes

The image of Walt Disney making a film about menstruation may seem funny today, but it was a natural enough outgrowth of Disney's contract work with the armed forces during World War II and of the liberal attitudes toward education shared by many immediately after the war. Why not use happy-go-lucky Disney animation to explain a taboo—but unavoidable—topic?

The Story of Menstruation was perhaps the first educational film with a woman narrator. *Educational Screen* called it "grace-

"Don't be droopy," she warns.

fully done" and "nothing to get excited about" and praised its "frank, pleasant directness that has proved to be the essence of wholesome good taste." No Disney characters were used, of course; the film featured a pert cartoon blonde with an oversized head. It also went beyond health education to reinforce gender roles, with a marriage scene followed by

She says that good posture is important.

a picture of a young mother with her baby, "suggesting the natural course of life."

Educational Screen called special attention to the film's cartoon approach as a "happy solution" to the showing of reproductive organs that eliminated "the ghastly effect of a realistic rendering." "No nude figures were shown," the magazine pointed out.

After each school screening, girls got a copy of a booklet, *Very Personally Yours*, which pushed Kotex products. This sales technique was later imitated by Modess when they sponsored their competing menstruation film, *Molly Grows Up.*

209

STREET SAFETY IS YOUR PROBLEM

Centron Corp. for Young America Films, 1952, 10 minutes

A promising title, but the folks at Centron were too kind to live up to its nasty potential. The film introduces young Fred Miller, who has an enemy "more dangerous than any savage." (A guy wearing an Indian headdress, waving a tomahawk, peers from around a building corner.) "Fred's enemy is—carelessness! Carelessness is as bad as a loaded gun! A gun aimed at Fred! A gun aimed at you!!!" But this film's all downhill after the first two minutes, full of the usual don't-play-in-traffic, cross-only-at-the-corner pedestrian advice—and not so usual warnings about not playing in piles of leaves on busy streets or under boxes in active driveways. "Protect yourself! You must think about safety all the time!"

STRESS

Nicholas Valla for University of Montreal, Institute of Experimental Medicine and Surgery, 1956, 11 minutes

This film is nothing more than a soapbox for the cockeyed theories of the University of Montreal's Dr. Hans Selye, who looks like Donald Pleasance and talks like a Nazi. The mad doctor explains his "new theory of disease" to earnest young Canadians in a lecture hall: "Civilization itself—just like germs and injuries—attacks the body, causing stress." In order to prove this theory, animated "pro- and anti-inflammatory hormones" are shown flowing through an artery, as well as live-action shots of rats being "physically and mentally disturbed" by being tumbled in a wire drum and nearly drowned in a big bowl of water. "The importance of stress now seemed clear," the narrator concludes. "Dr. Selye's theories have created a bright new avenue in the fight against man's oldest enemy—illness."

STUDENT GOVERNMENT AT WORK

Coronet Instructional Films, 1953, 10 minutes

According to this film's narrator, "The student council is an important part of the government of a school." It's soon clear why, with their crucial work on the talent assembly, the overdue library books committee, and the very important lunchroom investigation. Why are so many students being antisocial and eating in the halls? That could mean trouble! The student council—after receiving the go-ahead from their adult advisor and the principal—forms a committee to investigate.

With a sigh of relief, they discover that their fellow high schoolers aren't being rebellious or flaunting authority. The kids simply can't stand eating in the dirty, overcrowded lunchroom—problems that are easily solved by adding a second lunch period, deputizing lunchroom messiness monitors, and slapping a fresh coat of paint on the walls. "They respected the limits of their authority," the narrator comments approvingly. "But they also knew what things they *could* do."

SUBJECT: NARCOTICS

Denis and Terry Sanders for Narcotic Educational Foundation of America, 1951, 21 minutes

Dual narrators exchange somber commentary as staged scenes appear of junkies shooting up and breaking laws in downtown Los Angeles. Marijuana is "a powerful excitant" that produces "unpredictable emotional results," the narrators explain. They caution that "if you want to defeat your enemy, you must first know him," and blame drug addicts for degrading otherwise worthy chemical compounds. "All narcotics have legitimate medical uses...but in the hands of the addict their use is perverted to secure an escape from reality."

A grim, depressing *Why bother?* film (see also *Monkey on the Back*), supposedly created for police officers and "restricted from the general public and from all youth groups."

SUMMER OF '63
Sid Davis Productions, 1972, 21 minutes

In the early 1960s, Sid Davis began shooting a film about syphilis and teenagers titled *VD*. For reasons that remain obscure, he never sold it. Instead, he kept adding to it. He eventually hired a cast of grade-C actors and began shooting scenes with plot and dialogue. By 1970 *VD* had become a ninety-minute feature—Sid Davis's greatest work—and then it was taken away from him in a slippery distribution deal.

Sid Davis waited. In 1971 the film *Summer of '42* was a box office blockbuster. Sensing that the time was right, he hacked his *VD* footage down to twenty minutes, added a new prologue by one of its original—and now heavy and hairy—actors, and rereleased the mess as an educational film titled *Summer of '63*.

Here's what happens:

Monk and Cathy and Jim and Judy are the world's oldest seventeen-year-olds. They drive recklessly to a swimming hole rendezvous. Monk loses his license, Jim and Judy decide to get married. Cathy is jealous. Jim and Monk get drunk and pick up prostitutes. Jim gets syphilis. Monk spills the beans about the prostitutes. Judy gets mad and breaks off the engagement. Cathy moves in, Jim gives her syphilis. Jim finds out he has syphilis, breaks off with Cathy. Cathy gets mad and gives syphilis to Monk. Jim gets cured, gets back together with Judy. Jim tells the doctor about Cathy and Monk, they get cured, and it's back to 1972 with Monk—who is now a doctor!—summing everything up as he sits behind a desk in a white lab coat. "That's how it happened. It happened to Jim. It happened to Cathy. And it happened to me. In the summer of '63."

TAKE A LETTER...FROM A TO Z
Centron Corp. for McGraw-Hill Book Co., Gregg Division, 1967, 15 minutes

S

While gender equality was afoot in urban enclaves and on college campuses, the big world of business liked things just the way they were: men made decisions, women cleaned up afterward. That's painfully apparent in this secretarial training film. Although it tries hard to show that secretaries are indispensable and describes them in affirmative, feel-good terms as "intelligent communication specialists" who need "hours of study and specialized training" (particularly in Gregg shorthand), it also blithely accepts their subservient role in business. "He may originate the ideas to be communicated," the narrator declares, "but she is the one who specializes in putting those communications into permanent and perfect form."

The double standard shows up in scene after scene. Suit-wearing, serious-looking, boorish men sit in their important offices and give orders, while outside the secretary smiles, says tactful things to soothe "savage beasts" (other men in suits), and ensures that "her decision maker" remembers to go to the barber and rendezvous with his fishing buddies. In that respect, at least, men are shown to be as brainless as women—but they get the big paychecks and private offices. What do secretaries get? "The glow of shared accomplishments."

Sometimes they get more. A businessman eagerly jogs out of his office to pin a corsage on a well-tailored woman wearing a mink wrap. "It shouldn't be overlooked," the narrator says, "that many a *wife* was once a secretary to the man who orders the flowers for her furs." The wife gives a knowing wink to the young secretary, who looks on approvingly.

"Will *you* be the one that every bright young career man of tomorrow hopes to find?"

TAKE YOUR CHOICE
Jam Handy Organization for Detroit Society for the Prevention of Blindness, 1964, 13 minutes

Jeff is a careless teen who thinks he's "immune to danger." Jeff takes a number of rash risks with his eyesight, and then the soundtrack music shifts to a minor key to indicate he's bound for trouble. Jeff is blinded, bizarrely, by an overflowing test tube, and the narrator lays it on thick. "A moment of carelessness can last a lifetime. Is this where a fellow's luck and eyesight finally run out?" A montage of fun teen activities follows and then a scene of Jeff—blind—sitting in the dark at home, his carefully combed hair still perfectly in place. But don't worry. This "future" is mere cinematic speculation, for the hands of the clock suddenly spin backward and Jeff has covered his eyes in the nick of time and isn't really blinded by that test tube after all. Yay!

An uncredited blind kid taps his way through the background of several scenes—a whim of the producer or a demand from the sponsor?

THE TALKING CAR
Frederick K. Rockett Co. for AAA Foundation for Traffic Safety, 1953, 13 minutes

Jack, Mary, and Rags (a mutt that resembles an ambulatory mop head) are about to cross a suburban street corner. Suddenly they're yelled at by a 1953 Chevy convertible parked at the curb. "Well boil my radiator!" the car exclaims, scolding the kids for not waiting for the light to turn yellow, then red, then green again before they crossed. "When I see foolish things like that I nearly blow a gasket!"

Jack and Mary turn out to be two very safety-conscious and agreeable preteens. They spend the rest of the film discussing proper pedestrian safety habits with the car while staged footage shows kids thoughtlessly running into the shady streets of 1953 suburban Los Angeles and nearly getting run over. These are intercut with a static, head-on shot of the car, over which a pair of goggly cartoon eyes and a giant mouth are animated herky-jerky. It's a cheap, creepy effect made doubly weird by the car's overly jovial baritone (provided by Larry Thor).

Although this film was shot in Hollywood, its producers somehow managed to find two terrible child actors to play its leads.

TEEN TOGS
Georgia Agricultural Extension Service for Board of Regents, University System of Georgia, 1945,
10 minutes

Teenaged Barbara, who lives on a farm, receives a letter from her sister at college. Sis is inviting Barbara for a visit—but she can't go. She doesn't have the proper clothes!

Narrator Adelaide Hawley, who has great difficulty pronouncing *r*s, comments that poor "Bah-bruh" is "the pitch-uh of woe." But this film's message is one of hope; even the daughter of a poor Georgia dirt farmer can have a snappy wardrobe. Mother offers a suggestion: "Let us see the Home Demonstration Agent" (someone apparently affiliated with the Georgia Agricultural Extension Service). The HDA's advice is succinct: "Do your own sewing."

Barbara becomes a home fashion whiz, slicing up one of her dad's old suits to make an outfit for herself and fashioning a pinafore from printed feed sacks. Ms. Hawley follows along with a narration composed entirely of poorly metered rhyming couplets:
"Bah-bruh makes all her undies, a good way to be thrifty
Her remodeled suit is now what you'd call 'nifty.'"

Music director Ed Craig's strings play cheerfully in the background, blissfully unconcerned with matching the action or the verse.

By the end of the film, life has improved significantly for Barbara. She wears a sporty pant suit as she gathers eggs and shoos cows into the barn. Better still, her newfound knowledge has transformed her into "a true southern belle," and the film concludes with her being invited to a tea at the governor's mansion.
"Any girl who can plan and can sew for herself
Won't be found staying at home on the shelf."

The transitional device used between scenes by director J. Aubrey Smith is a repeated close-up of Barbara's feet, clad in loafers and white socks, pumping tirelessly on her sewing machine treadle.

No men appear in this film.

TEENAGERS ON TRIAL
RKO-Pathe, Inc., 1955, 8 minutes

When juvenile delinquency hit the headlines in 1955 (courtesy of *The Blackboard Jungle*), someone at RKO-Pathe had the idea to gut their 1947 juvenile delinquency film, *Who's Delinquent?*, and sell it to a new generation of anxious adults.

Teenagers on Trial dispenses with the plot of its predecessor but leaves in all its sensational footage. Some social themes are maintained: schools are still "understaffed and overpopulated," and "many parents are too busy earning a living to have time for their children." As a result, the narrator estimates that 2 percent of America's youth are juvenile delinquents. "They come largely from areas like this," the narrator remarks, as the camera shows black people in city tenements. However, "Any 'gang' would rather be a team. And these kids [no black people in this shot] live in a country where there is increasing teamwork—between schools and parents and law enforcement officers."

Although assembled from identical footage, *Teenagers on Trial* and *Who's Delinquent?* reach very different conclusions. In *Who's Delinquent?* the narrator cries, "Enough of bringing our children up to trial. Let's bring the *problem* to trial!" In other words, we admit that our kids are out of control; let's find a way to prevent their criminal behavior. In *Teenagers on Trial* the narrator says comfortingly, "Let's face the facts: two percent delinquent, ninety-eight percent all right. Let's put the problem on trial before we indict the teenagers!" Nothing to be afraid of after all.

TELL IT LIKE IT IS
Centron Corp. for American Vocational Association, 1968, 27 minutes

> *Tell it like it is, or I'll be long gone*
> *Tell it like it is . . .*
> *Where I'm goin', I don't need a snowin'*
> *No monkey biz*
> *I'm nobody's Dumbo, so cut your mumbo-jumbo*
> *Tell it like it is.*

Centron, producer of brilliant social guidance films like *The Sound of a Stone* and *The Snob*, also made this monstrosity. It's vocational education for a Brave New World, hosted by a sleazy teenager with an oily smile, a seersucker blazer, and a squint-eyed, puffy-cheeked face. His goal is to get us "moola-makers" excited about a career in "the action field"—what this film calls Distributive Management—which looks like nothing more than demeaning, entry-level retail-sales work.

He admits that "a lot of you can't see yourself going into the action field—yet," but he has a zealot's conviction that conversion to his worldview is inevitable. How about the idealist? Or the dropout? "*They'll* come around," the narrator says confidently. But they won't be "as far up" as they would be if they took "distributive education" courses in high school.

"D. E." class looks grueling. Its students spend most of their time stocking simulated display racks, practicing sales pitches for kitchen faucets—"Look at those solid brass fittings!"—and taking field trips to the local mall. The narrator smugly describes it as "a cut above the 'books, books, books' bit you usually associate with school." Boys are groomed as salesmen (and future executives) while girls learn how to design store windows and operate a cash register.

This film shouldn't get any more horrible, but it does—it whisks off to witness an abomination called DECA: the Distributive Education Clubs of America. The teens in DECA all wear matching black blazers, carry flags in processions, recite the DECA creed—"I believe in the future, which I am planning for myself"—and win trophies. "You get a lump in your throat, realizing that your thing is America's thing," the narrator says. "If you're serious about finding your own thing, then you have to tell it like it is!"

THE TERRIBLE TRUTH
Sid Davis Productions, 1951, 10 minutes

This was shot at the same time as *Name Unknown*. Stern judge McKesson returns as the scowling, unrelenting narrator, as does the girl—named Phyllis in this film—who was raped by the man with a hanky in his suit breast pocket.

The judge admits, as out of sync as ever, that he's baffled by drug use among young people. To find out what it's like to be "hooked," he visits Phyllis, a supposed

214

high school senior, who explains how when you smoke marijuana "everything speeds up to a hundred miles an hour!" In a flashback she meets Chuck (a "hype"), and in rapid sequence she becomes a junkie, then a dealer, then lets her hair go to hell. She goes through withdrawal—"It feels like your skin is being torn off!"—and, happily, reforms.

Judge McKesson proclaims that the Soviets are promoting drug traffic in the United States to "undermine national morale" and that the only way the spread of drug use can be stopped is to use "good sense." *The Terrible Truth* concludes with a screaming newspaper headline: AMERICA'S TEEN AGE DOPE 'FAD' ENDING!

A TIME FOR DECISION
Horizon Productions, 1966, 7 minutes

"A senior class president doesn't make any earth-shattering decisions," says this film's narrator. "He doesn't order an atom bomb dropped on Hiroshima. He doesn't commit troops to Korea or Vietnam."

Nevertheless, it's election time at Roosevelt High. The two candidates for senior class president are Larry Hope ("most of the 'in' students like him") and Frank Mueller ("a member of Quill and Scroll"). For some reason, this film wants the viewer to believe that Frank would make a better president, even though all he does is whine and sit in the library and projects all the dynamism of a puddle. Public-spirited Marge, however, is devoted to Frank's cause, and she approaches Jack Fulton, president of the Letterman's Club, for an endorsement. "I'm not gonna stick my neck out!" he replies. "Not on your life!" Idealistic Marge, the voice of her generation, is undeterred. "Don't you see?" she argues. "If nobody ever stuck their neck out, things wouldn't change! Why don't you do something about it?"

Too bad Marge wasn't running.

TOMORROW'S DRIVERS
Jam Handy Organization for General Motors Corp., Chevrolet Division, 1954, 11 minutes

This is ostensibly about the strange kindergarten through third grade driver ed classes at Garfield Elementary School in Phoenix, Arizona. It's actually about adults trying to program rebellion out of kids.

Happy childlike music plays. The narrator, Jimmy Stewart, talks about "self-control," "good driving attitudes," and "the need for rules and regulations" as six-year-olds pedal kiddie cars around a parking lot. "At a most impressionable time of life," Stewart explains, "an important rule of society is learned: laws are meant not to restrict, but to protect."

The cute kids serve as a sugary substitute for older drivers—one cuts off another on a curve, another weaves between lanes, a third runs a stop sign—while Stewart moans about "a few childishly inconsiderate drivers" and says that "bad driving habits are child-ish." Meanwhile, a kid in overalls peers under the hood of one car (at what, the pedals?) while "hot rodders" sit glumly on a bench, their driving privileges revoked. "Traffic violators," Stewart explains, "get tickets and are brought to trial before a jury of their classmates."

This is merely a setup for the second half of the film, which features the teens. A wrong-thinking juvenile driver has his license suspended and is sent to "attitude school," which otherwise seems exclusively populated by photogenic, fresh-faced girls. He undergoes "scientific tests" and learns that "laws and ordinances are passed by the people for their own common protection." The boy graduates, gets his license back, and in the very next scene he's wearing a suit and tie, politely holding a car door open for his date.

Only in America would driver education be seen as a linchpin of social engineering.

TOO YOUNG TO BURN
Sid Davis Productions for Federation of Mutual Fire Insurance Companies, Los Angeles, 1954, 26 minutes

In this film the same scary Sid Davis narrator from *Live and Learn* explains that "fire is very important to our civilization" and that "animals have never learned to regard fire as

a friend." Unfortunately—and unlike *Live and Learn*—all the scenes in which terrible accidents happen to children are shown using Magic Marker cartoon illustrations, not live actors.

There is one live-action scene in which a father lets his infant son burn his hand on a toaster—while Mom looks on—to teach him about fire and pain.

TOWARD EMOTIONAL MATURITY
Knickerbocker Productions for McGraw-Hill Book Co., 1954, 10 minutes

This important-sounding film pretends to teach deep psychological truths, but it's really just another broadside in the 1950s war against sexual desire in sexually curious teenagers.

It opens, the narrator explains, at the end of the last big dance, on the most wonderful spring evening of the year. Sexy Sally is in a convertible with her boyfriend, Hank ("*such* a nice guy"), who slyly suggests that they go up to Mountain Park and enjoy the moonlight.

Sally, thankfully, is an emotionally mature young lady who recognizes that "it isn't always easy to think things out in the heat of the moment." She recalls times when she was jealous and angry, and the narrator reminds her, "You never want to feel *that* way again." She remembers when she fell over her desk in terror when her weird (but very wise) psy-

chology teacher threw a rubber snake at her. She recalls the night she and Hank were caught in a pep rally that turned into an ugly, stone-throwing mob scene. This film wants to connect these creepy memories, these unpleasant manifestations of freakish behavior, with passion and sexual desire—well, they are all *emotions*, aren't they?

Sally understands perfectly. "Let's just go on home," she tells Hank, who merrily agrees, "You're the boss!" The narrator concludes, "No matter how deep the emotion is, you don't have to let it take you over." Sally and Hank exchange a warm goodnight hug.

TREASURES FOR THE MAKING
Pathescope Educational Films for General Foods Corp., Certo and Sure-Jell Division, 1951, 22 minutes

Ellen Douglas is getting hitched. "It'll be nice to be just a housewife where there'll be no great demand for talent or brains," she tells Susan, her kid sister. Susan—a home ec major—is aghast at this old-fashioned view of married life. "Does Bill know he's marrying a can opener instead of a wife?"

Susan explains that it takes both brains and talent to run a modern home. Recipes, for example, are "scientific"—and since this film was sponsored by Certo and Sure-Jell, all the recipes shown are for jams and marmalades. "It's not just liking to cook," Susan says. "It's accomplishing something!"

Much of this film is spent in flashback in Susan's student kitchen. She and her fellow apron-wearing classmates *ooh* and *ahh* in unison as their teacher plops wiggly phallic jellies from jars onto a plate for closeup inspection and slicing—scenes that stay with you long after entire other films are forgotten.

In the end, Ellen's fiancé is blown away by his sweetheart's newfound cooking skills. "I never realized she had such talent!"

TRIP TO WHERE
unknown producer for U.S. Navy, 1968, 45 minutes

A hotel room. Several young Navy men are sprawled about, tripping on acid. Groovy Hammond organ music plays on a reel-to-reel. Bill, the film's protagonist, sits in a daze. "Colors…a thousand colors are floating!" he mumbles. "Float with it, man," says Joe, the "guide" for the trip, who reads about "sparkling diamond highlights of the universe" out of a book he carries around. The room is shown through Bill's eyes: out of focus, multiple diffraction lense images, spooky Italian horror movie lighting, and dry-ice smoke covering the floor. Tooting slide whistles fill the music track. If acid trips really were this irritating, they wouldn't have been so popular.

Bill crawls out onto the window sill—"I'm one with the universe! I'm God and Jesus!" The gang hauls him back in and he freaks out. His pals turn into growling, many-horned monsters, then Russian cossacks, then motorcycle gang thugs wielding machetes. Bill breaks loose and stares into a mirror—and turns into a woman!

And this is just the first ten minutes of the film.

Bill recovers but, of course, there's never true recovery from acid in a 1960s drug film. There are always the dreaded flashbacks—and that's especially inconvenient for Bill, since he works as an air traffic controller on an aircraft carrier. The spooky slide-whistle music comes back every time he stares into his radar screen!

One would hope that Bill would put in for a medical leave, but instead Joe talks him into going to a pot party. "It'd be groovy," he insists. "If you're gonna reach a new level of awareness, you're gonna have to take some risks."

The pot party has nothing to do with the plot of this film, but it does give the filmmakers the opportunity to tar marijuana with the same brush of damnation as acid. Josh, a pot addict who wears a black turtleneck and a sissy poodle haircut, scoffs when red-blooded American boy Joe suggests that pot is a good way to score with chicks. "You can't do nothin' with chicks when you're smoking pot. It's a waste of good pot."

The film returns to the carrier, and poor Bill has just stared into his last radar screen. "I'm floating with it!" he cries as the slide whistle toots. "It's beautiful! Flight 207, I'm coming aboard!" Bill is carried down to sick bay. A Navy doctor sternly remarks that LSD "seems to interfere with ambition, reaching one's goal in life, and with being a responsible person." Joe is sent to prison. His defense—"I just thought it might be fun to turn them on, that's all. I mean, like, for kicks"—isn't much help. Bill has developed "a psychotic mental disorder" and apparently will spend the rest of his long life in a nuthouse.

THE TROUBLE MAKER
Centron Corp. for McGraw-Hill Book Co., 1957, 12 minutes

Bret Waller plays Mel Stone, in what was either serendipity or a brilliant piece of casting. He is perfect for the role. Short, with close-cropped hair, an acne-scarred face, squinty eyes, and a leer instead of a smile, he falls somewhere between a pest and the Antichrist and embodies the description *weaselly*.

Creepy Mel hovers on the edge of every scene in this film, waiting for his chance to hop in and spread nasty half-truths and innuendo among the more attractive, good-hearted teens. He finally pushes things too far when he shows up at the Victory Dance and accuses the noble quarterback and his recently injured pal of losing the big game because they broke training. "I think you're just plain jealous!" says the noble quarterback's equally noble cheerleader girlfriend. "You're botherin' us. Beat it!" growls another teen, shoving Mel out into the center of the gym floor. Alone, surrounded by enemies, Mel tries to take everyone down with him. "That's right...stick together, all of you!" he cries, his voice echoing in the darkness. "Why do you always make it look like I'm in the wrong? Why is everybody always against me???"

By an odd justice, Bret Waller played the partying teen in *The Snob* whose brutal comments send Sarah—an equally unlikeable character—over the edge. Waller was an artist as well as an actor and reportedly became a curator at the Metropolitan Museum of Art in New York City.

UNDERSTANDING YOUR IDEALS
Coronet Instructional Films, 1950, 13 minutes

Teenager Jeff Moore wants to be popular (see *Shy Guy*), but thinks he can achieve popularity by having a car and "fancy clothes" (see *How to Be Well Groomed*). However, his shallow world crumbles when Dad won't let him borrow the car to take his date to the class party. "How can you be popular without a car?" he protests to his girlfriend. "You don't know what popularity means!" she replies, storming off.

Jeff is thoroughly confused. "If you can't be popular with a car and the right clothes, how can you be popular? I'm all mixed up." Dad sits him down for a father-son chat about the need for "clearly defined ideals," citing as examples the Ten Commandments and the construction of hydroelectric dams. "You see, when ideals are sound and clear, they can help us to do some wonderful things."

Jeff has seen the light. "I wanted to be popular. But I never asked myself what it means." He vows to adopt new ideals—sincerity, honesty, and good sportsmanship—because he realizes that these are the true keys to popularity. "Jeff is on the right track now," the narrator says. "Yes, the way out of our difficulties is easier to find if our ideals—like headlights—are strong and clear."

218

VANDALISM
Sid Davis Productions, 1953, 10 minutes

On the streets of southern California, Sid Davis takes great delight in showing white, suburban, "smart-aleck" teenaged boys committing pranks and winding up in the slammer. *Vandalism* takes the open-minded position that most suburban juvenile delinquency is childlike, thoughtless behavior, and not intentionally wicked. However, such actions, if unpunished, lead to "habit-forming wildness," something that cannot be tolerated.

> **"There's a difference between good fun and being stupid."**

"You're talking about these kids as if they were criminals!" protests a teen voice on the soundtrack. "Well, what is a criminal?" replies the narrator. "Someone who breaks the law."

High schoolers Ben and Dave, for example, "are at the age when they should start learning some of the responsibilities that go along with the privileges in a country like this." Instead, they spike the punch at a Halloween party, let air out of automobile tires, and steal another car for a joyride. "Of course, it isn't really *stealing*," the narrator says, his voice dripping sarcasm. "It's just a Halloween joke."

The film ends with the boys being arrested, and a Sid Davis screaming newspaper headline: YOUTHS STEAL CAR FOR "GAG"; JAILED. Sid Davis's browbeating peroration is heartfelt: "Sure, you may get away with irresponsibility and let somebody else carry your load—for a while. But eventually it's going to catch up with you. And being young, underage, isn't going to be enough of an alibi."

WARNING FROM OUTER SPACE
Professional Arts for Marin Medical Society, 1967, 11 minutes

This overproduced oddity is, believe it or not, an antismoking film. A starship from Galaxy Zeta is cruising past earth when its "all-seeing Z Screen" picks up images of earthlings— and they're smoking. The alien crew, who wear turtlenecks with oversized collars made of sheet aluminum, kidnap five human smokers and tell them of the near destruction of the Zeta race by similar smoking shenanigans. The humans are empathetic but unconvinced, and the alien captain shrugs his shoulders and returns them to earth before zooming back out into the smogless cosmos.

Too much creative license doesn't necessarily make a good film, and this one proves it. Its producers had to build a spaceship set, find a location that resembled an alien planet (it looks like they used an abandoned Mother Goose kiddie park), and explode flash pots whenever someone is "beamed" to the alien ship. All this for an antismoking film? The Marin Medical Society must have had cash to burn in 1967.

Perhaps this film's most bizarre touch is that all its narration—and all the dialogue as well—is spoken in rhyming couplets dubbed in by the narrator. No actor ad-libbing allowed.

THE WAY TO A MAN'S HEART
unknown producer for National Live Stock and Meat Board, 1945, 32 minutes

Jane Heywood stands at the train station in Scotsville. She wears a large, silly-looking hat and unattractive, thick-rimmed glasses. Her blouse is buttoned tightly around her neck; her hair is oily and pinned close to her head. She's worked hard, the narrator remarks, to get here: winning a graduate scholarship in chemistry at Scotsville and lining up work to earn her room and board in the home of Dr. Steven Ward—the "wonderful" Dr. Ward, coos the envious brunette in a tight sweater who drives Jane to his house. Jane asks, "How is the chemistry department here?" The brunette sighs, "You *are* the studious type."

Jane loses her attraction to chemistry quick enough. Soon all she can do is stare pie-eyed at the professor, who shares the house with his aging mother, as he apparently has done all his life. Perhaps it's his bulging Adam's apple that turns Jane on, or his sunken eyes, his jug ears, his cadaverlike complexion, his monotonal voice, his wooden demeanor, or his hair that's even oilier than Jane's. For whatever reason, she's hooked. And when the professor snubs the first meal she cooks for him as not being up to his standards, is she offended? No; she brands herself a failure and is ready to run back home in shame!

Scotsville College, it appears, is an all-girls' school filled with desperate, horny women (pickings were slim during the war). Poor Jane is the only one on the entire campus—faculty and students included—who wears glasses. Dr. Ward, it turns out, is a professor of nutrition, although all he seems to do is promote "animal foods" and extol the virtue of "variety meats." "Nutrition is a matter of degree," he pronounces.

Mother Ward convinces Jane to stay and attend an experimental cookery class. It certainly is cutting-edge; all the students wear white nurse outfits while Miss Phoebe Taylor lauds the benefits of low-temperature meat basting and exposes the fallacy of "searing." Jane listens and learns—"a mighty bright girl!" the narrator chuckles—and soon is devoting all her time to the Ward kitchen, not the college lab. "That's the one sure way to a man's heart!" the narrator cheers.

As the film ends, Jane and Dr. Ward are seated at the dinner table; the end of another perfect meal. Now Jane looks positively yummy: her lips are full and moist, her décolletage bewitching, her hair is thick and flowing, and her glasses are nowhere in sight. Jane tells the professor her definition of love: "It's the kind of feeling that would make a man want to help his wife with the dishes," as she gets up and walks deliberately into the kitchen. The professor, displaying all the emotion of a brick, stares into space for a few seconds, and then slowly gathers together some coffee cups and follows her. Music up and out.

THE WELL MANNERED LOOK
Jam Handy Organization for duPont & Co., 1964, 22 minutes

This production tries to palm itself off as a social guidance film about "standards of dress and good grooming," but it's really a plug for clothing made out of duPont plastic fibers. The narrator declares that "appropriate dress" improves school spirit and gives a school "a better reputation." He also warns against "the tendency of a few to create bad impressions that harm the welfare of the many." Just what are these bad impressions? "Fads, gimmicks, and extreme styles," says the narrator, as caricatures appear of teens wearing cotton T-shirts and denim blue jeans.

Thankfully, the well-mannered teens in this film—nerdy guys in skinny neckties and chunky girls with page-boy hairdos—have the good sense to wear "durable" nylon, Orlon, and Dacron, which have "wrinkle recovery" and "crease retention."

WHAT ABOUT ALCOHOLISM?
Centron Corp. for Young America Films, 1956, 11 minutes

Most of this film takes place in a high school classroom where a group of teens loudly declaim their opinions on alcoholics. Hothead Ed insists "they're all spineless and sooner or later they'll all wind up on the skids, believe me!" Bleeding heart Bill thinks "most alcoholics want to be diligent members of society," but they "spend too much money on liquor and finally go out of control." The teens' advisor is always present, but he stands in the shadows at the back of the room and never moves or speaks.

As the film ends the teens are even more confused than when they began, and it's uncertain what, if anything, can bring alcoholics "back to responsible citizenship."

WHAT ABOUT JUVENILE DELINQUENCY
Centron Corp. for Young America Films, 1955, 11 minutes

Hot jazz blasts on the soundtrack as a gang of high school punks roughs up a bald guy in a Buick. Later, at the soda shop, they discover the bald guy was the father of Jamie, one of the absent members of the gang. Jamie gets mad, snarls (nearly every teen in this film snarls at some point), rips his lightning-bolt insignia off his jacket, and joins forces with the good kids to put an end to juvenile delinquency. The punks race after them in an exciting (for an

educational film) car chase. They all end up at a town council meeting where the good teens tell the adults, "Teenagers aren't all delinquents," and complain that the proposed city curfew treats them "as if we're a bunch of *freaks* or something." The film ends as the narrator asks, "What would *you* do?"

This film reduces a complex social problem to a narrative melodrama, but it moves.

WHAT ABOUT PREJUDICE?
Centron Corp. for McGraw-Hill Book Co., 1959, 12 minutes

"This is the story of Bruce Jones, who walked in the shadow of hate and suspicion. The shadow of what he was because of his background." A waist-down tracking shot follows the tattered jeans and scuffed shoes of Bruce as he shuffles along a sidewalk, while the freshly pressed chinos and spick-and-span saddle shoes of his peers stride arrogantly in the opposite direction.

Bruce is never actually shown. The title crawl explains that "since he is a symbol for any or all of the minority groups, he will not be seen or identified." Plenty of Bruce's white, middle-America classmates are shown, however, as they bitch and moan about the "undesirable element" in their midst. "I don't know why they let people like him go

to our school anyway," gripes one. "My dad made it plain I'm not to associate with him," adds a second. "He's not like us and he never will be," proclaims a third. Bruce is suspected of everything from starting fights to stealing sweaters. Then, on the night of the big dance, the teens learn that two of their friends have smashed their car into a bridge abutment, but their lives were saved when Bruce came by and pulled them from the burning wreck! "The gas tank exploded," one of the teens elaborates. "Bruce was burned severely."

W

The same kids who vilified Bruce suddenly make a U-turn toward tolerance. A series of shots ensues of them in the hospital emergency room, looking repentant, while voice-overs convey their shame. "How will I ever be able to face myself after what I've done to him?" asks one. "I just hope I can somehow work out a new set of values to judge him by in the future," thinks another. "You hear about other people's prejudice, but you never feel guilty until you realize it's you! You're the one who's prejudiced!" concludes a third.

"This trip to the hospital," the narrator says, "could be the first step for these students of East High toward tearing down the false barriers which their own bias and prejudice have built." The big Centron question mark appears. "What do *you* think?"

WHAT ABOUT SCHOOL SPIRIT?
Centron Corp. for Young America Films, 1958, 11 minutes

A dewey-eyed blonde named Sally from Westport shares a Coke with Jimmy from Lawrence. She discovers that he spent his Saturday with his classmates working for the United Fund and sighs, "You know, you've really got it here at Lawrence. The right kind of school spirit."

Jimmy offers up an aw-shucks grin and attributes his school's civic-mindedness to the leadership of clean-cut, jug-eared Bob Corby, president of the senior class and captain of the basketball team. "Oh..." Sally replies, "*that* Bob Corby..."

Jimmy remembers how it was in the old days: "Whenever we won we really cut loose. Snake dances snarling up traffic, racing up and down streets blaring car horns and yelling, it's a wonder somebody didn't get killed." And it got worse. "Sometimes noise wasn't enough. Sometimes it was 'kid stuff' such as painting the school initials in places where they had no business to be. If we had had any sense we'd have known that all this carrying on was a discredit to the school."

But, Jimmy recalls, Bob stepped in and taught everyone that school spirit was "more than just noise." Then Bob "got really sick" and there was "no foolishness at all after that."

"It was a thing that carried over," Jimmy reflects. "When you get right down to it, a classroom is a kind of team, too."

Jimmy thinks back on recent events. "There are times when all the spirit in the world doesn't help. Sometimes you've got to lose." Still, Bob "showed that you can lose like a champion, too." By dying, that is.

Sally draws the line at crediting Lawrence's school spirit to the spirit of dead Bob. "Can't you see? The spirit was there all the time!"

Jimmy turns to the camera and shrugs. "Well, how can you argue with a woman?"

WHAT IT MEANS TO BE AN AMERICAN
Frith Films, 1952, 22 minutes

This is possibly the most muddled, meandering account of representational democracy ever put on film. "In what way does an American enjoy a way of life that other countries do not have?" asks narrator Don McNamara as several shots show leaves blowing down an empty street. Producer Emily Benton Frith—who apparently had just taken a cross-country auto trip—makes use of her endless footage of mountains, lakes, oil wells, and exciting state capitals such as Frankfort, Kentucky, and Helena, Montana. "In Europe and in the Orient," McNamara declares, "motor trips are not possible for the average family."

Next comes an extended visit to the Carrs, "a typical American family," who apparently live on a farm the size of West Virginia. Between trips to the orchard and horse-back riding by the mountain range, Dad teaches his kids badminton and breaks up a quarrel over potato chips. "Even small children feel free to speak their own opinion in an American home."

Then it's on to a home construction site. "The men work hard, but there is a carefree atmosphere— not found in countries controlled by a dictatorship." A group of harbor workers "say what they think, with no fear of interference." Shown next are the belching smokestacks of a Pennsylvania steel mill and a South Carolina match factory. "Notice the cars of the workmen. Workmen in foreign countries do not go to their jobs in cars." Nor, according to McNamara, do they own washing machines or irons. Frith reinforces this message with shots of home appliances filmed in American storefront windows.

What It Means to Be an American is nativism at its most basic, with its repeated assertions that every good behavior is actually "typically American" and that the "American way" is in all ways superior to lifestyles in other countries. Still, it's hard to get really mad at the woman who made *Mother Mack's Puppies Find Happy Homes.*

WHAT MADE SAMMY SPEED?
Sid Davis Productions, 1957, 11 minutes

This film opens with a long shot of an accident scene. "Under this ambulance sheet lies Sam Robertson, age seventeen. What made Sammy speed? Why did this have to happen?" The rest of the film aims to find out.

A stone-faced police investigator visits all of Sammy's acquaintances in an attempt to learn the truth. He finds out that Sammy was "a conscientious and responsible youngster" but that he also had a fatal flaw—an "attitude." He discovers that Sammy was "scornful of careful drivers and always told 'woman driver' jokes." He learns that Sammy used speeding to "make up for failures in his life."

Sammy's girlfriend, tramp that she is, confesses that she led Sammy down the road to ruin, admitting that she found his driving "manly and courageous" and that it gave

her "a thrilling sense of power." As punishment, she not only has to witness Sammy's death but receives gashes in her face in the fatal accident.

The film returns to the accident scene, where the grim police officer concludes with this remarkable peroration: "Sammy's speeding, then, was an emotional outlet. And a tragically ill starred one. For it was a compensation for a feeling of insecurity and inferiority. Unhealthy thrill seeking. Immature defiance of authority. And a lack of a sense of responsibility!" Cut to a shot of the investigator standing in the middle of the road watching the ambulance disappear into the distance.

WHAT MAKES A GOOD PARTY?
Coronet Instructional Films, 1950, 11 minutes

The world portrayed in this film is so innocent it's embarrassing. Jean, Nora, and Eileen are hanging out in their pj's and decide to throw a "coming-out" party to introduce college boy Steve to the rest of the gang. But, whoa, let's not be impulsive, the narrator cautions, for "a successful party needs planning and skill." Accordingly, every detail of the get-together is mapped out, from the refreshments (hot chocolate and sandwiches) to the "well-chosen games" (charades and "rhythm"). "Everyone's out to have fun and to help others have fun," the narrator says.

The party itself is an adult-scripted fantasy. Not even teenagers in 1950 were this cornball. All the boys wear suits and, more to the point, everything is done as a group: entertainment, eating, talking. When Nora pulls Steve aside for a private chat, Jean immediately spots them and drags them back for the hat-making contest. "Keep the party fun for all," the narrator commands, and the gang soon has a grand time singing *Jimmy Crack Corn* around the piano.

The narrator offers a final suggestion: "Part of a good party is knowing when to go home"—and the kids do just that.

WHAT TO DO ABOUT UPSET FEELINGS
Coronet Instructional Films, 1964, 11 minutes

Jimmy, Susie, and Paul are students in Mrs. Robinson's class. All are upset for one reason or another. By a remarkable coincidence, Mrs. Robinson is showing a film about what children should do when they're upset. "Let's stop the film!" she exclaims—something real teachers rarely did in real classrooms. As the film-within-a-film freeze frames (without bursting into flames), Mrs. Robinson explains that the upset children in the film-within-a-film "didn't get a good night's sleep or eat a good breakfast." She then encourages her students to "do something sensible" instead of sulking or getting angry.

Jimmy, Susie, and Paul learn from their encounter with modern visual instruction. Once out of class, the three are confronted with situations that would have rendered them hopelessly upset only hours earlier, but "then they remember the film they saw in school," face their difficulties with calm, and go home to bed.

WHAT TO DO ON A DATE
Coronet Instructional Films, 1951, 10 minutes

Goony Nick Baxter wants to take Kay—"a swell girl"—out for a date, but he's afraid she'll say no. He finally works up the courage to ask her to a movie (*Wagon Train*), but she's already seen it. What to do? Nick decides to ask if she wants to help set up the scavenger sale at the community center—a nice, safe, group activity—and Kay accepts eagerly. "I sure didn't think she'd go to a place like that for a date!" Nick says to himself afterward.

"A group...doing things together," the narrator says approvingly. "Pretty good idea for a first date!" Safely shielded from any one-on-one opportunities, Nick and Kay hang crepe paper, dust lamps, and have laughs with the gang. Over Cokes and sandwiches, in one of the most memorable scenes in any social guidance film, they discuss their future plans:

NICK: "I thought all girls wanted fellahs to take them to fancy places. Spend lots of money."

KAY: "Not this girl."

NICK: "You know...I like to go on bicycle trips. Do you?"

KAY (*through a mouthful of sandwich*): "Mmm-hmm. And miniature golf. Do you like that?"

NICK: "Yeah! And weenie roasts and square dances."

KAY: "And baseball games and taffy pulls. I think they're swell."

NICK: "Say...you like to do *lots* of things, don't you!"

The Kay in this film is not the same Kay who later starred in *More Dates for Kay*, for which Nick should be thankful.

WHAT'S ON YOUR MIND
unknown producer for National Film Board of Canada, 1946, 10 minutes

Postwar North America was fascinated with abnormal psychology. After all, hadn't mass mental illness brought about Nazism and the blind obedience of Imperial Japan? In the stress-filled atomic age, could the same thing happen here?

This fast-paced film doesn't answer those questions, but it does feed the viewer's morbid curiosity while cloaking its sensationalism in the mantle of mental hygiene. The producers used lots of underlighting and filled the music track with nervous, discordant strings to create a mood somewhere between a funhouse and a psycho ward.

"Today's psychiatrists believe that many of the world's ills will be solved only by mature, emotionally stable citizens."

"This man is a catatonic schizophrenic," says the film's bombastic narrator, Lorne Greene, as an obviously staged scene shows a guy in black leotards, his eyes turned upward, wandering around a tile-lined room. "In a world changing overnight, men long to escape the fear of atomic destruction, of everyday living!"

In rapid succession the film cuts to a car running over a pedestrian, a distraught family waiting in line for postwar housing, a riot between union strikers and police, and a woman throwing herself off a bridge. "For some the urge to escape grows so extreme, they make the final exit!"

How can the human mind possibly cope with to-day's "strains of living"? Canada, it turns out, wields a big broom in postwar psycho-tidiness. The inner workings of Montreal's Allen Memorial Institute are shown, where the employees wear white lab coats and the patients undergo psychodrama and electroshock sessions—"It jolts people back to sanity." *What's on Your Mind* ends with a shot of normal-looking kids in Toronto, playing with blocks. Greene concludes, "Psychiatrists hope for a new generation, free from hidden fears and resentments. A generation able to face life realistically—and handle it unafraid!"

WHEELS OF TRAGEDY
Safety Enterprises, Inc., 1963, 27 minutes

More bloody mayhem from the folks at Safety Enterprises, Inc., with the cooperation of the Ohio Highway Safety Patrol. As in *Signal 30* (1959) and *Mechanized Death* (1961),

Wheels of Tragedy uses footage of genuine dead accident victims to drive home its message of "human failure." But in this film, director Dick Wayman takes the approach a step further by hiring local dinner-theater actors to portray the victims in the last seconds of their lives. For example, two guys in a Ford with a cracked muffler argue—"I said I'd make Columbus by nine and I'm gonna make it!"—before the carbon monoxide seeping through the floorboards puts them to sleep and they slam into the back of a truck. "It was pretty gruesome," says the film's patrolman narrator as the camera obligingly shows close-ups of bodies with their heads smashed to a pulp, lying in pools of blood. "Chalk it up to human failure."

Other examples of human failure in this film include a trucker who succumbs to "highway hypnosis" and crushes a car in front of him, and three teens who accidentally drive off a bridge. "Frank, you're going too fast." "Relax. Just let me drive, willya? Just sit back and let me Ahhhhhhhgggggggg!!!"

WHEN YOU ARE A PEDESTRIAN
Progressive Pictures, 1948, 10 minutes

A nameless "ex-pedestrian" announces that he's dead, killed by a driver named Joe Smith. "It hurt pretty bad at first," he reflects, as a bloody corpse is shown on an autopsy table followed by a series of pictures of mangled cars and dead kids. "Statistics don't bleed or scream with pain," the dead guy explains. "You can't cripple a statistic or smash its face to a jelly."

"Here is death!" he cries. "Raw and ugly death!"

Street sequences (shot in Oakland, California) show a man in a suit dodging apparently unsuspecting cars; elaborate feltboard animation depicts pedestrians being mowed down; and some odd shots appear of robotic, paramilitary safety-patrol kiddie

guards. As the film ends, Joe Smith is told he must pay the ex-pedestrian's wife $50,000, which makes everybody miserable except the narrator. "Well, I'll be seeing you!" he says cheerily as the credits roll— apparently convinced that everyone will follow in his footsteps by not following the lessons laid down in this very odd film.

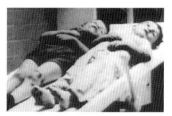

WHERE THE GIRLS ARE
unknown producer for U.S. Air Force, 1969, 23 minutes

Where the Girls Are chronicles the sexual downfall of Pete Collins, a likeable guy with a cute girlfriend, who takes a tour of duty in Southeast Asia. "Julie was worth waiting for no matter where they shipped me," Pete asserts, but this virtuous state of mind doesn't last long.

Pete falls in with Ernie King, a leering hipster who apparently knows every bathhouse on the subcontinent and who always seems drunk or hungover. As cocktail lounge music fills the soundtrack, several montages are shown of Asian girls in short skirts and tight dresses, and faced with this kind of stimulation (and Ernie egging him on), Pete succumbs to temptation.

In the end, Ernie pays a high price for his philandering: "Pete—after we went out that time—you have any trouble trying to take a leak?"; and when Pete returns home, the doctor tells him that he can't get married because he has syphilis. "You can't promise a girl like Julie you'll be true to her and show up with a case of syphilis," Pete concludes.

WHERE THERE'S SMOKE...
Ib Melchior for Sid Davis Productions, 1957, 10 minutes

Sirens wail and somber chimes ring. A nameless, grief-stricken family watches as a house is engulfed in flames. "This is Johnny's and Laurie's home," the narrator announces. "And fire is destroying it."

Too bad for Johnny and Laurie, but after all, people who break the rules get what they deserve. A series of shots—actually visually interesting, which is rare for a Sid Davis film—shows curtains and trash cans and ironing boards and towels bursting into flame because of careless disregard for safety rules. But the crime committed by Johnny and Laurie's family is not carelessness, it's arrogance! They try to put the fire out themselves instead of immediately calling their fire department. Those few seconds of selfish independent action cost them their home. Although firemen dutifully race to the scene and spray water all over the place, the house goes up like a torch.

WHO ARE THE PEOPLE OF AMERICA?
Coronet Instructional Films, 1953, 11 minutes

The narrator declares that Americans are "a mixture of the people of the world" and that "much of that which is American is of the world." A montage showing spaghetti, baseball, and a jukebox demonstrates that "these are some of the things we share as Americans. For we have become Americans through the process of sharing." This film consists purely of stock shots from previous Coronet films (along with the obligatory cheap animated lines and arrows converging on a map of the United States), but it's all incidental eye candy to hold the viewer's attention while the narrator delivers his message. "Playing together, growing together, learning together. America is a land whose people shared what they knew."

Mel Waskin, Coronet's senior scriptwriter, claimed he wrote this film and then assembled it "rhythmically" at home using footage from the Coronet stock library. According to Waskin, this film brought tears to his boss's eyes when he first saw it.

WHO'S DELINQUENT?
Jay Bonafield for RKO-Pathe, 1947, 16 minutes

Grantwood is a postcard-perfect community of tree-lined streets—with girls in jail, boy car thieves, and twenty-six children in reformatories.

Old Man Everhart, who runs the town newspaper, vows to get the scoop on juvenile delinquency after a couple of teens run down a cop in a stolen car. His reporters discover

227

that Billy Marvin, one of the joy riders, lives with his widowed mom in what looks like a garage. "A sad home," the narrator says, "never visited by social workers or juvenile authorities." They visit the overtaxed juvenile court and the underfunded, understaffed, overpopulated schools, where both kids and teachers must contend with "an impossible load of work." They tour urban slums populated with black people. These sad conditions "across the track," among the "human tools" that helped win the war, affect us all, the narrator points out. Staged scenes show kids stealing bikes and breaking windows, older kids shoplifting and shooting craps, and still older kids stealing cars and busting open railroad boxcars. "Nightlife in rural precincts has altered considerably since taffy-pull days," the narrator growls as the camera pans a bar filled with kids, all under eighteen, all having a grand old time smoking cigarettes and drinking beer. "Our kids cruise around to outlying honky-tonks," the narrator complains. "Real dives that our town police would never license." Who knew that teenage life in 1947 was so wild?

The town gets worked up by Everhart's investigative journalism and convenes a meeting. "Our town is obsolete," the narrator declares. "We need overhauling in everything touching youth." Grantwood will henceforth drop its "drowsy policy of 'do-nothing' and get down to brass tacks."

"This is democracy doing its homework!" he cries as the stock music builds to a crescendo. "And this, our youth, is why no community can afford to come up with the wrong answers!"

"Who is delinquent—our children or us?"

WHY PUNCTUATE
Centron Corp. for Young America Films, 1948, 10 minutes

Teenaged Tommy writes a letter to his dad without punctuation. His dad finds it funny, but the narrator cautions that soon his writing will be read by "more critical correspondents." Two teenaged girls in party dresses appear as the narrator exclaims, "He may be judged by the letters he writes!"

"It doesn't take the girls long to find out about Tommy," the narrator says as the girls shake their heads sadly in unison and drop his letter to the floor. "He writes as a child, and that's how he's considered; just a child." But the girls have one more letter to read, one that's correctly punctuated. "Here's a different story," the narrator cheers, "a letter from a right guy!" The girls smile to each other approvingly. "And what a reception it gets!"

WHY STUDY HOME ECONOMICS?
Centron Corp. for Young America Films, 1955, 10 minutes

High schoolers Janice and Carol, sisters, are deciding which classes they want to take next semester. Janice says she wants to take some courses in home ec; Carol is aghast. "Why in the world do you want to take home economics?" she scoffs, but Janice is not easily dissuaded. "Why? Because that's something I'm gonna need to know. If I'm gonna be a homemaker the rest of my life, I want to know what I'm doing!"

To shore up her opinion, Janice visits Miss Jenkins, the home ec teacher. Miss Jenkins explains that home economics isn't just baking and sewing; it teaches "the fundamental principles of food buying" and "the psychology of clothing." "Present-day textiles cannot

be judged with confidence just by casual examination," Miss Jenkins cautions as girls peer through microscopes and stretch fabric swatches on a mechanical rack. If Janice decides not to get married ("at least not right away," Miss Jenkins chuckles), she can apply the knowledge gained in home ec to college courses such as chemistry and bacteriology.

"Home economics training teaches ways of developing democratic practices within the home," Miss Jenkins adds, but she doesn't have to say more to convince Janice. "Anyone who's going to be married and a homemaker would be foolish not to take home economics!"

WHY STUDY INDUSTRIAL ARTS?
Centron Corp. for Young America Films, 1956, 10 minutes

Joe is a shop geek (and a terrible actor) who likes "the smell of fresh wood chips" and "the dull 'tap-tap' of tools on leather." Bill, his buddy, is a fan of Joe's handiwork—"Hey, this looks like furniture you'd buy in a store!"—but he doesn't think that a course in industrial arts would do him any good. However, after some lengthy harangues from a couple of male authority figures (the industrial arts instructor and a basketball coach), Bill turns into

> **"You'd have to look far and wide to find a job that doesn't, in some way or other, use industrial arts training."**

a shop convert. "With the large amount of construction work that's taking place in our country's expansion, we need many more young men who are trained to design our future."

WHY STUDY SOCIAL STUDIES?
John F. Criswell for Gateway Productions, 1961, 10 minutes

Betty and her stern father sit at the breakfast table. Betty's dad, the narrator says, is going to teach his daughter how people all over the world contribute to their morning meal. Of course, he's going to use visual aids to drive the point home.

Dad has a map of the world nailed to the wall, and he's tied strings to everything on the table. Slowly, deliberately, Dad thumbtacks the end of each string to the country of its origin: bananas go to Honduras, napkins are tacked to Ireland, etc. Poor Betty's breakfast is lost in the tangled thicket of strings, but Dad has successfully illustrated his point.

In a Midwestern twang the narrator declares that "history is an exciting story of people and the things they did in years gone by," while the screen shows footage of bored Indians shaking maracas as they walk in a parade. He also explains that "father and mother are the leaders of the family government," although it's unclear exactly how this relates to social studies.

WHY TAKE CHANCES?
Sid Davis Productions, 1952, 10 minutes

This film is almost a twin of Sid Davis's classic *Live and Learn,* a series of vignettes of bad accidents happening to careless kids, introduced by a narrator whose deepest expression

of sympathy is "Too bad." Sid Davis tries to soften the blow by inserting wacky music and goofy drawings of kids being hurt, but there's also ample footage of real children writhing in pain. Jimmy is the principal victim as he runs into a tree playing football, steps on a rusty nail, flies a kite in a rainstorm, and "talks his friends into digging a cave in a hillside." Fans of Sid Davis films can easily guess what happens next.

WHY VANDALISM?
Encyclopaedia Britannica Films, 1955, 16 minutes

Jeff Turner and his pals Don and Ed are three teens in a dark, ugly city. Jeff lives in a home that "is lacking in love and affection," where it looks like no one's washed the dishes in a month. All three are filled with "a desperate urge to get even," the narrator comments, his voice filled with careworn wisdom and pity.

After scorning the movie offered at the community center—"Yuck! Those *free* movies"—the boys impulsively break into the high school through an open window. Jeff guides them to the science lab so he can cuddle his favorite fluffy bunny, but their "feelings of resentment are too great to be controlled completely" and they end up trashing the place. The bunny dies in the mayhem, all three punks are caught, and a judge sentences them to be turned over to doctors and social workers who, it is hoped, will reprogram them to be "happy" and "normal."

This film deserves credit for recognizing long-simmering anger as a cause for juvenile delinquency and for pointing out that vandalism is often capricious, not evil. But the oh-so-wise tone is enough to make you want to put a bullet in your head.

WHY WE RESPECT THE LAW
Coronet Instructional Films, 1950, 13 minutes

Kent feels guilty about stealing wood to build a backstop for a baseball diamond. He decides to ask a lawyer for advice. He gets a lecture instead. "The issue, Kent, is not a few dollars' worth of lumber. It's your attitude toward law itself!"

The lawyer tells Kent that "law is in harmony with the universe" and shows what life would be like if there were no laws—very bad. Next, he narrates a flashback through the life of another teen thief who began by stealing pennies from his mother and ended up in jail. "You mean that my taking a couple of boards could lead to something like *that?*" asks Kent. "Couldn't it?" replies the lawyer. Kent is humbled and the lawyer strikes a deal with the lumberyard to have Kent work off the cost of the stolen wood.

Lawyer-brokered deal making is one of the reasons Americans *don't* respect the law, but that isn't mentioned in this film.

WINKY THE WATCHMAN
Hugh Harman Productions, 1945, 10 minutes

This cartoon opens in the real-world waiting room of Dr. Allen, a dentist. Dr. Allen tells a group of kids and their parents the fable of Winky the Watchman, a cartoon dolt who is always falling asleep while guarding the wall of a fabulous city.

The wall, actually a row of giant teeth, is attacked and ravaged by "Bad-Uns" while Winky is slumbering. The Bad-Uns are black, nasty things with horns. Their faces look like a cross between Mussolini and Telly Savalas. Winky finally wakes up, opens the city gates, and out charge the "Good-Uns," Casper the Friendly Ghost types who ride horses shaped like blobs of toothpaste and who speak with British accents (it *was* 1945). The pale Good-Uns massacre the unarmed Bad-Uns mercilessly, strafing, machine gunning, and hacking them to pieces with swords. The bloody victory saves the city, and Winky promises never to sleep again, ever.

"Remember," the dentist says as the film ends, "the Bad-Uns are always waiting to attack your wall."

WISE USE OF CREDIT
Sutherland Educational Films, 1960, 11 minutes

Silver-haired, suit-wearing "Mr. Money" sits in his very neat office. The wall behind his large desk holds shelves of books—but not too many—so it's clear he's worthy of respect, not a weirdo egghead.

In another part of the world, John Nelson and Judy Naler chat with their friends in their school yard. Mr. Money presses a button on his desk and—*boink!*—John and Judy are magically transported out of the yard and into Mr. Money's office, which they accept in stride—"Hey! It's Mr. Money!" Yuppies before their time, they are the kind of teens who genuinely enjoy a visit with Mr. Money. Judy, for example, is shown a copy of her dad's credit report. "Hey! It goes way back to before I was born!" she squeals with delight.

Mr. Money turns on "the learning machine" (a futuristic TV) with his desk-mounted remote control and the camera dollies in to show happy, fun animated diagrams and cartoons encouraging everyone to borrow money. "Gee, there sure are a lot of things I'd like to buy for better living!" says John, a real lackey. Judy would like to be a lackey too, but her character is too dumb. "Gee, Mr. Money—do girls have to learn all this about credit too?" she asks. "Well, Judy," Mr. Money replies in a tone normally reserved for small children, "women do most of the shopping when they get married and very often spend most of the family income." "Well, sure!" John adds, catching on quick. "If a guy has to work hard to earn money, well, a wife ought to learn to get the most out of it!"

"There's the bell!" cry John and Judy as the film ends. "We don't want to be late for class!"

WORTH WAITING FOR
Wetzel O. Whitaker for Brigham Young University, 1962, 27 minutes

This isn't a film about sex, it's about marriage. Which, until the 1970s, meant the same thing.

Joe is seventeen, Julie is sixteen. They want to get married—which is not so odd, considering that this is a Mormon film—but none of the people they know agree with them. Gloria, Julie's friend, asks, "Are you sure you know what you're doing?" but Julie says that she wants to have babies now, when she'll be "young enough to still be pals" with them. "I want to be a *mother* to my children," Gloria snorts.

Phyllis Stanway, Julie's perky home ec teacher, is another doubter. A self-proclaimed "old maid at twenty-six," she has a thirty-year-old lawyer for a boyfriend and is planning a ski vacation in Chile. "The Andes are beautiful this time of year," she explains with relish.

Julie's hopes are buoyed when she runs into Viv at a school function. Viv wears a mink, tells Julie that teen hubby Rex is in the oil biz, and flashes pictures of her lovely home and baby. Julie drags Joe out to see Viv and Rex on a whim—and discovers that the home and the mink belong to Rex's mom, Rex works pumping gas, and the baby screams incessantly.

As Julie and Joe drive back in Joe's snazzy Studebaker Hawk (it's not explained how he can afford that), they reconsider their decision. "Save this for me," Julie tells Joe, handing back her engagement ring. "It can be my graduation present—next year." The moral: marriage for Mormons is bad at sixteen but okay at eighteen.

YOU AND YOUR ATTITUDES
Keaneleigh Productions, 1947, 11 minutes

In this film eleven minutes are spent with the Barrett family—Mom, Dad, Tom, and Betty—as they endlessly discuss the validity of their respective attitudes on family finances, other people's problems, and Greek restaurants.

BETTY: "Dad, how do we know when we're forming attitudes without realizing it?"
DAD: "I think the first thing to do is to make a complete analysis of yourself!"

Tom and Betty are much too old to be playing teenagers in this obscure little liberal-minded film, with its clumsy jump cuts and flubbed lines.

YOU AND YOUR BICYCLE
Progressive Pictures, 1960, 11 minutes

Shot on what looks like a very tight budget, this film shows kids riding bikes in Oakland, California. The narrator is full of cautionary advice, such as, "Follow a straight line and avoid being run down," and "An unexpected turn or stop can mean sudden death." No one is ever shown being killed, a disappointment, but there is one brief, crudely animated cartoon sequence in which a kid whose head looks like a dollop of soft ice cream flies over his handlebars and lands on his face.

YOU AND YOUR FRIENDS
B. K. Blake for Cowles Magazines [Look], 1946, 10 minutes

This follow-up to *You and Your Family* opens at "a nice, friendly party," where three teen couples dance in somebody's living room. Big band music wahs and honks on the soundtrack as the narrator instructs the viewer to watch the kids carefully and decide: "Would I rate them plus or minus as friends?"

Most of the action takes place around the snack table: Frank speaks ill of Eddie—"He's a drip"—while Mary defends him—"I think he's tops!" Betty acts antisocial; Ethel can't keep a secret, etc. The problems are typical, the kids have good and bad qualities, and

the narrator constantly butts in to ask the viewer's opinion, making this film and its predecessor two of the few social guidance films that went easy on the guidance and encouraged discussion. "If you have any problems like those you've just seen, talk them over. Because the only way to have a friend is to be one. And friendship is one of the most precious things in life."

YOU AND YOUR PARENTS
Coronet Instructional Films, 1949, 13 minutes

Teenager Dick Robinson runs away from home after his parents yell at him for coming home late—but first he stops to say goodbye to Mr. Martin, his club leader. Mr. Martin lures him inside with a piece of cake and the two quickly settle into a reasoned discussion on the need for self-discipline and the need for relaxing authority when self-discipline is displayed. It's all very soothing and visually reassuring—Dick wears a suit, Mr. Martin wears a silk robe and an ascot—and by the next morning Dick understands that Mom and Dad only wanted the best for him all along. "If that's the way my parents feel about me, I think I get the idea!"

YOU CAN'T STOP ON A DIME
Sid Davis Productions, 1954, 10 minutes

This is pretty tame stuff for Sid Davis. Most of it is a filmed version of a standard parking lot traffic safety demonstration that shows how much distance it takes to stop a person, bicycle, or car in motion. There are some odd moments of kids looking left, right, then left again in unison as the same perky music loops over and over and over again. Unintentional surrealism, courtesy of robotic 1950s safety rules and Sid Davis being too cheap to buy more than one piece of stock music.

YOU'RE GROWING UP
Sid Davis Productions, 1956, 10 minutes

This film follows a number of kids as it outlines "the four major periods of growing up," from birth to age twenty. In one classic Sid Davis touch, a baby scalds her hand on a hot stove. "Though the experience may hurt, it helps to avoid pain the next time." Another sequence features Jill, Sid Davis's daughter, as a young teen who's given a pair of new shoes for her rapidly growing feet. She gets so happy she breaks

"Growing up is a strange and exciting experience."

233

into a spontaneous hully-gully in the living room. And when she and her parents go to the drive-in, the movie on the screen is *Gang Boy!*

By the time you hit twenty, the narrator concludes, "you should be able to accept help gracefully from others" and "be thinking about the future, a career, and family."

YOUR FAMILY
Coronet Instructional Films, 1948, 11 minutes

Young Tony Brent learns to pitch in with extra work when the family needs it (and when it serves his own interests of getting dinner on the table). "Doing things together is fun!"

Pretty standard stuff, although this film is memorable for Mom, who wears a great heart-shaped apron and has eyebrows that have been plucked into nonexistence. "Dinnertime is happy time for this family!" the narrator cheers. Here's how they spend it:

"They talk about the good things that happen each day, sharing their fun with each other. Nancy tells us something pleasant that her music teacher said today. Mother says how helpful Tony was this afternoon. Tony tells of a new trick that Fluffy learned. Father tells of helping a man whose hat blew off and went sailing down the windy street."

The Brents spend their after-dinner hour watching home movies of themselves.

YOUR JUNIOR HIGH DAYS
Centron Corp. for McGraw-Hill Book Co., 1961, 11 minutes

This is an indoctrination film for twelve-year-olds. It's pretty straightforward—increased responsibility, goal setting, etc.—but it is fun to watch this film straddle the line between 1950s groupthink and 1960s individualism. One moment it's asserted that people with good personalities "make the effort to go along with their friends in what they do, what they wear, and the way they talk," and the next that "you are worthy of respect! You are still you!"

The narrator challenges the audience to "be yourself. Find out what is best for you," then offers them a choice of the school paper, marching band, or photography club.

YOUR PERMIT TO DRIVE
General Motors Photographic, 1952, 11 minutes

This odd film consists of a continuous stream of traffic and driving footage—most of it shot from an open convertible—overlaid with narration provided by an unseen talking driver's permit.

"I am your permit to drive an automobile," it begins. "I am only a card in your wallet or purse, yet I unroll before your eyes a magic carpet—the millions of miles of highways and byways that crisscross the nation." According to this General Motors vision of America, "The automobile has brought with it a new way of life, a new standard of living, matched by no other nation in the world."

But the rosy scenario also has a few thorns. "This year," the permit says, "I will be among the last papers of tens of thousands"—mostly "eighteen- to twenty-four-year-olds"—"who will have no further use for me." The permit is perplexed, at first. "Over and over I ask myself, why? Is it the supposed thoughtlessness of youth that takes such a toll? Or is it my fault? Have I allowed myself to be taken for granted?" Then the permit suddenly realizes who is to blame—the drivers—and becomes outraged. "I am a privilege and an obligation! I try to tell people when they write their names across my face that they are signing a pledge—a pledge to be the kind of driver they want others to be. We owe to each other the courtesy—the fair play—each of us expects!"

Next comes the plea for 1950s conformity. "As a nation, we set great store by sportsmanship. Almost all of us, at some time, play the game." Sadly, the permit notes, our nation's highways have their share of "poor sports." "They are the reckless, who cause the accidents that maim and kill! Offenders, whose invasion of the rights of others may lead to curtailment of their own rights." For emphasis staged shots are shown of a smug young man in a loud plaid sport coat having his permit revoked by a judge. The permit reiterates, "I am your permit to drive, not your right to drive. You are entitled to drive only as long as you abide by the rules."

General Motors had too much riding on the automobile for this film to end on a sour note. "Perhaps the poor driver never learned the proper way to drive," the permit reflects. "You have more opportunity than he. You have the opportunity to learn the right way to drive." Finally, just in case the audience isn't salivating enough about the prospect of driving, the permit delivers a rousing peroration: "I, your permit to drive, am the 'open sesame' to a lifetime of new experiences. I bring wings to your feet. A freedom of motion you will learn always to cherish!"

YOUR STUDY METHODS
Coronet Instructional Films, 1964, 11 minutes

This is an incredibly tedious film, narrated in voice-over by an elementary school teacher who wears an ill-fitting striped suit. Well-organized students John, Alice, Bill, Roger, Gail, Dave, Steve, and Brenda go to the library, "pick out key thoughts," work with others, and make notes and outlines. "Laying out a graph with reasonable neatness makes it easy to read—and attractive, too." This film features many overly organized desktops and looseleaf binders, and the fact that a detail like that is noticeable provides a clue as to how dull the film really is. "I hope the methods used by Brenda and the other pupils of my class have given you some ideas on how you can make your study methods more effective."

YOUR THRIFT HABITS
Coronet Instructional Films, 1948, 11 minutes

Irresponsible Jack is envious of the camera that sensible Ralph has just bought. How can he possibly save the money he needs to buy one for himself? "Are budgets just for parents?" the narrator asks sarcastically. "If he'd do without extravagances, he could save every week!" Jack concedes that he should learn to budget, so he devises a "camera-graph" and attempts to follow it. This isn't always easy, but the narrator is always on hand to flay Jack verbally whenever he veers from his narrow, approved path. "Too many movies! Too much candy!" he chides. "You can't have everything you want!"

YOUTH IN CRISIS
The March of Time, 1943, 19 minutes

This March of Time theatrical release was recut and distributed to schools in the spring of 1944. It "depicts what is happening to our young people because of the excitement of war, the mental and nervous instability of some of our draft-rejected young men, and teenage flouting of parental authority." While not a social guidance film—it yelled rather than persuaded, as did most films of its time—it does show why social guidance films would soon exist.

"The grim story of what the war is doing to America's youth!"

According to the narrator, a ten-year-long decrease in juvenile delinquency "has been completely and startlingly reversed. Everywhere, children with working parents are being left without adequate supervision or restraint!"

"Freed from parental authority, youngsters are venturing into new and unwholesome worlds. Experiments with new sensations [cut to shots of kids smoking dope] are tempting more and more teenaged youngsters along dangerous paths." The peddling of obscene books, "a furtive and despicable occupation," has become a "lucrative sideline for unscrupulous shopkeepers in some high school neighborhoods."

Boys were not only free from parental oversight, they had paying jobs and the additional freedom that money provided. "Feeling himself a man, the teenaged boy feels entitled to act as he believes older men do." Too often this translated into "moral laxity." And the girls? The narrator paints a portrait guaranteed to traumatize any mom and dad: "To many young girls, even those in their earliest teens, war is opening up avenues of unaccustomed excitement. To them, any man in uniform seems a hero, and in towns crowded with footloose soldiers or sailors, it is easy for them to get passing attention they could not normally expect. But too many youngsters, thinking of themselves as 'Victory Girls,' believe it is a part of patriotism to deny nothing to servicemen." (As *Educational Screen* put it, "They have no 'no' in their vocabulary.") "The adolescent girl, with experience far beyond her age, is beginning, like her brother, to reject parental discipline."

MOTHER: "Betty! Do you realize what time it is?"
BETTY: "Oh, Mother, don't be such an old fuddy-duddy!"

"Profoundly shocking" were the figures that showed arrests of girls under twenty-one up 350 percent between 1941 and 1943, and "offenses against common decency" by girls under twenty-one rising 89 percent in 1943 alone. "Our young people are getting out of hand everywhere!" complains a matron to J. Edgar Hoover.

Children must learn to "accept responsibility and discipline" and "understand the cooperative terms on which society exists," the narrator commands. He also suggests the busy-hands approach to social engineering: "The average youth is in no danger of becoming a delinquent so long as he has something to keep him busy." As teen boys make models of enemy planes for air-raid wardens, the narrator declares, "Youth given a part of the all-out war effort—selling bonds, collecting salvage, operating victory gardens, organizing 4-H clubs—will prevent most of the shocking delinquencies."

> "I think it is most true that an effective audio-visual program grows out of a rebellious spirit—rebellion against the failure of the school and its profession to accept the inevitability of progress."
>
> —GODFREY ELLIOT, EXECUTIVE VICE-PRESIDENT, YOUNG AMERICA FILMS (1947)

EPILOGUE

Things change. The civil rights movement, the Kennedy assassination, Vietnam all chipped away at the fixed social order championed in mental hygiene films. Absolutes were no longer absolute; society became divided, fractioned, factioned. The concept of change took root.

Mental hygiene films could not change. In both style and philosophy they were wed to the past. Teenagers, their principal audience, no longer believed them. Young people of the 1960s demanded "truth" in their visual education, not a carefully crafted, scenario-driven product. Kids wouldn't believe anything less blunt than what they saw on television news: people being hosed in Birmingham, beaten in Chicago, shot in Newark and Saigon. They demanded real people talking to the camera telling their side of the story—not some scriptwriter's idea of what that story should be.

No physical obstacle prevented mental hygiene films from making this change. The technology—lightweight cameras, portable sound equipment, more sensitive film stock—had been widely available since the late 1950s. But there was a philosophical roadblock: mental hygiene films engineered opinion; they did not objectively report it. A few productions—*LSD-25* (1967), *Tell It Like It Is* (1968),

Breath: "An original and amusing cartoon for adults that shows a man and a woman breathing in and out. Open to many interpretations."

Catch the Joy: "Beautifully photographed film illustrating the world of dune buggies. It conveys a sense of poetry in motion."

The Fish Teacher: "A delightful bit of fancy, in which French schoolgirls transform their teacher into a fish."

The Hangman: "The film uses stark, stylized paintings and jazz music to illustrate the murder of a whole town by a self-appointed hangman simply because no one dares protest."

Help! My Snowman's Burning Down: "This zany experimental film opens with a man sitting in a bathtub on a pier at the Hudson River. Images and episodes get increasingly funny. Young adults and all adults will find hilarious."

The Jump: "A little man in the clutches of mechanization performs monotonous

Marijuana (1968)—faked television documentary style to give an illusion of validity. But these new techniques of deception were unfamiliar to an older generation of scriptwriters, editors, and directors. The approach never caught on. The square peg would not fit in the round hole.

Mental hygiene films were all but gone by 1970.

Ironically, what arose in their place was not hard-hitting TV-style 16mm documentaries. Instead, classrooms of the early 1970s were awash with vague "discussion" films that provided even less substance than their mental hygiene predecessors. Young 16mm filmmakers were more interested in self-expression than accurate portrayals of life. Young teachers and film librarians were quick to mock the efforts of past producers but slow to criticize the indulgences of their peers. Freedoms were abused; new prejudices replaced the old. It was as if America's visual education establishment had tumbled back into the Middle Ages—or 1945—its course charted by a ruling class of shortsighted, arrogant twenty-five-year-olds.

It was a cruel lesson.

series of movements in a world that is void of humanity."

Junkdump: "A vivid portrayal of one day in the life of a husband and wife who live and work in a city dump. Excellent film for students of the film as art or for ecology oriented discussion."

Para 1000: "A Joycean delirium of colors and sounds of reality and unreality; visions of hippies at play. Psychedelic lighting and colors produce an eerie and striking glimpse of pop culture and the mod generation."

7362: "Highly acclaimed psychedelic abstract film. Hints at the schizophrenic condition of our 20th century mechanical-conformist society. Uses, in part, Rorschach tests in motion."

That's Me: "A comedy-drama in which Alan Arkin plays a guitar-strumming Puerto Rican. Shot on location in Central Park, with script improvised. Can be used for guidance, 'generation gap,' or counter-culture discussions."

film descriptions from the
1971 Camden, New Jersey,
Regional Film Library catalog